"Daniel Satinsky has made an important contribution to one of the great stories of our times – the emergence of Russia after the collapse of the Soviet Union and the nation's white-knuckle transition of Cold War relics into the institutions of modern democracy and capitalism. Satinsky delivers a thoroughly researched and highly readable account of America's role in the modernization of Russia, and the extraordinary cast of US academics, bankers, business executives, companies and everyday citizens who played a part. *Creating the Post-Soviet Market Economy: Through American Eyes* is a deeply compelling read for anyone interested in exploring the real story behind the historical significance and high drama of that time, and for understanding the complicated and fascinating mechanics of modernizing a country."

Boris Jordan, *International Businessman, and founder of Renaissance Capital*

"I feel that I speak for many in saying that this book is a trip down memory lane. This is a time of mixed emotions for those of us who dedicated our lives to American–Russian relations and while it might be in some ways painful to revisit this period and try to understand what went wrong, a lot did go right. This book helps us put that into perspective. This reflection on such an intense period of change is long overdue. I appreciate the challenge of trying to write on this subject at this particular moment in history, but it is precisely what is needed."

Renee (Stillings) Huhs, *Founder of SRAS*

"I like the voices presented, and I like the messages. Two stand out. The first is that you give Russians agency; lots of it. This is how it was, but far too many people here ignored that reality. Second, it shows how those of us who engaged with Russian society achieved more than those for whom it was another assignment or some sort of abstraction."

Blair Ruble, *Distinguished Scholar, Woodrow Wilson Center*

"This book uniquely captures a foundational period in US relations with post-Soviet Russia. We need to closely study the events, actors, and dynamics that Daniel Satinsky painstakingly chronicles to help understand how we got to where we are today. Hats off for its timely publication."

Trevor Gunn, *Adjunct Professor, School of Foreign Service at Georgetown University*

Creating the Post-Soviet Russian Market Economy

This book captures the essence of the period when Russians and Americans collaborated in creating new structures of government and new businesses in completely uncharted conditions. It presents the experiences of key American participants in late Soviet and post-Soviet Russia during a time when Americans thought anything was possible in Russia. Using an analytic framework of foreground ideas (Western, liberal, and neo-liberal) and background forces (Russian cultural influences, nationalism, and lingering Soviet ideology), it examines the ideas and intentions of the people involved. First-person interviews with consultants, businesspeople, and citizen diplomats help capture the essence of this turbulent reform period through the eyes of those who experienced it and present the importance of this experience as a piece of the puzzle in understanding contemporary Russia. It will be an invaluable resource for students of international relations, Russian Studies majors, researchers, and members of the general public who are trying to understand the evolution of the current antagonism between the United States and Russia.

Daniel Satinsky, J.D., M.A.L.D., Consultant, Author, and Associate of Davis Center for Russian and Eurasian Studies at Harvard University. He is co-author of *Hammer and Silicon – The Soviet Diaspora in the U.S. Innovation Economy*. He participated in joint ventures in the Soviet Union and business in Russia until 2014.

Routledge Studies in US Foreign Policy
Series Editors: Inderjeet Parmar, *City University*, and
John Dumbrell, *Durham University*

This new series sets out to publish high-quality works by leading and emerging scholars critically engaging with United States Foreign Policy. The series welcomes a variety of approaches to the subject and draws on scholarship from international relations, security studies, international political economy, foreign policy analysis and contemporary international history.

Subjects covered include the role of administrations and institutions, the media, think tanks, ideologues and intellectuals, elites, transnational corporations, public opinion, and pressure groups in shaping foreign policy, US relations with individual nations, with global regions and global institutions and America's evolving strategic and military policies.

The series aims to provide a range of books – from individual research monographs and edited collections to textbooks and supplemental reading for scholars, researchers, policy analysts and students.

American Presidents and Israeli Settlements since 1967
Michael F. Cairo

Foundations, US Foreign Policy and Anti-Racism in Brazil
Pushing Racial Democracy
Elizabeth Cancelli, Gustavo Mesquita and Wanderson Chaves

The United States' Residual Hegemony: A Complex-Gramscian Examination
A Complex-Gramscian Examination
Rashad Seedeen

Creating the Post-Soviet Russian Market Economy
Through American Eyes
Daniel Satinsky

For more information about this series, please visit: www.routledge.com/series/RSUSFP

Creating the Post-Soviet Russian Market Economy

Through American Eyes

Daniel Satinsky

Routledge
Taylor & Francis Group
LONDON AND NEW YORK

First published 2024
by Routledge
4 Park Square, Milton Park, Abingdon, Oxon OX14 4RN

and by Routledge
605 Third Avenue, New York, NY 10158

Routledge is an imprint of the Taylor & Francis Group, an informa business

British Library Cataloguing-in-Publication Data
A catalogue record for this book is available from the British Library

Library of Congress Cataloging-in-Publication Data
Names: Satinsky, Daniel M., author.
Title: Creating the post-Soviet Russian market economy :
through American eyes / Daniel Satinsky.
Description: New York : Routledge, 2023. |
Series: Routledge studies in us foreign policy |
Includes bibliographical references and index.
Identifiers: LCCN 2023006760 (print) | LCCN 2023006761 (ebook) |
ISBN 9781032021591 (hardback) | ISBN 9781032021607 (paperback) |
ISBN 9781003182153 (ebook)
Subjects: LCSH: Russia (Federation)–Economic conditions–1991- |
Russia (Federation)–Foreign economic relations–United States. |
United States–Foreign economic relations–Russia (Federation) |
Russia (Federation)–Commerce–United States. |
United States–Commerce–United States. | Post-communism–Russia (Federation)
Classification: LCC HC340.12 .S276 2023 (print) | LCC HC340.12 (ebook) |
DDC 330.947–dc23/eng/20230315
LC record available at https://lccn.loc.gov/2023006760
LC ebook record available at https://lccn.loc.gov/2023006761

ISBN: 978-1-032-02159-1 (hbk)
ISBN: 978-1-032-02160-7 (pbk)
ISBN: 978-1-003-18215-3 (ebk)

DOI: 10.4324/9781003182153

Typeset in Times New Roman
by Newgen Publishing UK

This book is dedicated to a future time when Americans and Russians can once again mingle freely, work jointly, respectfully exchange views, and learn from each other.

December 2022

Contents

Acknowledgments

I want to begin by acknowledging the foundational contributions made by the 106 people interviewed for the book. In the end, I was only able to include quoted information from 66 of them. However, I learned from each interview in ways that shaped the overall book. All the people interviewed generously shared their unique experience and their insight into this formative period of modern Russian history and their own personal contributions to that history. My apologies to those who were interviewed but not included in the book. There was simply not enough room to include everyone, but every interview contributed to the final product.

I identified interview subjects through the networks of people developed over my many years working in Russia and through the connections shared with me by others. Almost every person I interviewed suggested someone else to talk to, but a few people were especially important in helping me to reach key individuals who were outside my own personal networks. In particular, I would like to thank Bernie Sucher, Fred Berliner, Jim Hickman, Joel Schatz, and Chris King for the doors that they opened for me and the contributions they made to the book.

I also want to acknowledge the early advice and counsel that I received from colleagues and friends with whom I have worked on business and business promotion projects for their sound advice and for access to their contacts. In particular, I want to thank Renee Huhs, Todd Lefko, Pat Dowden, and Kendrick White.

Anya Kucharev provided invaluable advice and institutional knowledge about citizen diplomacy. She is one of those people who are indispensable but rarely recognized for her role in the behind-the-scenes implementation of history-making events. Anna revealed to me the breadth and complexity of the citizen diplomacy movement, which has been insufficiently studied and recorded.

Arik Burakovsky and Chris Miller of the Fletcher School Russia and Eurasia Program were also important in the early stages of research for the book through providing support for Fletcher graduate student, Natasha Hill, to catalogue the complex network of US government and private aid programs active in Russia in the 1990s.

Special thanks to Ralph Halpern for his editing assistance and his critical perspective as an informed general reader who is not a Russia specialist. Also special thanks to my lifelong friend George Robinson, who provided moral support and guidance during times in the writing process when I thought I might never finish the book.

It is also important to acknowledge the Russian friends, colleagues, and acquaintances that I made during the late 1980s and 1990s who taught me so much and who did their best to disabuse me of many facile and superficial assumptions about Russia, and, frankly, about life in general.

I am sure that I have been like many other writers who try the patience of their family, spouse, or significant other with their book project obsessions. Like many of them, I want to recognize the support of my wife Dinah and of my family over the years that I pursued my obsession with this book.

Lastly, I want to state clearly that the choice of quotes, the analytic framework, and the conclusions drawn from this project are all mine. Any errors of fact or analysis are also all mine.

Daniel Satinsky
December 2022

Introduction

How do foreigners, particularly Americans, understand Russia? Stereotypes are easy and abundant. From the Russian Revolution of 1917 until the end of the Soviet Union in 1991, Russia was the main geopolitical and ideological foe of the United States, dubbed the "Evil Empire" by President Ronald Reagan. Then, unexpectedly, the Soviet Union was dissolved by President Boris Yeltsin and Russian reformers who sought the material success of the United States and Europe. As of the time of writing of this book, Russia has declared through its invasion of Ukraine that it is at war with the West and the United States. Russia has reverted to the status of strategic foe of the United States, accompanied in the popular media with revived and reinvigorated Cold War stereotypes, tropes, and memes. Once again, Americans are confronted with the question of how to understand Russia and its malevolent destruction of Ukraine against the background of its recent period of integration into the globalizing world and adoption of a market economy with all the social changes that this process brought. It is difficult to view Russia today except through the lens of the war in Ukraine. However, it is necessary to look deeper into the years of the reform period to understand how we got here and what might be possible in the future.

This book presents the experience and conclusions of the many Americans who were active in Russia in the 1980s and 1990s. These citizen diplomats, businesspeople, and government aid program staffers became experts in Russia through their personal experience interacting with Russians in practical circumstances and joint activities. Their point of view and insights have not been part of our understanding of Russia. Instead, the only voices heard on Russia are from expert policymakers and academics that have frameworks that contain within them fundamental flaws, clouding our understanding of this vast and complex country.

There are two such frameworks that bookend the 30 years from the end of the Soviet Union to the present that represent the accepted wisdom of expert opinion of the time than appeared in the leading US foreign policy journal, *Foreign Affairs*, one from Zbigniew Brzezinski in 1992 and the other from Fiona Hill and Angela Stent in 2022.

DOI: 10.4324/9781003182153-1

Zbigniew Brzezinski was the national security advisor to US President Jimmy Carter and one the leading foreign policy strategists of his time. In an article in Foreign Affairs in the fall of 1992, titled "The Cold War and its Aftermath," he stated that:

> The Cold War did end in the victory of one side and in the defeat of the other. This reality cannot be denied, despite the understandable sensitivities that such a conclusion provokes among the tenderhearted in the West and some of the former leaders of the defeated side. ... Most important of all, the Soviet Union itself has crumbled and central Eurasia is now a geopolitical vacuum. ... Indeed, the economic and even political destiny of what was not long ago a threatening superpower is now increasingly passing into de facto Western receivership.[1]

As will be illustrated by the testimony in this book, the end of the Cold War was an ideological defeat for a socialist alternative to modern capitalism, but it did not in fact signal a "de facto receivership" as Brzezinski concluded. In fact, the post-Soviet period in Russia was a repetition of Russian historical patterns of modernization begun by Peter the Great with Russian reformers carrying out top-down modernization and tapping Western technological and managerial expertise for their own purposes, under their own direction in that process.

The period of reintegration of first the Soviet Union, and then Russia, reintegrating into the US-led globalized economy has ended, beginning with the Ukrainian Maidan revolution in 2014 and definitively with the Russian invasion of Ukraine in February 2022. Fiona Hill and Angela Stent correctly locate this period within the historical context of Peter the Great's modernization through importing European expertise in their article "The World Putin Wants," in the September/October 2022 issue Foreign Affairs, as follows:

> Regardless of whether he prevails in Ukraine, Putin's mission is already having a clear and ironic impact, both on Europe and on Russia's 22 years of economic advancement. In asserting Russia's imperial position by seeking to reconquer Ukraine, Putin is reversing one of the greatest achievements of his professed greatest hero. During his reign, Peter the Great opened a window to the West by traveling to Europe, inviting Europeans to come to Russia and help develop its economy, and adopting and adapting European artisans' skills. Vladimir Putin's invasions and territorial expansions have slammed that window shut. They have sent Europeans and their companies back home and pushed a generation of talented Russians fleeing into exile. Peter took Russia into the future. Putin is pushing it back to the past.[2]

However, they also have some mistaken characterizations. The closing of this window began much earlier than they identify. It was a slow process that began after the 1998 economic crisis and accelerated through the 2000s to the final closing of the window to the West in 2022. Further, characterizing closing the window to the West as a return to the past ignores the fundamental changes that began in the late 1980s and accelerated in the 1990s that point to a distinctively Russian future that differs from its Soviet past. It may not be a future that Americans would prefer, but that ethical, moral, or even ideological view is irrelevant to gaining a realistic understanding of Russia.

There are clues to that realistic understanding that can be gleaned from the Americans who actively engaged with Russians in the unique historic period of the 1990s as both eyewitnesses and as active participants in the creation of a new Russian market economy. Russia in 2022 is far from Russia in 1991, as the stories of the Americans in this book will confirm. Unfortunately, their experience and insight are rarely acknowledged or consulted in any analysis of the further evolution of Russia in the 2000s. This book is a contribution to correcting that oversight.

Methodology

When I began this book, my intention was to preserve the history of the 1990s interaction between Americans and Russians that I knew about through my own personal experience. The methodology that I intended to employ would rely on in-depth interviews with Americans active in the Soviet Union and then Russia in the late 1980s and 1990s. This was familiar territory from my own life and experience. I first visited the Soviet Union with a group of attorneys in 1984 and later worked in several Russian American joint ventures, trade promotion organizations, and business consulting until roughly 2014.

The interviews that form the basis of the book were completed between January 2020 and August 2022, with almost all of them completed prior to the Russian invasion of Ukraine on February 24, 2022. I conducted 106 interviews and used material from 65 of them in the final manuscript. The people interviewed were deeply engaged in Russian life in the 1980s and 1990s. These interviews were rich with experience and insight that provided much more information than could possibly be included within the confines of the book. I owe thanks to all who agreed to give me an interview and apologies to all those who spoke with me but were not included in the final text.

It is important to note that the people interviewed are all very strong personalities with their own opinions and recollections of the past. Not all of them liked each other and not all of them remembered things the same way. Some are the subject of controversy. However, within broad parameters, they conveyed a consistent picture of the period, with their differences being footnotes to their collective lived experience. As a general matter, the people interviewed found success in Russia and developed an emotional bond with the Russian people and culture. Their experiences are much less well known than those of people who did not develop the same level of comfort with Russian life, business environment, and culture.

The interviews for the book were concentrated primarily on Americans, with some Europeans and Russians included for context and perspective. The focus on Americans is not intended to diminish the importance of Europeans and multinational agencies in the events and institutions discussed in the book, but there was simply not room to include them. Equally important are the experiences of Russians working with foreigners, encountering the foreign concepts and institutions introduced in this period. They are also deserving of separate treatment but similarly cannot fit within the limits of this volume, with a few exceptions that have been included.

The point of view of the book also differs from traditional academic analysis and from the narrative about Russia that comes from Russian émigrés who are usually members of the highly educated intelligentsia in Moscow or St. Petersburg who interpret Russia to foreigners. While the émigré or English-speaking academic view is certainly important and authoritative, it does not always correspond to the point of view or experience of the non-English speaking majority of Russians. As a Russian friend in Yaroslavl advised me in 1991, "Moscow is not Russia." All the interviews were conducted in English but virtually all the Americans interviewed either could speak Russian when they arrived or learned Russian over the years of living in Russia. This language ability gave them the ability to deeply integrate into Russian life and facilitated the insight that they provided. A good number of those interviewed also were active outside of Moscow and St. Petersburg in the Russian regions.

An area of caution was flagged by one of my interviewees. He warned me about "survivor bias," meaning interviewing only people who had been successful in business and in integrating into Russian society, not those who failed in business or who did not appreciate Russian culture. These successful survivors have quite a different perspective than their peers who did not successfully navigate the Russia of the 1990s. Most general accounts of Russia in the period under discussion focus on the negatives and problematic nature of the country. Presenting the positive experiences of people interviewed can provide a bit of balance, without distorting the overall picture. However, the reader should consider this "survivor bias."

Real-Life Experiences and Stereotypes

The standard big picture overstories or stereotypes about Russia in those years are often focused on the notion of the "Wild East," with anecdotes and accounts of unchecked rampant corruption, violence, and lawlessness. This narrative parallels the American "Wild West" narrative in which there was little law and disputes were resolved by guns or personal violence. In post-Soviet Russia, the narrative of the Wild East focused on mafia wars, the lack of functioning legal norms, and the creation of an extravagant, flamboyant group of super-wealthy oligarchs. Some of these stereotypes were anchored in true events and characteristics of Russian life in these years. However, the stereotypical view is far from the full picture.

Focusing on Russian social, political, and economic dysfunction makes for great stories, page-turning fiction, and exotic journalism, but it is far from the complete story of those years. As with any period of historic and dramatic change, there is a complex story of collapse of the former economic order and opportunity in constructing the new that are simultaneously present, as Russian society went through convulsive change and then found a new equilibrium. The shifting balance away from Western liberal models toward a hybrid Russian nationalist model of society is far more relevant to understanding the current conflict with the West.

Deciding on an organizing structure for the book meant slightly violating the initial intention of letting the interviews speak for themselves. The original framework proved to be impossible because real people act out of a variety of motives and not according to some framework that is simple and easily understandable. Americans came to Russia in the 1990s for a variety of reasons including adventure, ideology, religion, money, and sex. This was a dynamic, chaotic, and constantly changing period. This messy combination of motives, experiences, and their Russian context required a coherent framework for readers who had not been in Russia but who want to understand what really happened. Hopefully, the focus and structure chosen will provide that framework.

Focus and Structure

The focus of the interview excerpts is on how Americans individually and through US government-funded programs participated in the transformation of the Soviet planned economy to a Russian market economy. Within the broad scope of academic and journalistic writing on this period, there is already a substantial body of analysis of the political and geopolitical factors in the transformation of the Soviet Union to the Russian Federation. A great deal has also been written about the Russian natural resource sector and its transformation. Therefore, my focus has been on sectors of the economy less related to the transformation of existing Soviet structures and more on sectors that did not exist in Soviet times in finance and service sectors, like real estate, restaurants and hotels, entertainment and media, telecom and international law firms.

The book is not a complete history of the Soviet Union and Russia in the 1980s and 1990s, but the topics covered need to be placed in a historical context and timeline. So, I have created a selected list of pivotal events for reference purposes as Box I.1. The reader not familiar with these events may need to refer to this list at different points in the book.

Box I.1 Pivotal Events

Citizen Diplomacy:

- 1979. Esalen Institute sent James Hickman and Mary Payne to an international conference on the unconscious in Tbilisi, Georgia, where they met Joseph Goldin, key enabler of citizen diplomacy on the Soviet side.
- November 4, 1980. Ronald Reagan elected US President in a landslide victory over incumbent President Jimmy Carter.
- 1980. First World Conference on Sports and Modern Society in Tbilisi, Georgia led to the formation of the Esalen Soviet-America Program, which organized dozens of cooperative US–USSR programs involving young political leaders and high-ranking government officials, scientists and artists, astronauts and cosmonauts, and leading entertainers from both countries.
- September 1982, Labor Day weekend. First ever live satellite two-way broadcast between the United States and the Soviet Union at the rock and roll "US Festival," initiating a decade of space bridges between the two countries that were seen by millions in both the United States and the Soviet Union.
- March 8, 1983. US President Ronald Reagan pronounces the Soviet Union to be an "Evil Empire" and the "focus of evil in the modern world."
- March 23, 1983. President Ronald Reagan announces the US strategic defense initiative, what came to be called the "Star Wars" program.
- May 30, 1983, Memorial Day. Second US Festival.
- September 1, 1983. Soviet aircraft shoot down Korean Airlines flight 007, killing all 269 passengers.
- September 16,1983, Sharon Tennison and delegation of 20 people, plus PBS crew depart San Francisco for her first trip to the Soviet Union with a citizen-to-citizen delegation, which was the forerunner of hundreds of such exchanges to follow.

Gorbachev Period:

- March 11, 1985. Mikhail Gorbachev becomes General Secretary of CPSU.
- June 6, 1985. The first computer conference between the United States and the USSR was organized by Joel Schatz and Oleg Smirnov of the All-Union Scientific Research Institute for Applied Automated Systems (VNIIPAS).
- 1987. Gorbachev initiated the policies of Glasnost (openness) and Perestroika (socialist reconstruction).

- January 1, 1987. New Soviet "Law on Joint Ventures" enacted allowing Soviet entities to pair with foreign companies for foreign trade.
- June 30, 1987. New Soviet "Law on State Enterprises" enacted giving more autonomy to state enterprises, including freedom of export, right to form joint companies with foreign partners, and the right to have their own foreign currency accounts.
- May 1988. New Soviet "Law on Cooperatives" enacted allowing independent, worker-owned cooperatives.
- September 1989. Boris Yeltsin visited the United States on a trip organized and managed by Esalen Institute.
- November 9, 1989. Fall of Berlin Wall.
- December 1990: US President George Bush starts to provide economic assistance to Russia.
- June 12, 1991. Boris Yeltsin elected president of the Russian Soviet Federative Socialist Republic (RSFSR).
- August 1991. Coup attempt against Gorbachev was successfully resisted by forces led by Boris Yeltsin.
- September 6, 1991. The Soviet Union recognized the independence of the former Soviet Republics of Lithuania, Latvia, and Estonia.
- December 8, 1991. The Belavezha Accords were negotiated and agreed upon by President Boris Yeltsin and First Deputy Prime Minister Gennady Burbulis, representing the Russian Federation; Chairman of the Parliament Stanislav Shushkevich and Prime Minister Vyacheslav Kebich, representing Belarus; and President Leonid Kravchuk and Prime Minister Vitold Fokin, representing Ukraine, which declared the Soviet Union no longer existed.
- December 21, 1991. Representatives of 11 of the 12 remaining Soviet republics, excluding Georgia, signed the Alma-Ata Protocol, which confirmed the extinction of the Soviet Union and established the Commonwealth of Independent States.
- December 25, 1991. Gorbachev resigned and confirmed the formal dissolution of the Soviet Union.

Yeltsin Period:

- December 3, 1991. President Yeltsin signed a decree ending price controls on wholesale and retail goods, except for some essentials like sugar, salt, bread, gasoline, vodka, and milk, that took effect on January 2, 1992.
- December 3, 1991. The Committee on State Security (KGB) was restructured, and its functions were divided among several different independent agencies, including the Federal Service of

Counterintelligence (FSB), Foreign Intelligence Service (SVR), Federal Agency for Government Communications (FAPSI), Federal Protective Service, Federal Border Service, and others.

- July 1, 1992. The Russian ruble became a fully convertible currency.
- December 1992–June 1994. The Yeltsin Administration conducted voucher privatization of state property through coupons issued to every Russian citizen, with 15,000 firms privatized.
- September 21–October 4, 1993. President Yeltsin suspended the Russian Supreme Soviet (Parliament), accusing it of obstructing political and economic reforms. Vice President Alexander Rutskoy called Yeltsin's decree unconstitutional and Supreme Soviet voted to impeach Yeltsin and confirmed Rutskoy as President. On October 4, Yeltsin crushed the Soviet with a military assault on the Soviet, led by tanks.
- December 12, 1993. President Yeltsin pushed through a new Russian constitution by referendum, replacing the 1978 Soviet Constitution and creating a strong Presidency with sweeping power to enter decrees.
- November 1994. President Yeltsin strengthened the powers of the Russian equivalent of the US SEC, the Federal Commission on the Stock Market (FCSM). Anatoly Chubais, the first deputy prime minister in charge of the economy, was appointed as the top official of the new commission.
- April 12, 1995. President Yeltsin signed a law reorganizing the Federal Counterintelligence Service (FSK) of Russia as the Federal Security Service of the Russian Federation (FSB).
- 1996. Loans-for-Shares. President Yeltsin adopted a "loans-for-shares" program with some of the largest state industrial assets designated for auction in return for loans to the government by commercial banks, with ownership ultimately passing to these banks.
- July 1996. President Yeltsin won a narrow second round election victory over the Communist Party candidate, Gennady Zyuganov.
- July 25, 1998. President Yeltsin names Vladimir Putin as head of the FSB.
- August 17, 1998. The Russian government devalued the ruble, defaulted on ruble-denominated domestic debt instruments and declared a moratorium on repayment of foreign debt.
- August 9, 1999. President Yeltsin fired Prime Minister Sergei Stepashin and named Vladimir Putin as Prime Minister.
- New Year's Eve, 1999. Yeltsin announced his resignation from office and named Vladimir Putin as acting president until a March 26, 2000, election.

Chapter Topics

Chapter 1 describes the citizen diplomacy movement of the 1980s and the growing contact between Americans and Russians in face of the threat of nuclear war that is a prelude to the post-Soviet interaction. These direct contacts led to the first civil society exchanges and the first Soviet-era Russian–American joint ventures during the Gorbachev period.

Chapter 2 covers US government aid programs and private agency programs in support of the Yeltsin era political and economic reforms after the dissolution of the Soviet Union. The chapter describes American support for the transition to a market economy and training provided for the nascent Russian civil society.

Chapter 3 focuses on the privatization of state property and the creation of capital markets to replace state planning mechanisms. This process was driven primarily by Russians but relied heavily on US government-funded consultants and American private entrepreneurs. New institutions like a stock exchange, investment banks, and private equity funds were created with US government support and private collaboration between Russians and Americans. It includes an overview of the importance of the 1996 Presidential election and the loans-for-shares program and the significance of the August 1998 financial crisis.

Chapter 4 describes the dramatic changes in the institutions of everyday life that came from the creation of new private sector businesses in sectors that either did not exist in the Soviet Union or which had very different purposes. It covers the development of new businesses in real estate, restaurants, and hotels, media and entertainment, telecom and the entry of international law firms that all contributed to fundamental changes in how Russians live, eat, entertain themselves, and communicate.

Chapter 5 summarizes the significance of American participation in Russia and emphasizes the ongoing impact of Americans on the Russian economy. It suggests lessons learned from the 1990s that are important for future US–Russia relations.

Analytic Themes

Equally important to the structure of the book are four themes that repeat throughout the book. The first is the impact of almost 75 years of the Soviet Union on the institutions, values, culture, expectations, and style of life of the generations who matured under that system. The second is the pattern in Russian history of looking to the West for expertise in modernizing perceived Russian backwardness. The third is the question of political control and agency, i.e., the balance between Russian and foreign control of the reform process. The fourth is the necessity of evaluating change, success, and failure in a historical context for a country that has existed and survived so much over the period of its existence.

Transformation from Soviet Planned Economy to Russian Market Economy

To better understand the transformation from the Soviet planned economy to the reformed Russia market economy, it is important to understand some very simplistic, but fundamental aspects of the Soviet economy. These basic foundations of the Soviet economy are central to understanding the profound nature of the Yeltsin era transformation and the challenges facing both the Russians who led it and the foreigners who assisted them.

First and foremost, in the Soviet period, private enterprise was illegal. So-called "speculators," people who engaged in private business, were prosecuted as criminals. Of course, there was influence pedaling of various sorts and exchange of favors, but this informal side of socialism was quite different than ongoing private business. As a result, there was little or no widescale experience with how to start and operate a private business until adoption of the Soviet Law on Cooperatives in May 1988.

There was also the related notion that the wealth of the country belonged to Russians as a whole, the patrimony of the Russian people. This feeling was expressed in widespread opinion that successful businesspeople in the 1990s had to be crooks. Regarding foreigners, I often heard ordinary Russians ask, "Why should foreigners be allowed to come to Russia and make money from Russian land and resources?"

Second, in the planned economy, the function of money was completely different than in a market economy. In the planned economy, money was an input allocated by the planning agencies. It was not an independent indicator of value or measure of success. Therefore, while there were banks in Soviet times who had an instrumental role in transfers of money per planning directives, there were no financial institutions as we know them in a capitalist market economy that served an important market function. The Soviet Law on Cooperatives allowed for the beginning of private banks as we shall see in Chapter 1. The real growth in new institutions of Russian capital markets was heavily influenced by Americans as will be described in Chapter 3.

Third, there was no private ownership of land. People were registered as occupants of apartments, giving them certain rights, including inheritance, but they did not own the apartment or building. The same was true of country dacha plots that were allocated and registered but ultimately were not individually owned. Therefore, there was no experience with renting, buying, and selling real estate. The evolution of the new Russian real estate sector in the 1990s will be covered in Chapter 4.

Fourth, media, movies, restaurants, retail stores, telecom, and other services were all state owned. These types of enterprises existed under the Soviet Union, but with different purposes and forms than in a market economy with private ownership. In general, these enterprises were subjugated to state political objectives and were quite different in form and content from analogous businesses in Western consumer society. This is another sector of the Russian economy in which Americans played an important role as will be described in Chapter 4.

Fifth, the planned economy of the Soviet Union was a separate and all-encompassing economic system, with its own accounting systems, legal system, operational procedures, distribution networks, scientific institutions, and means of distributing consumer goods. These separate processes and procedures existed in parallel with processes and procedures in the Western-led global market economy. Integration into the global economy required mastering the standards, processes, and procedures of the Western-led global market economy. This transformation is an aspect of integration of Russia into the global economy that will be covered in Chapters 2 and 4.

Russian Historical Pattern of Modernization

There is a well-established Russian historical pattern of borrowing Western expertise to modernize its economy that echoes through the Yeltsin period under consideration. Strong leaders, like Peter the Great and Joseph Stalin, have implemented top-down modernization, featuring state-led industrial policy, importation of foreign experts and machinery to bridge the gap with Western competitors, along with educational reform to prepare Russian experts for the newly modernized economy. It is a repetitive pattern that consciously or not reoccurs in the 1990s with importation of foreigners interviewed for the book who were later replaced by Russians who assimilated Western expertise through work experience or education.

Peter the First or Peter the Great, Tsar/Emperor, 1682–1725, initiated a top-down, coercive, state-led economic development in Russia that was facilitated by foreign expertise. Peter implemented a comprehensive industrial policy principally to support his military ambitions. In those times, Russia was an agricultural society with only a tiny industrial sector, but Peter's military ambitions required industry to equip his army and navy.

In pursuing the creation of the new industrial sector, Peter required technical and managerial expertise that simply did not exist in Russia. Peter tackled this problem by establishing a new educational system in Russia and by recruiting foreign experts. The Pulitzer Prize winning biographer of Peter the Great, Robert K. Massie, wrote, "None of Peter's work in developing the national economy would have been possible without the foreign experts and craftsmen who poured into Russia between the time of Peter's return from the West in 1698 and his death in 1725. The Tsar engaged more than a thousand foreigners during his first visit to Amsterdam and London, and thereafter Russian envoys and agents at foreign courts were urgently commissioned to search out and persuade local artisans and technicians to enter Russian service."[3] The pattern of Russian economic reform, relying on foreign models and experts, became well-established from this historical period forward.

Joseph Stalin's modernization was not a literal repeat, but the general outlines were analogous, with a strong centralized state needing to modernize its industry and to support its military.

The Soviet state created a vastly expanded educational system to create a new cadre of "Red experts and engineers" and to lead the cultural transformation into the "Soviet Man" to carry out the ambitious scope of Soviet transformation of Russian industry. In his study of the industrialization of Russia, William L. Blackwell highlighted the important role of foreigners. "During most of the Stalinist industrialization drive, Russia, in one way or another, had to rely heavily on the technology of the West. Western knowledge, in the form of books and research, was assimilated on a large scale in the technical schools and institutes."[4] More importantly, the Soviet Union relied on "the time-honored practices of importing machinery ..., sending students to study abroad, or contracting with foreign technicians to come to do the job ..."[5] Blackwell goes on to explain that "The United States came to be venerated as the ultimate repository of advanced technique, and as many as 5,000 American engineers have been estimated to have been employed by the Soviet government during the 1930's. Some of this number were experienced engineers; others, politically sympathetic skilled workers ..."[6] These skilled workers included two of the Reuther brothers, who were instrumental in later creating the United Auto Workers in the United States and whose descendent was a key person in the first real estate joint venture in Moscow in the 1980s, as we will see in Chapter 4.

The involvement of Americans in Soviet industrialization was not limited to individuals but included a roster of prominent US companies. "The Soviet government, for its part, made no secret of the many large American firms that had contracted to build factories, dams, shipyards, refineries, roads, apartment houses, and even new cities in Russia. Ford, General Electric, Sperry, and RCA are among the more prominent American concerns in a list of 25 appended to the English edition of the First Five Year Plan."[7] This history repeated itself with the movement of multinational companies into Russia during the course of the 1990s.

At the same time, there were important differences from prior Russian experience with modernization. The top-down modernization of the Yeltsin period was carried out by a weak state, not a strong one. Russia went into an economic depression; oil prices were very low and the rapid decline of the role of the Communist Party opened the country to many competing regional and sectoral power centers. Yeltsin did not have the levers of coercion that were wielded by Peter the Great or Stalin to force compliance with his agenda.

On the other hand, there were factors that favored modernization. As opposed to the socially backward conditions of the Russian population in the Peter the Great and Stalin periods, Russia had a highly literate well-educated population, an existing industrial base and its own established institutions of science and technology. Russia of the 1990s differed dramatically from the peasant dominated, poorly educated population during the first two periods of rapid modernization. These differences gave modern Russia the potential to much more rapidly reform and modernize, with less overt state coercion. However, as we shall see, state coercion of the prior periods was replaced in the 1990s by private violence and cronyism in the disorderly process of dividing up former state property into private property and creating the institutions of a market economy.

It is not clear that either the political leadership of Yeltsin era Russia or the foreigners who rushed into Russia after the dissolution of the Soviet Union were themselves conscious of this historical background. Nonetheless, the Russian leadership was facing similar problems and implemented similar solutions as in the times of Peter the Great and Joseph Stalin. The use of this framework is useful in understanding some of the patterns of change during the 1990s.

Political Control and Agency in the Reform of Russia

Americans are used to putting themselves in the foreground in almost any scenario. In this case, Americans and other foreigners were important players but not the decisive actors in constructing the new Russian market economy. Foreigners, including Americans, had an important role in providing tools, concepts, expertise, and money that played an important ancillary role in how the Russian market economy developed, particularly in the industry sectors covered in this book. However, it is important to place this role in its proper perspective. As many of those interviewed stated, foreigners were guests in Russia and ultimately Russian elites decided how their society should be organized.

In the Yeltsin era, there is an implicit question of who or what interests were driving the shape and directions of Russian market reforms? Were events and policies driven by Russians or by foreigners, particularly Americans? If by Russians, then there is a further question of which Russians, given that there were many contending power centers and interests in Russia at that time. Putting these questions another way, who was responsible or, depending upon your perspective, who was to blame for the 1990s and their consequences in the 2000s?

The point of view of this book is that what happened in Russia in the 1990s was primarily driven by Russian interests and Russian interest groups. Foreigners were invited into Russia and penetrated very deeply into Russian life, economy, and culture, financed by powerful foreign institutions like US Agency for International Development (USAID), the World Bank, and many diverse aid programs financed by foreign governments and private institutions. As much as they were able to teach, lecture, train, cajole, and harass Russian officials into following their lead, the ultimate decisions on the shape of reform in Russia were made by Russians. As different interest groups jostled for power in post-Soviet Russia, the primacy of various individuals and centers of power shifted over time, but these changes were increasingly independent from foreign influence.

As we shall see, individual Americans and other foreigners came to Russia in the Yeltsin period for a variety of reasons. From the perspective of history, regardless of their personal motivations, they played a role in modernizing Russia in the 1990s analogous to previous waves of foreigners in Russia in the Peter the Great and Stalin eras. On an institutional level, American policymakers were never completely clear on their priorities in Russia, with changes throughout the period. What is clear is that there was a massive financial commitment to shaping the new Russia into a country with values, economic structures, and institutions compatible with America. This financial commitment politically and economically supported the Russian reformers and facilitated the historical pattern underlying Russian reform.

Russian History of Resilience

The early 1990s saw the largest influx of Americans into Russia in history. Americans encountered a confused half-Soviet, aspiring market economy that presented huge opportunities and huge dangers. Most of us who were active in Russia then thought that we were witnessing a new era of historical change in Russia that was different than anything that had occurred in the past. The Soviet Union had "lost" the Cold War and was in an era of irreversible fundamental change that required them to adapt to our rules and ways of doing business. Most of us read this history incorrectly.

I remember distinctly when the scope of Russian history was driven home to me most decisively. In 1993, I made a business trip to Uglich. It is a city of around 35,000 people located on the banks of the Volga River in the Yaroslavl' Region, 180 miles or so north of Moscow. At the entrance of the city, there is a small sign indicating that Uglich was founded in 937.

The idea of a place being in existence for more than a thousand years was difficult to assimilate. Not only has Uglich existed that long, but it has played an interesting role in Russian history. It is the site where Ivan the Terrible killed his youngest son in 1581. It is also the historic homeland of the Smirnoff family of vodka fame, who fled during the Russian Revolution and Civil War in 1919. In Soviet times, Uglich became the site of the Chaika Watch Factory, the largest watch manufacturer in the Soviet Union.

With the dissolution of the Soviet Union, Chaika lost its exclusive markets in the former Soviet Republics and its state sources of capital, while facing aggressive international competitors. The workers were not being paid and the factory had no funds to modernize its equipment. During my visit, the general director broke out the vodka at noon and shared his business plan that a Russian consultant had created for him with a template taken from the Internet. His goal was to use this business plan to raise money that would replace the money that had been allocated by the centrally planned economy with either foreign or domestic investment to make the plant competitive. He offered me the opportunity to solicit investors based on his business plan.

The problem was that the business plan had no chance of receiving funding from any foreign investor. There was no mention in the plan of the most elementary information that any investor would want to know, including when and how they would profit from this investment. In his conception of things, investors were supposed to just put money into the factory, with no promise of shares in the company or interest-bearing loans to secure the investment. The general director wanted to preserve his enterprise just as it was in Soviet times, but without any outsider shareholder interference. I politely thanked him and left knowing that he faced a tough road ahead attracting any foreign investment.

As I was leaving Uglich, I thought again about the founding date of 937 and all the historic difficulties that the inhabitants of Uglich have faced in the millennium or so of its existence. It occurred to me that despite the lack of Western business skills and understanding of capital markets, maybe these folks would figure out something after all. I did not know how and still do not to this day. But I do know that they managed to preserve Chaika as a maker of high-end, jewel-encrusted watches for a niche market. It was somehow accomplished in a Russian way.

Along the same lines, I remember also quite distinctly a famous article in *The Atlantic Monthly*, May 2001, by Jeffrey Tayler with the title, "Russia is Finished," with the subtitle, "The unstoppable descent of a once great power into social catastrophe and strategic irrelevance." The assumptions of this article ignored again the historical fact of Russian resilience and resurgence over time. The same historically blind assumptions about the fate of Russia continued throughout the 1990s and the 2000s, even in the face of Russia's renewed importance both economically and politically.

The point of this story is that Russians have persevered through countless ups and downs of fate and are resilient and self-reliant. It is a mistake to look at Russia as it is at some point of time and assume that it will stay that way without change. Therefore, an historical perspective and narrative is critical not only to explain the trajectory of Russia in the years under consideration, but as a necessary corrective to overly conclusive projections of its future. Hopefully, it will be a contribution to a better future.

Notes

1 Zbigniew Brzezinski, "The Cold War and Its Aftermath," *Foreign Affairs* (Fall 1992), www.foreignaffairs.com (www.foreignaffairs.com/articles/russia-fsu/1992-09-01/cold-war-and-its-aftermath paid subscriber access only).

2 Fiona Hill and Angela Stent, "The World Putin Wants – How Distortions About the Past Feed Delusions About the Future," *Foreign Affairs* 101, no. 5 (2022): 122.

3 Robert K. Massie, *Peter the Great – His Life and World* (New York: Alfred K. Knopf, 1980), 774.
4 William L. Blackwell, *The Industrialization of Russia – An Historical Perspective* (New York: Thomas Y. Crowell Company, 1970), 130.
5 Blackwell, *The Industrialization of Russia – An Historical Perspective*, 130.
6 Blackwell, *The Industrialization of Russia – An Historical Perspective*, 131.
7 Blackwell, *The Industrialization of Russia – An Historical Perspective*, 131.

1 The Permeable Iron Curtain

Citizen Diplomacy and American Soviet Joint Ventures

"Live from Moscow. It's Saturday night," my friend, Rick Lukens, and I screamed as the popular Soviet rock band, Arsenal, blasted its signature song over the airwaves. Behind us, in the USSR's best television studio, danced several hundred 18–25-year-old Russians and some Soviet Communist Party officials to celebrate the historic event – the first ever live by satellite interaction between people from the United States and the Soviet Union.

It was Labor Day weekend, September 1982. On the world stage, 60,000 nuclear warheads were poised to initiate Armageddon if leaders of either the US or the USSR (Union of Soviet Socialist Republics) believed the other country was about to launch a nuclear missile. On the California stage, the Australian band, Men at Work, rocked the fan-filled 60-acre amphitheater. While in the Moscow studio stage, ecstatic young Russians cried from joy because, as one 19-year-old rocker said 'I am shaken to the core. Something has changed inside me … I feel a spiritual uplift.

(James Hickman, First Director, Esalen Institute Soviet American Exchange Program, Interview on November 21, 2021)

The story of large-scale interaction between Americans and Russians begins in the shadow of the height of the Cold War with the citizen diplomacy movement. In the 1980s, there was legitimate fear that the United States and Russia would exchange nuclear attacks on each other under the military doctrine of "Mutually Assured Destruction." In a speech to the National Association of Evangelicals on March 8, 1983, US President Ronald Reagan declared that the Soviet Union was an "evil empire" and the "focus of evil in the modern world." This was the era in which President Reagan labeled the Soviet Union as the "Evil Empire." Also in 1983, US scientists developed a model of the impact of 100 or more nuclear explosions creating a worldwide "nuclear winter." Fear of nuclear war led to the growth of broad and diverse grass roots peace organizations who engaged in what came to be called "citizen diplomacy" with the Soviet Union. The citizen diplomacy movement believed that through breaking the communications barriers between the West and the

DOI: 10.4324/9781003182153-2

Soviet Union and through people-to-people contact, war could be avoided. The activists of this movement broke new ground using new technologies like the satellite telecommunications that enabled the rock and roll concert exchange of the US Festival in 1982, supplemented by increasing personal contacts and travel by peace activists to the Soviet Union. This period was a prequel for the much broader and deeper interactions between Americans and Russians to follow in the 1990s. It was a movement that sowed the seeds of American promotion of civil society organizations and American–Soviet joint ventures as private sector prototypes that blossomed in post-Soviet Russia.

The citizen diplomacy movement was a broad and deep involvement of great diversity, which makes it difficult to capture concisely. There is no general history of this movement, so the accounts here will feature only certain aspects relevant to the events that follow in the 1990s. It arose at a time when there were relatively strong independent peace organizations in the United States coming out of the opposition to the Vietnam War, ongoing counterculture organizations that also developed in the 1970s that were exploring alternate views of life and reality and a different set of sources of information in the pre-ubiquitous Internet era.

The term "citizen diplomacy" began to be recognized in diplomatic circles as a separate forum of international relations. In a seminal article in *Foreign Policy* quarterly (Winter 81–82), Joseph V. Montville, a Foreign Service officer in the State Department defined the official channel of government-to-government relations as "track one diplomacy" and the unofficial channel of people-to-people relations as "track two diplomacy." Montville argued that the second track is "a supplement to the understandable shortcomings of official relations."[1] What remains of citizen diplomacy in current times is often referred to as track two diplomacy.

Perhaps the most visible of the citizen diplomacy organizations was the International Physicians for Prevention of Nuclear War that was founded in 1980 by Dr. Bernard Lown, Harvard Medical School, inventor of the defibrillator, and by Dr. Evgeny Chasov, personal physician to Leonid Brezhnev. By 1984, this organization had grown to 70,000 affiliated members in 43 countries. However, there were many more similar or related organizations with the same objectives at that time. This chapter will describe the activities of the most relevant organizations that impacted the post-Soviet period.

California Dreaming – Counter-Cultural Roots of Citizen Diplomacy

California is the recognized center of the counter-cultural movements of the 1960s and 1970s. There was an atmosphere of openness and questioning, along with an active peace movement that supported the movement to prevent nuclear war through mutual understanding. There was also a network of people with inherited wealth, like Henry Dakin in San Francisco and Harriett Crosby in Washington, DC, with her circle of like-minded "Doughnuts," who provided financial support for the citizen diplomacy initiatives. The pioneering activities of the Esalen Institute and the space bridge activities moved citizen diplomacy from the margins of society into the mainstream with lasting impact.

Esalen Institute – Human Potential Research Morphs into Citizen Diplomacy

Esalen Institute was a groundbreaking leader in setting the stage for literally hundreds of citizen diplomacy organizations in the 1980s. Founded in 1962, it is a key institutional component of the human potential movement, sometimes popularly referred to as New Age philosophy. The Esalen connection with the Soviet Union began in the 1970s when one of its co-founders, Michael Murphy, visited the Soviet Union as a guest of the Soviet Academy of Sciences. He was aware that there were overlapping areas of research in parapsychology and human development for which there may be common ground.

Then, in 1979, Michael Murphy dispatched two young researchers, James Hickman and Mary Payne, to represent Esalen at the "International Symposium on the Problem of the Unconscious" in Tbilisi, Georgia. This conference was the first official recognition of the idea of the unconscious by official researchers in the Soviet Union and was part of their own research into human potential.

Jim Hickman was a former draft resister and parapsychology researcher who was aware of Soviet research into human potential. He first went to the Soviet Union in 1972 and spent several years collaborating with parapsychologists in the Soviet Union, particularly studying energy fields around living systems before becoming affiliated with Esalen.

In preparation for the trip to Tbilisi, Michael Murphy reached out to Anya Kucharev, whose parents had been forced out of the Soviet Union and came to the United States as displaced people after World War II. She was teaching Russian at a military school in the area and was exploring Esalen and its philosophy. Anya introduced Michael, Jim Hickman, and Mary Payne to a number of Soviet émigré intellectuals in the Bay Area as a kind of cultural preparation for the trip to the Soviet Union. She became more and more involved with Esalen's Soviet program as a cultural and linguistic go between.

Almost always in the background, Anya played a key role in the success of many of the space bridges and other Esalen affiliated activities. As Anya expressed it in our interview, "… if you look at history and how it's made, it's made by individuals who connect, whether they fight or they fall in love, personal relationships are important." Anya was a connector of people in this sense and the source of considerable insight on the citizen diplomacy movement.

During the 1979 Tbilisi conference visit, Hickman met Joseph Goldin, one of the principal Soviet organizers of the conference, who was to play a critical role on the Russian side fostering citizen diplomacy. In most English-language sources, Goldin appears as a somewhat mysterious figure, who is variously described as a visionary, dissident, and entrepreneur who somehow had very good connections in the Soviet scientific and media circles.

A more complete picture of Goldin as a key figure on the Soviet side appears in a February 2016 post in Russian in *Live Journal* by A.V. Sazikov that includes an extensive biography and evaluation of Goldin's role on the Soviet side for many of the key citizen diplomacy activities of this period.[2] Goldin's participation in these activities is an example of a pattern that repeats over and over again, where success depends not only on the intentions of the US side, but on mutual interests of both sides. These interests did not have to be the same, but they needed to be close enough to allow for enthusiastic joint activity.

According to Sazikov, Goldin was a graduate PhD candidate at the Institute of Biophysics of the Soviet Academy of Sciences and while there began research into human potential and hidden human reserves. He became the scientific secretary of a Commission for the Complex Study of Man organized within the Soviet Academy of Sciences, which was exploring human potential and human reserves. As Anya Kucharev explained, "this was a group that was looking at the fact that they were in stagnation, when they had so many brilliant people. We know that it was the Brezhnev period of stagnation and all that, but how do we [Soviets] bust out of that without winding up in jail. So, this Commission was their vehicle for very far thinking on this topic." Goldin's business card had a graphic on it that read "Expedition to the Hidden Reserves Center."[3] At some point in his career, he had been in the merchant marine so knew about the broader world from personal experience. He also was a screen writer and became acquainted with people in the film industry and in theater through this activity.

For his part, Goldin proposed a global project of a "Mirror for Humanity" for exchanges that would help the world avoid nuclear war and nuclear winter. Vladimir Posner, who later was to be a key figure in moderating US–Soviet space bridges, remembers, "He considered that if all the large cities of the world constructed gigantic television screens allowing people to not only see each other, but discuss and converse, this would help prevent war. Joseph was a dreamer from one side – a romantic-idealist and from the other side an absolute pragmatic who knew exactly how to achieve his wishes."[4]

Goldin promoted his ideas for global communications not only within the Academy of Sciences but also among high-ranking government officials, importantly gaining support from Anatoly Dobrynin, the Soviet Ambassador to the United States, which became important in the history of the space bridges.

In the opaque world of the Soviet Union, Goldin appeared to the Americans to be a determined visionary without any visible official position of influence, but nonetheless he was instrumental in introducing Hickman and other citizen diplomacy pioneers to influential people in the Soviet government as a kind of "fixer" who got things done and got connections made. Behind the scenes, Goldin had standing and political capital within the Soviet Academy of Sciences as a representative of a trend of thinking among others who facilitated citizen diplomacy on the Soviet side. He ultimately served as a board member for Esalen and later lived in California for several years.

Returning to the beginnings of citizen diplomacy, Hickman came back from the 1979 Tbilisi conference after a several weeks stay in the Soviet Union and convinced Michael Murphy and his wife Dulce that the overlapping research interests with Soviet scientists and the opening for private, non-governmental communication channels was worthy of institutionalized support. Convinced of the importance of these channels, Dulce Murphy founded the Esalen Institute Soviet American Exchange Program (later called Track Two), in 1979, with Jim Hickman as the first director. The initial contact between Americans and Soviet counterparts around research into esoteric areas of auras and hidden human potential became a wide-ranging citizen diplomacy effort through the new Esalen Institute Soviet American Exchange Program.

Esalen became the centerpiece for several important private exchange channels with the Soviet Union, including the space bridge era that will be described below. It also engaged in bringing several high-level Russian political figures to the United States. In 1988, Esalen brought Abel Aganbegyan, one of Mikhail Gorbachev's chief economic advisors, to the United States. In 1989, Esalen brought Boris Yeltsin on his first trip to the United States and arranged meetings for Yeltsin with then President George H. W. Bush as well as many other leaders in business and government.

The trip included a famous unplanned stop at Randalls grocery store on the way to Johnson City, Texas, that reportedly had a huge impact on Yeltsin's views on socialism in his own country. After wandering the aisles looking at the abundance of meat, produce, and staple goods, he stated in his biography, "When I saw those shelves crammed with hundreds, thousands of cans, cartons, and goods of every possible sort, for the first time I felt quite frankly sick with despair for the Soviet people. … That such a potentially super-rich country as ours has been brought to a state of such poverty! It is terrible to think of it."[5] Two years later, Yeltsin resigned from the Communist Party. The relative impact of this visit to Randalls grocery store on that decision is an open question, but the exchanges organized by Esalen for top-level Russian leaders undoubtedly had an impact on their thinking and actions.

These leadership exchanges are only a part of the story. Hickman was also active in promoting path-breaking musical exchanges, including for John Denver, Paul Winter Consort, and Billy Joel. He and US Astronaut Rusty Schweickart also played an instrumental role in organizing a series of Astronaut/Cosmonaut Dialogues between 1982 and 1985 that resulted in the formation of the Association of Space Explorers in 1985, an organization that includes all the people who have flown in space.

All these activities broke barriers and the accepted beliefs of the time, not to mention causing suspicion from the security services of both countries. Hickman and his colleagues at Esalen, already considered to be cultural oddities in the 1980's United States, were not deterred by doubters and sought to do what was considered impossible. Perhaps the most outstanding example is the initiation of a series of dialogues between Americans and Russians over satellite TV, space bridges.

Space Bridges – Citizen Diplomacy Takes a Technological Leap

The combination of activist citizen diplomacy and leading-edge technology concentrated in California led to a series of "space bridges," a term derived from the Russian word "telemost." These space bridges were live satellite-linked TV broadcasts, with the opportunity for direct dialogue between Americans and Russians broadcast to mass audiences in each country. The narrow confines of previous citizen diplomacy were expanded to include millions of people in an unprecedented exchange between people in the Cold War adversaries.

In the 2021 interview with Jim Hickman, he discussed the origin of space bridge TV transmissions between the United States and USSR and explained, "Well, it wasn't one person's idea, it was a variety of people who brought the idea into, you know, into this world in a sense, and through a wide variety of sort of synchronicity events." The key people involved on the US side were all loosely connected through circles around Esalen, including Jim Hickman, Kim Spencer, and Evelyn Messinger.

Kim Spencer, Evelyn Messinger, and several of their activist producer friends, David Hoffman and Paul Greenberg, had formed a non-profit company, Internews Network, with the intention of pursuing satellite broadcast opportunities, initially on Public Broadcast Stations. Kim Spencer produced the first independent live satellite TV broadcast, when he put together a broadcast of the May 6, 1979, Three Mile Island protest in Washington, DC. Then, in 1980, Kim and Evelyn worked on a live satellite PBS broadcast on Thanksgiving called "America at Thanksgiving" with families across the United States talking to each other via satellite in a program moderated by Art Buchwald. The broadcast was groundbreaking in providing a real opportunity for dialogue between the families that was totally new and unexpected, providing Kim and Evelyn the inspiration for thinking about other uses of this technology, including for promotion of dialogue with the Soviet Union. As Kim Spencer remembers it, "Evelyn was editing, and we were looking at this footage. Evelyn said wouldn't it be amazing if we could use this technology to get Russians and Americans to talk face to face by satellite, connecting Russians and Americans face to face. We could call it 'the second kitchen debate' [following the first 'kitchen debate' between Nixon and Khrushchev during Nixon's visit to Moscow in 1959]."

The idea of using satellite technology to bridge the gap between people in the United States and the Soviet Union was beginning to bubble up among a number of people. While Evelyn Messinger is generally credited as the co-creator of the space bridge concept in the United States, in the interview in April 2021 for this book, she said that she had the idea of creating a space bridge at the same time as Joseph Goldin, without actually knowing Goldin. Accordingly, she thought of herself as the American co-creator.

Around the same time, Stephen Wozniak, Apple computer designer, was initiating the US Festival as "a celebration combining innovative communications and computer technology with the universal language of music and song to encourage cooperation and understanding among young people throughout the world." The festival featured the rock & roll superstars of the day, The Police, The Grateful Dead, Jackson Browne among others, alongside a high-tech fair that emphasized the balance between serving oneself and serving others – in other words, serving "us."

Hickman recounted that in a late-night brainstorming session with Wozniak and the Festival executives Richard Lukens wondered: "Would it be possible to have the Russians participate via live satellite link-up?" Though seemingly remote, the possibility excited the production team as a dramatic example of the festival's theme. The Festival Producers, Peter Ellis, and Peter Gerwe, endorsed the concept and encouraged its development. Richard Lukens was familiar with the Esalen Institute Soviet American Exchange Program and he knew Jim Hickman, the director of the Esalen program, so he approached Jim with the idea of a satellite link-up.

At the time, Hickman knew almost nothing about the technology, but he did have excellent connections in Russia through Joseph Goldin and an indomitable adventurous spirit. On the Russian side, in addition to Joseph Goldin, there were several young technicians, producers, and media figures who enthusiastically embraced and implemented the idea. Of course, in the background on the Russian side were the so-called "men of the 60s," reformers who were beginning the changes that were later articulated in Gorbachev's policies of glasnost and perestroika.

Hickman decided to bootstrap a project he was engaged in to assemble astronauts from both countries to discuss the psychological and spiritual impact of their experiences in space as an opportunity to discuss the space bridge idea with Soviet officials.

"With guidance and significant work from Joseph Goldin, Rusty and I visited Moscow several times to further the Astronaut/Cosmonaut project within the Soviet bureaucracy. One such trip coincided with the US Festival proposal. Because Cosmonauts represented human space flight, which was the greatest scientific accomplishment in Soviet history, they were extremely respected and influential. To the Soviets, a US Astronaut coming to Moscow for discussions was a very serious matter. As this gave us access to the corridors of power, we intended to leverage this on behalf of the US Festival. Perceptions and attitudes were the crucial elements we would use in attaining a positive decision."

The idea of a space link between America and Soviet Union during the US Festival was similar to Joseph Goldin's idea of putting up big screens on the main streets of Moscow so he supported the idea and became a critical door opener for the project, including introducing Hickman and US Astronaut Rusty Schweickart to the Soviet Vice Minister of Communications.

Hickman continued, "Toward the end of that Moscow trip, Rusty met with a very powerful Soviet leader who was charged with deciding whether to hold an astronaut-cosmonaut meeting – what would become the Association of Space Explorers or ASE. Today, ASE is the official organization of all people who have flown in space with over 400 space fliers from 38 countries participating."

"When later that day, we met with Vice Minister of Communications Henrikis Jushkevitchus to discuss the US Festival, he called the party member with whom Rusty had met earlier and confirmed our credibility. That moved the project along significantly." According to Sazikov's account, Goldin's Commission for the Complex Study of Man of the Soviet Academy of Sciences became a Russian co-sponsor of the first space bridge.[6]

Returning home from Moscow without any definite decision from the Soviet officials regarding the space link, Hickman called Kim Spencer, who was to produce the US side of the link and alerted him that it might happen. There was complete silence from the Soviet side until about a week to 10 days before the festival was to take place. Hickman prepared for an annual family vacation and checked with the US Embassy in Moscow from a pay phone on the dock before the family houseboat trip. The Embassy informed him that they had been trying to reach him and that the project had been approved and that Hickman was expected in Moscow the next day. He dropped the family vacation plans and flew to Moscow with Rick Lukens to produce the Moscow side of the space bridge.

In 2007, *RIA Novosti* interviewed Yuli Gusman, Russian producer of the first space bridge, about his recollection of this historic event on the 25th anniversary. Gusman, who was an established Soviet movie producer at the time, was sitting in the office of Nadezda Alexandrovna Sevruk at the State Committee on Television and Radiobroadcasting ("Gosteleradio") late on a Friday afternoon. In walked Joseph Goldin, who knew Nadezda Alexandrovna but had never met Gusman. Goldin was carrying a letter from the Soviet Ambassador to the United States, Anatoli Dobrynin to Sergey Lapin, Chairman of Gosteleradio, proposing support of a space bridge with the US Festival in California. Lapin had approved the letter and issued orders for implementation, including making Sevruk responsible for the program content. The problem was that the space bridge was scheduled for the following Monday. Lapin had put his stamp on the letter, assigned cadre, and left for his dacha for the weekend. Goldin proposed that he and Gusman organize the program and they did so over the weekend before it was to take place, including recruiting students to be in the audience and getting leading Russian musicians to participate. Gusman's main concern, as he recounted it, was creating the proper atmosphere in the studio.[7]

In his memoir, Hickman describes the experience as the link went live, "The 300,000 rock 'n roll fans at the 'US Festival' in southern California were electrified when the images from Moscow first arrived over the 60-foot diamond vision video screen that was suspended 100 feet above the stage."

"US President Carter and Soviet Premier Brezhnev had only a teletype machine for direct communication, yet people from both countries demonstrated that satellite telecommunications could create a live musical bridge that cut through the fears and beliefs holding the world hostage to catastrophic technologies and differing economic philosophies."

In the 2021 interview, Hickman filled in some of the details about that first space bridge and its significance. "What was important was the first thing had happened. And you know, we had been told, several times by both the CIA and the CIA office head in the Embassy and other specialists in Embassy that it wasn't possible. You know, this could never happen, we are wasting our time."

"So, this is what I say to people, don't always listen to the experts, because they have an idea of what can and cannot be done. I didn't believe what could or could not be done. I was just following the energy. What I say is I was just a midwife of the whole thing. I was connecting people and the idea was surfacing."

"Then 15 minutes or so into the show, Bill Graham, who was producing the thing on the US side said, you know, this is propaganda. It's being broadcast from the Soviet Embassy in Washington. This isn't true, and he just disconnected the feed."

"So, the technical people in Moscow came to me and said that Bill Graham just disconnected the feed. And I said, okay, don't tell the Russians. As far as they're concerned, we are still going. They can see the crowd and did so until it finished. You know, a few people, probably in San Bernardino knew what happened, but most everyone else was not paying attention. You can imagine it was 200,000 kids at a rock and roll festival and suddenly there are Russians dancing up there on the screen. Bill Graham thought that this was disinformation."

"The Russian state news channel did a three-minute segment on the satellite bridge that brought this to the attention of the entire Soviet Union." This was the breakthrough that legitimized the project on the Russian side.

Reflecting on that period and their motivation at that time, Kim Spencer told me that "We thought that dialogue was essential and that it was important for Americans to see Russians as real people. And that you know, in some way was sort of the beginning of the track two sort of diplomacy. We as citizens were trying to move around barriers and do things that governments couldn't do through official track one diplomacy."

After the aborted first space bridge, there was a much more organized and planned space bridge program set up for the second US Festival. Setting up the second festival required Jim Hickman and Rick Lukens spending about six months negotiating with Soviet officials who wanted a one-million-dollar fee for the second festival but were moved off this position by the intervention of Soviet Academician Evgeny Velikhov and other influential Russians. In the end, according to Hickman, the Russians' main concern was that the broadcast was not going to be a propaganda ploy to discredit them. Meanwhile, Jim Hickman was lobbying California Congressman George Brown to also become involved and bring credibility on the US side.

The second space bridge was produced on the American side by Peter Gerwe, who will appear again later in this book in Chapter 4, with the technical support of the Internews team, who will appear again in Chapter 2. The moderator on the Russian side was Vladimir Pozner, who was a relatively unknown figure in Russian TV at that time. However, he was part of the circle of avantgarde thinkers around Velikhov and Goldin and through them he became acquainted with Michael and Dulce Murphy of Esalen. He also became acquainted with Jim Hickman, who lobbied to have him become the space bridge moderator. Pozner became a familiar figure on US TV in future space bridge programs, as well as becoming quite well-known in the Soviet Union. This second space bridge was conducted in a separate tent on the grounds of the US Festival and included both official exchanges with public figures and musical performances.

Evelyn Messinger was working in the equipment trailer doing production and described the impact of this space bridge on her personally. "Okay, so we all have technical tasks, and I am working in this trailer, and it was like 100 degrees in the trailer. You know, just working, working, working and I want to participate where the thing was happening. I went and sat in the audience, and I tell you that changed my life. I mean you know what it was like, the evil empire and all that. It was the height of the evil empire, and nobody had talked to each other for how many years. And suddenly, there they are and there we are! I remember the Russian cosmonaut and Rusty Schweickart, the US astronaut brilliantly because they were taking you up into the bigger picture and space and all that. And they knew each other already, the cosmonaut and the astronaut. But the person that blew everybody away was Evgeny Velikhov [physicist and scientific leader in the Soviet Union], who was supposed to be just a bureaucrat, but he said some really amazing things about the importance of peace. So, I think that really changed everything and in a way that was the start of the whole thing, and it was a big success."

The US Festival space bridges led to a multitude of space bridges that gradually expanded the audience size for these programs in both countries. As Evelyn Messinger explained, "then one thing led to another, and the next thing you know Internews was asked to create a space bridge with scientists on both sides talking about the concept of a nuclear winter that could follow from a nuclear war, a concept introduced by Carl Sagan. The Nuclear Winter space bridge aired on CNN in October 1983. There was a big leap after each of these space bridges, with each one leading into new and more important subjects with more people seeing them. For the one on nuclear winter, there was a lot of tension. It was really important for the Russians to do this, and they wouldn't use our name for the topic. We called it 'the world after nuclear war,' and they called it 'the world against nuclear war.' I guess their bosses told them they had to do that. …"

"We had these very dark, kind of gloomy sets on both sides. I was producing the American side and Kim was in the Russian side. In the middle of the show, there was a lunch break in Washington. Well apparently, the Russians huddled in the Moscow studio decide whether they were going to say yes and agree to the American scientist's view of Sagan's concept of nuclear winter. After the break, the Russian scientists said: 'Yes, it's important we have to fight against the possibility of nuclear war because of nuclear winter.' Kim

Spencer witnessed the discussion among the Russian scientists. Up until then the official Soviet line was that "when you hear the sirens you go down into the subways, you'll be safe." … "The scientists debated whether they should say what they really believe, which was nuclear winter was a possibility, there was not a way to survive a nuclear attack – both sides were going to go down. It was late in the evening in Moscow, so they decided that they wouldn't call their bosses. They were just going to say what they believed, and they did. The next day the headlines around the world were that Soviet and American scientists agree about nuclear winter. That would not have happened without the space bridge – because it allowed the scientists to speak without consulting any government minders." The space bridge was broadcast unedited to over 100 million viewers on Soviet TV and on CNN in the United States. This and many space bridges were front page news in Pravda. The space bridges were simply a sensation across the USSR. In the United States, most space bridges were reported under the culture beat and received much less attention but did appear in the mass media. The exception was Carl Sagan's Nuclear Winter conference in Washington DC which was widely covered.

The successful Nuclear Winter space bridge led to a series of townhall style space bridges between ordinary citizens in both countries moderated by Phil Donahue and Vladimir Pozner. One of the most memorable exchanges in the series took place on the 1986 Women to Women space bridge broadcast from Leningrad and Boston. An American woman stated that sex featured prominently in many US TV commercials and asked whether the same was true in the Soviet Union. Ludmilla Ivanova leaped in to defend her country by saying, "We have no sex in the Soviet Union. We have only love." By the time that she finished saying no sex in the Soviet Union, her next phrase was drowned out by laughter from both audiences. She was later chastised by the Communist Party for having used the word "sex" in public, but the phrase itself became a well-known and often repeated saying of the time. Any Russian over 50 and many younger ones will be familiar with this as somehow emblematic of Soviet times.

The space bridge format continued to grow both in scope and visibility. Evelyn continued, "Our Internews partner at that time, David Hoffman, approached California Congressman George Brown, who had participated in the second US Festival space bridge and whose district included San Bernadino County where the US Festivals took place, with the idea of a space bridge between the US Congress and the Supreme Soviet. Brown teamed up with Republican Congresswoman Claudine Schneider, who went to Moscow to meet their counterparts in the Kremlin. The idea was then pitched to all the American networks. Eventually ABC News agreed, leading to a series of telebridges moderated by Peter Jennings and Leonid Zolotarevsky, an anchor for Gosteleradio, Soviet State TV. Ultimately, this series earned Internews a national Emmy Award for technical direction and a nomination for outstanding news and documentary achievement."

Throughout this period of the increasing scope and reach of the space bridges, the Internews principals developed unique relationships with their counterparts in Soviet media and familiarity with operating in the Soviet Union. As Kim Spencer explained, "And you know, it was a great opportunity to get to work on all these programs. It kind of created a new profession of designing and executing two-way TV exchanges. I think I produced 13 of those space bridges and to travel there a lot during the Soviet period, making friends with key players at Gosteleradio. We had to trust each other because of all the technical difficulties of live TV and the communication problems we had to overcome with the ostensible enemy." This trust and experience led to a new phase in their involvement with the developing independent media in post-Soviet Russia that will be explored in more detail in Chapter 2.

Box 1.1 Partial List of US–USSR Space Bridges

1982, Labor Day. First US Festival was produced by Unuson and organized by Jim Hickman and Joseph Goldin.

1983, Memorial Day. Second US Festival, "Linking US Together." Hosted by Sam Keen and Vladimir Pozner. The discussions featured Rusty Schweickart, an American astronaut and a Russian cosmonaut, political leaders, and live rock music on both sides. It was produced by Unuson and organized by Jim Hickman and Joseph Goldin.

1983, July 20. "Moscow Calling San Diego: Children and Film." Organized by Helene Keyssar, Department of Communications, University of California San Diego and initiated by Joseph Goldin, Vladimir Pozner, Michael, and Sheila Cole. The Soviet partners were Gosteleradio and the Moscow Film Festival.

1983, October. "The Moscow Link." A full-day space bridge that linked a scientific conference about Nuclear Winter in Washington DC, organized by Carl Sagan and Paul Ehrlich, with leading Soviet scientists in a Gosteleradio Moscow studio, led by Sergei Kapitsa and Evgeny Velhikov. The 3-hour program aired several days later on CNN and WTBS Atlanta cable superstation. Produced by Internews Network and Gosteleradio.

1984, December 13. "Beyond War Award." In a live link from San Francisco to Moscow. awarding of the Beyond War Award to the founders of the International Physicians for the Prevention of Nuclear War. Hosted in Moscow by Vladimir Pozner. Live to 75,000 Americans at satellite downlinks across the United States, and later broadcast on Gosteleradio Channel 1, reaching a Soviet audience of millions.

1985, May. "Remembering War: A U.S. – Soviet Dialogue on World War II." This space bridge, organized by Helene Keyssar in San Diego, focused on the similarities and differences of World War II in the historical memories of Soviet and American citizens. The program was seen by an estimated 150 million Russian prime time viewers and about 20 million Americans on PBS.

1985, December 2. "Peace Child." Live two-way performance of a children's play with casts in Moscow and Minneapolis. Hosted by John Denver at the Minneapolis Children's Theatre and by Vladimir Pozner before a large studio audience in Moscow. Produced by David Woollcombe, Evelyn Messinger, Kim Spencer, and Gosteleradio. The recording was broadcast on WCCO Minneapolis and by PBS stations on December 25, 1985.

1985, December 29. "Citizen's Summit." Russians and Americans in Seattle and Leningrad, from all walks of life, talk frankly, moderated by Phil Donahue and Vladimir Pozner. Produced by KING-TV Seattle and Gosteleradio.

1986, May 20. "Citizen to Citizen Summit II. Women to Women." This included women in Boston and Leningrad and was moderated by Phil Donahue and Vladimir Pozner.

1986, September 11. "Chernobyl & Three Mile Island Citizen's Summit." Scientists and policymakers met via space bridge to discuss the implications of the Chernobyl and Three Mile Island nuclear reactor disasters. The 2-hour link between a studio in Moscow and a gathering at the University of San Francisco also included satellite hook-ups to other locations in the USSR. Organized by Esalen Institute Soviet-American Exchange Program, producers Jim Garrison, Evelyn Messinger, and Kim Spencer.

1987, April. "Congress Bridge." Parts 1 and 2. The first "face-to-face" meeting of members of the US Congress and the USSR Supreme Soviet, in Washington DC and Moscow studios. Produced by Internews Network, this 3-hour link-up in April 1987 was a practice session for the "Capital to Capital" series that began broadcasting live in both countries later that year. Participants were Georgy Arbatov, Adina Blokhinova, Vadim Zagladin, Nikolas Vlazenkivov, Georgy Kalashvili and Kiril Lavrov of the USSR Supreme Soviet and US Congress members George Brown (D), Clay Shaw (R), Alan Cranston (D), Claudine Schneider (D), Jim Leach (R), and Tom Downey (D). The hosts were Leonid Zolotarevsky, an anchor for Gosteleradio, Soviet State TV, and William Ury, the Harvard-based conflict mediator and author of "Getting to Yes."

1987, July 18. "Together to Mars." The principals on the US side in Boulder CO were Carl Sagan, Thomas Payne of NASA, and other leading Mars-mission scientists. Gathered at a Moscow exhibition park under a full-scale model of the Soyuz-Apollo docking in space, the Soviet team was led by the popular Soviet scientist and TV host Sergei Kapitsa and cosmonaut Valery Kubasov. Produced by The Planetary Society, Internews, and Gosteleradio.

1987. "Media and Communications – American and Soviet Journalists in Debate" Linking two panels of journalists in San Francisco and Moscow, moderated by Peter Jennings and Vladimir Pozner. Produced by the Center for Communications, Internews, and Gosteleradio and aired on PBS.

1987. "Capital to Capital." Dialogue between members of USSR Supreme Soviet and US Congress live from the USSR Supreme Soviet and from the US Congress. There were six episodes focused on different themes, including security, human rights, regional conflicts, and the environment, that were broadcast by ABC and by Soviet state TV. Hosted by Leonid Zolotarevsky and Peter Jennings.

Space bridges were enormously successful in opening communication and dialogue between ordinary people and later between political leaders of the United States and the Soviet Union on a massive scale. What began as an experiment by peace activists somewhat on the fringe of American mainstream society ended up reaching millions of people in both countries. The thesis of the peace activists that communication would lower the risk of war arguably proved to be successful in contributing to glasnost in Russia and to support for a series of summit meetings on the US side. As such, this new form of communication made a tangible contribution to ending the Cold War.

Professor Helene Keyssar of the University of California, San Diego, created the 1985 space bridge program "Remembering War: A U.S. – Soviet Dialogue on World War II." Reflecting back on this experience and on space bridges generally, she wrote in a 1994 article that "In the face of mutual distrust, pinning hopes for a less dangerous future on politicians seemed irresponsible. We were looking for an alternative way of contacting 'the other side.' This is what space bridges offered."[8] In evaluating the impact of space bridges in achieving the goals of the initiators, she writes, "First, and most generally, space bridges made a difference in Soviet-American perceptions of each other, but the nature of that difference is other than what was imagined or intended by those who worked on them. A common expectation among sponsoring groups, producers, moderators, and participants was that through these programs, Americans and Soviets would 'really get to understand each other better' and that this would lessen our fear of each other."[9] However, she concluded that "A diminution of fears of the other turns out not to be the same as an increase in understanding. Analysis of the content of the space bridges and of audience responses makes this difference clear and, in fact, suggests that space bridges, at times, confirmed or augmented misunderstandings and confusions."[10] The difference between communication and understanding, probably most memorably illustrated by the exchange about sex in the Soviet Union, is an ongoing theme in relations between Americans and Russians, owing in part to language, translation, and different cultural contexts for certain words and concepts.

People to People Contact

Alongside the technological revolution in communications that space bridges brought, a growing number of programs of direct contact between the people of the United States and the Soviet Union also began to erode barriers between people of the two Cold War adversaries. These programs included a growing number of Sister City organizations, an expanding number of direct exchanges through organizations like Project Harmony and the Center for Citizen Initiatives (CCI), as well as an under the radar expansion of Rotary Clubs in the Soviet Union.

Sister Cities

The traditional citizen-to-citizen contacts through the Sister Cities began to develop in the 1970s after a meeting between the USSR Twin Towns Association and Sister Cities International in 1973, which set up the rules for developing sister cities between the United States and the USSR. By 1977, there were five sister city partnership and this number rapidly expanded in the 1980s. At the time of the 1989 US–USSR Sister Cities Conference, there were thirty-six recorded sister city partnerships.[11] These sister city relationships provided an opportunity for people in each country to get to know each other. They became a human platform for many joint activities in the Perestroika period and further expanded with the dissolution of the Soviet Union.

This access was particularly impactful for people in the smaller towns and cities. Moscow was paired with Chicago and Leningrad (later St. Petersburg) was paired with Los Angeles. People in these cosmopolitan centers had a variety of ways to interact with foreigners that far exceeded what was available to Russians in the provinces. Partnerships between cities like Trenton, New Jersey, and the Lenin District of Moscow (1987); Eugene, Oregon, and Irkutsk (1987); Burlington, Vermont, and Yaroslavl (1988); and San Diego and Vladivostok (1991) had a great deal of impact as venues for extensive exchange between ordinary Americans and Russians. These organizations became vehicles for the rapid expansion of post-Soviet contacts and activities, including business contacts. The intensity of these relationships began to diminish by 2014 and then were all suspended because of the Russian invasion of Ukraine in 2022.

Project Harmony

Project Harmony was formed in 1984–1985 by three people in Vermont, Charles Hosford, an architect, Kathy Cadwell, a high school social studies teacher, and David Kelly, a lawyer to promote peace through citizen diplomacy. Charles Hosford provided the background on how they grew from a small group wanting to promote peace to an international organization focused on citizen exchanges.

Amidst all the crises of the time, they decided that if governments could not find a way to defuse tensions, then they would do it through citizen diplomacy. None of them had ever been to the Soviet Union. They had no family background or relatives in the Soviet Union. None of them spoke Russian. They brainstormed what they could do to promote exchange and came up with music as a common language. Kathy convinced her principal to allow the advanced chorus group from her high school to be the first group for their projected exchange. This musical connection is why they named their organization "Project Harmony."

With the tentative approval of the School Board and the Principal, they had to find a Russian partner. Charlie Hosmer recounted, "Dave Kelly and I decided we're going to make some contacts and we went to the UN. The Soviets had a cultural attaché there by the name of Valentin Makarov. We just went to New York and knocked on his door. He asked what we wanted, and we told him that we wanted to take a group of kids to the Soviet Union. He said that he had a 12-year-old who is interested in coming to the States thought that he could work something out with them through a Soviet organization called 'Sputnik,' a youth travel bureau." After a period of negotiations and preparation, Project Harmony took their first student choral group to the Soviet Union in November 1985. This was followed by a visit of a Soviet youth delegation with home stays in Vermont.

Project Harmony began to rapidly expand their school exchanges with the assistance United States Information Agency Samantha Smith Grants. "We tapped into the US Information Agency (USIA) and began a massive relationship with them. The Samantha Smith grants initially funded what were called direct school exchanges. ... There was an explosion of interest in Russia and Russian culture and the opportunity for nonprofit groups to engage that culture just went crazy. ... At one point we had nearly 100 schools involved with direct school exchanges. We're talking from Palo Alto, California, to Maine to Rhode Island to New Jersey to New York. I mean all over the place. This was by 1990. ... These led to semester study programs. ... We were sending staff full time to Russia. We opened an office in Moscow. ... We established a sister state relationship between Vermont and Karelia."

The story of Project Harmony will be continued in Chapter 2 as they continued to expand into a major organization promoting citizen exchanges in post-Soviet Russia.

Center for Citizen Initiatives

In parallel with the activities of Esalen Institute, Space Bridges and San Francisco/Moscow Teleport, the CCI, created by Sharon Tennyson, was part of the growing citizen diplomacy movement sparked by escalation of tensions between the two superpowers and fears of a nuclear exchange. Located initially in the San Francisco social activism incubator founded by Henry Dakin, CCI and Sharon Tennyson sought to break down tensions by bringing delegations of Americans to Russia and then later delegations of Russians to the United States.

By 1989, CCI began to develop entrepreneurship programs. According to the CCI website, "CCI developed and ran five different business training programs between 1989 and 2009 for some 6,500 Russian entrepreneurs who were hosted pro bono by American civic clubs (Rotary, Kiwanis, etc.) in over 500 American cities in 45 states. Thousands of American companies stepped in and provided training."[12] The impact of CCI was broad and widespread throughout the years after the dissolution of the Soviet Union as an administrator of USAID-funded programs.

Rotary Clubs

Rotary International (RI) is the umbrella organization for a worldwide network of local Rotary Clubs that engage in humanitarian service activities. As soon as relations between the United States and the USSR began to thaw, RI began to move into Eastern Europe, first establishing a club in Budapest, then Warsaw and other Polish cities. During visits to Spain and India, Gorbachev visited Rotary Clubs and became favorably disposed toward the organization. In November 1989, Gorbachev invited the President of RI, Hugh Archer, to Moscow. After a series of visits and the necessary approvals by the Soviet government, the Rotary Club of Moscow was officially chartered on June 5, 1990.[13]

There is some discrepancy in the record as to which city formed the second Rotary Club in Russia, but it was either Leningrad (now St. Petersburg) or Irkutsk in Eastern Siberia. The website of the Rotary Club Saint Petersburg states that their club was presented their charter on October 24, 1990, only a few months after the Moscow club was awarded their charter. The Charter Ceremony on that date was attended by both Russian and foreign dignitaries, including Anatoly Sobchak, Chairman of the Leningrad City Executive Committee, and Tom Bradley, Mayor of Los Angeles, sister city of Leningrad.[14] Vladimir Donskoy, first President of the Irkutsk Rotary Club, and historian of the Rotarian movement in Russia, states that Irkutsk was the second club chartered. In 1988, Irkutsk had become a sister city of Eugene, Oregon, and ties with Rotary were developed through this sister city connection. When the RI delegation came to charter the Moscow Rotary Club in 1990, they continued to Eastern Siberia to Irkutsk to establish the Rotary Chapter there. Very quickly, the Alaska Rotary clubs became involved in fostering new clubs in Eastern Siberia and the Rotarian movement exploded and contributed to formation of the new Russian market economy and civil society in heartland of Russia in ways that are not generally recognized.

Business in the Era of Citizen Diplomacy

During the Soviet period, there were very limited contacts between US-based multinationals and Soviet enterprises. The business ties that existed were mostly in trading and equipment supply. As the reform of the Soviet economy began under Gorbachev, the door was opened for new business activities through passage of the Law on Joint Ventures as of January 1, 1987, which allowed Soviet entities to form joint ventures with foreign partners. Later that same year, a special Party Plenum approved a new Law on State Enterprises that came into effect on June 30, 1987, which gave state enterprises greater autonomy to export and form partnerships with foreigners, along with strengthening the independent power of the enterprise general directors. These laws were followed by the Law on Cooperatives in May of 1988 that allowed independent worker-owned cooperatives. All these pieces of legislation were intended to assist in the modernization of Soviet enterprises and assist them in gaining access to foreign technology and foreign management techniques.

With this legal opening to cooperate with foreigners, powerful individuals on the Soviet side began searching for reliable partners to help them take advantage of the new opportunities. At the same time, American entrepreneurs who had an interest or background in the Soviet Union also began to explore potential business with Soviet partners. This mutuality is critically important in understanding this period. The successful joint ventures that developed in this period depended upon the American or foreign side having a powerful Soviet partner, whose motives and interests are often ignored with the story of those times told only through the eyes of the American participants. The critical role of powerful Soviet business leaders in the late Gorbachev period joint ventures will become obvious, particularly in the formation and operation of companies like Dialog and Perestroika that will be described later in this chapter.

Before delving into the purely business-oriented joint ventures, it is worth noting the growing overlap that began to occur as entrepreneurial business ties began to grow out of citizen diplomacy activities. Several American citizen diplomats began entrepreneurial businesses motivated by the idea that economic ties between the United States and the Soviet Union would contribute to de-escalation of political tensions. The connection between citizen diplomacy and business activity is not a linear story in which one thing follows another. It is a story of connections and relationships that merge and morph from one thing into another.

Culturally, Russians typically prefer to collaborate with people that they know personally and feel that they can trust. So, in this early period, business collaboration arose out of connections formed through citizen diplomacy activities or other kinds of personal connection. These early Gorbachev period business relationships were in many ways the harbingers of the new Russian market economy that was to emerge from the dissolution of the Soviet Union.

The San Francisco entertainment lawyer Lizbeth Hasse is a case study in the merging of citizen diplomacy and business collaboration. In 1988, she met an Estonian filmmaker at the Telluride Film Festival, co-founded by Tom Luddy, a Russophile who is responsible for acquiring much of the Russian and Georgian collection at the University of California Pacific Film Archive. Hasse's meeting with the Estonian filmmaker led to an invitation to come to Estonia to speak with the Estonian Filmmakers Union about film rights and distribution. As part of this trip, she then went to Moscow where she became acquainted with Andrei Smirnov, actor, director, and then head of the Soviet Filmmakers Union and where she gave similar talks and workshops.

In 1989, she became involved with a project of the Oakland Children's Hospital to share surgical techniques for open heart surgery on children with Russian doctors. This project became Heart-to-Heart Global Cardiac Care. She explained that "the point was for US cardiac surgeons to train doctors throughout the Soviet Union in pediatric cardiac surgery procedures for newborns and young children. We started with our initial mission to St Petersburg, then called Leningrad. I came along to organize media because media was very interested. I knew media people there at that point, news people and TV, and Heart to Heart needed somebody non-medical to kind of coordinate the media while they were doing their own work. So, I came along for that, later set up Heart to Heart's legal structure, and now I've been on the Board of Directors of that group for almost 40 years. Heart to Heart developed 6 self-sustaining centers for pediatric cardiac care throughout the Soviet Union and saved the lives of over 30,000 kids [worldwide]while passing on the medical education."

This project led to further contacts in diverse areas as Hasse described, "It was 1990, and I put together a space bridge. I was approached by some ecologists from St Petersburg, who I met at Henry Daikon's center in San Francisco. They were very upset about a dam being built across the Baltic that was to block part of the Baltic Sea just outside of St Petersburg and the environmental effects of it. They wanted to try to have a space bridge with San Francisco activists about environmental activism, and to learn how activism is done."

Producing this Bay-to-Bay space bridge between San Francisco's NBC affiliate and Leningrad TV, then led her to become involved with the beginnings of independent media in the USSR and later in post-Soviet Russia. "I met a lawyer in Leningrad, Viktor Manakhov. He was helpful with some Heart to Heart issues and he invited me to speak a few times at his law faculty. He was interested in free speech issues and communication. We worked together and he became my co-director of a multi-day conference in Novgorod of a lot of independent news and filmmaking groups trying to become independent TV companies. These were smaller companies from different regions in the Soviet Republics who came to learn about how to organize independent media, as well as a French contingent of media and film people. There were over 200 small Russian companies there that formed what they declared to be the first independent broadcasting association in the CIS. It does not exist anymore." In brief, this illustrates how Liz Hasse's humanitarian contacts led directly into the nascent private media sector in post-Soviet Russia as will be more fully explained in Chapter 2.

San Francisco/Moscow Teleport

At the same time as satellite TV space bridges were allowing American and Soviet citizens to see and speak to each other directly and were creating new perceptions of each other, Joel Schatz, a social entrepreneur and peace activist, was bringing emerging Internet technology and email messaging to the Soviet Union as a means of direct individual communication and as a facilitator for business contacts.

Joel Schatz was an energy advisor to the Governor of Oregon and peace activist, who established the first commercial Internet email connections between the Soviet Union and the United States, the first Internet image transfer between the two countries via video telephone and then later the first official Soviet–US telecommunications joint venture.

In some ways, Schatz was similar in background to James Hickman in that he had no professional training in computers or telecommunications technology, but his drive to initiate communications and his ability to think outside of standard channels was much more important than technical skill. Schatz was a former military intelligence analyst for the US Army, who later trained in psychology and communications and conducted longitudinal research in human development at the University of Colorado School of Medicine. He then went on to a 5-year job as state energy adviser in Oregon. From 1983 to 1987, Joel was a representative of ARK Communications Institute.

As he explained in our interview, "I made my first trip to the USSR in early 80s [August 1983]. My motivation was not business, but concern about growing prospects for nuclear war. There were approximately 50,000 thermonuclear warheads aimed at US and USSR population centers, and only 33 international telephone trunk lines between our countries! Considering the bona fide threat of nuclear war … the virtual absence of communication between the peoples of both countries seemed utterly dangerous and incomprehensible. That is why I invited myself to Moscow to propose the creation of a reliable email network to connect our nations – to initiate active cross cultural creative communication exchanges among scientists, educators, businesspeople, investors, politicians, doctors, journalists, artists, et.al."

Joel wrote a letter to the Soviet Mission to the United States saying that he and his wife, Dianne, wanted to come to the Soviet Union. In that letter, he explained that he and his wife were working on what he described as "an interesting piece of art which eventually became posters and coloring books, called Peace Trek. It was about the evolution of the arms race into a peaceful world. We were conducting workshops all over the United States and Canada to gather ideas of this project, and I wanted input from the Russians." At this point, Joel Schatz and his wife were just individuals interested in peace and dialogue with the Soviets.

Joel received the invitation he needed for a visa to visit the Soviet Union. In planning for this first trip, he hired Anya Kucharev, Russian-speaking staff member of Esalen, to be their translator because they did not trust the official translator that would have been provided by the Soviet tour agency, Intourist.

The actual trip took place in August 1983 and Anya introduced Joel and Dianne to Joseph Goldin in Moscow soon after they arrived. This is the same Joseph Goldin who was key to the space bridge for the US Festival and who had developed a working relationship with Esalen. Goldin became a critical door opener for Joel over the next few years as he worked toward establishing more efficient communication between the peoples of the United States and the Soviet Union. Joel describes Goldin as a person who basically changed his life.

In 1984, Goldin introduced Joel to Evgeny Velikhov, the Vice President of the Russian Academy of Sciences. Velikhov appears repeatedly as a key figure on the Soviet side during this period of citizen diplomacy. He was a participant in the 1984 second US Festival space bridge and made a very strong impression as Evelyn Messinger recounted. Velikhov became Joel Schatz's patron in the Soviet Union, opening bureaucratic doors for his subsequent pioneering computer-based and satellite telecommunication ventures.

Reflecting on Velikhov and his role in opening the Soviet Union, Joel stated that Velikhov "knew that the Soviet economy was so stuck that it couldn't survive without international investment and technology from the West. And he knew he couldn't get investors to come into the Soviet Union if they couldn't communicate with their home office while in Moscow. At that time, it took you know, a week or two to make an international phone call. ... I wanted to bring electronic mail and open the system at that time. We weren't even talking about an improved telephone system, that was a couple of years later."

"My motive was not to make money. It was trying to open two-way communication between the peoples of both countries. So, I oddly enough, my timing was so perfect. Everything I tried to do to open the system, I got the green light. Velikhov became my sponsor, and he just cleared the way for me for anything I needed on the Soviet side, including later when I needed permissions for an immediate Intelsat satellite link."

The Soviet Union had already been searching for a partner for x.25 telephony cooperation in the West. As early as 1982, they had established a test connection to Austria. So, it appears that when Joel showed up expressed interest in establishing an email connection, he became a prospective partner to accomplish their existing goals.

In 1985, Academician Boris Rauschenbach, preeminent Soviet physicist and rocket engineer, referred Joel to Oleg Smirnov at the All-Union Scientific Research Institute for Applied Automated Systems (VNIIPAS) to act as his partner in the Soviet Union. Together, they started the first US/USSR computer teleconference on June 26, 1985, through a working computer link between VNIIPAS and the New Jersey Institute of Technology. As Joel told the *LA Times* in a 1987 interview, "Computers represent a break with history. They are by definition a planetary-scale technology. Their decentralized quality of communication is changing the architecture of international boundaries."[15]

Joel and his Russian partners used this new technology for a broad range of purposes and exchanges including "social and cultural exchanges between recovering alcoholics and political cartoonists in both countries; scientific research exchanges on the effects of Chernobyl, the exploration of outer space, and the spread of AIDS; commercial joint ventures in design, film and television; electronic mail services, and a series of formal and informal electronic conferences."[16]

Schatz and his Soviet partners began experimenting with using slow scan television, a 1960s technology that sent pictures over the copper phone lines, operating at very low speed. As primitive as it was, this technology allowed individuals to share documents and pictures, pointing the way to future new uses of technology to promote communications. This technology was in line with Joseph Goldin's vision of global communications through gigantic interactive TV screens in major cities around the world, strengthening the connection between the two sides around exploring emerging technologies for purposes of peace and understanding.

Shortly thereafter, the new email link was shut down by the Department of Commerce. Joel then employed a lawyer from San Francisco that he described as a "pit bull" who pointed out that the link did not violate any US law, and so by October 1985, the link was back in operation.

These early contacts were then folded into San Francisco/Moscow Teleport (SFMT), a non-profit that Joel founded in 1987 with funding support from San Francisco philanthropist Henry Dakin, through his Washington Research Institute.[17]

At this point, George Soros enters the picture. Joel was working on a humanitarian mission to bring Polina Osetinskaya, a young piano prodigy to San Francisco. George Soros' office manager in Moscow was also working on behalf of this young girl and he offered to introduce Joel to Soros as described by Joel. "Because of the trust built between us as we were trying to save this little girl, he told me that he worked for a billionaire, and asked if I needed money? I said sure and he said his name is George Soros, here's his phone number. Tell him, I sent you." In 1988, Joel called Soros and he was invited over to meet him at his office in New York City.

Joel told Soros that he wanted to connect the United States and the Soviet Union by computer. "I wanted to introduce first scientists and then businesspeople and educators and physicians, writers and artists by electronic mail and to open up the system for two-way communication."

Joel described Soros' reaction to his plan, "He asked well how much money do you need? I said, well, I don't know I don't have a corporation, and I don't have a business plan yet. He said you will need lawyers, you know some equipment, etc. I said, okay half a million dollars. He said, okay, here's my deal. I'll give you a quarter million dollars, if you find somebody to match me in 24 hours, goodbye, So I left his office."

"I came from the nonprofit world and government work so that seemed to me to be like $50 billion. I had no clue what to do. But I did know another guy in New York, another rich guy named Alan Slivka. So, I called him, and I went over to see him at his office on Madison Avenue. I told him the story and he said okay, I'll consider it, but I need about a month to decide. I said no. I'll give you 10 minutes because I'm going to lose a quarter million dollars. ..., And he took his glasses off and bit them. I remember that and then he said, 'okay I'm in.' So, I called George back and told him I found the other matching funds and he asked what took so long? ... These two guys wired $500,000 to my personal checking account at Wells Fargo, nothing was signed. George just said, 'go to work.'" With this new investment, the non-profit SFMT was converted to a for-profit, commercial company in 1988.

Then, in 1989, SFMT and VNIIPAS registered a Soviet joint venture called SovAm Teleport. At that time, SovAm Teleport was the only private telecommunications system operating with the approval of both the United States and Soviet governments to open commercial digital communications between approved customers from each country. Joel Schatz recounted that his first customers were probably the KGB and the CIA. Major Soviet agencies, including the Space Research Institute, the Ministry of Health, Mir Publishing, Komsomolskaya Pravda, Novosti Press, the Society of Soviet Designers, the National Center of Data Communications, Sovinfilm, Gosteleradio, and the Soviet Cultural Foundation became clients. On the US side, Sovam Teleport rapidly gained clients among international companies with offices in Moscow like GE and Control Data Corporation, US government agencies like the Library of Congress, and with major media organizations like *Time Magazine*.

The email connection also became important in facilitating the many citizen diplomacy exchanges and space bridge programs that developed in these years. Suddenly, private communications between the United States and the Soviet Union became easy and accessible, leading to the facilitation of exchange between the two countries on all levels. "The word spread, and we can barely keep up with the demand. ... When Western businesspeople realized that they could actually work out of Moscow, their investments increased for all kinds of business."

This new form of communications made the front page of the *New York Times*. Joel recalled the reaction to that *New York Times* article. "After the February 19, 1989, front page New York Times article was published I received a really angry call from the Department of Defense requesting that I come immediately to the Pentagon to explain my activities. I was there the following day along with three attorneys in tow, as a precaution! There were about twenty people in the room."

"I then told them I was simply following President Reagan's recent policy to improve cooperation among educators, scientists, medical researchers, et. al. in the U.S. and USSR – and I was simply helping to provide a two-way communications channel for this purpose."

"Finally, I was told that this new channel might facilitate a breach of national security by allowing Soviets to tap into all American public databases with the possibility of insights that could threaten our national security."

"I told them that Soviets could access US computers from many countries outside the USSR … and if this was a real concern, they had two options: cut off all telecom circuits between the U.S. and the rest of the world, which could cripple the global economy – or classify all U.S. public databases so Soviets (and Americans) would be deprived of access to all public data."

"A National Security Agency guy then told me I was a real smart ass … and abruptly concluded the meeting!"

Undeterred, Joel continued to expand his communications services business operations in 1990 when SFMT joined with Moscow Main Trunk Lines Control Center and GTE International Communications to form a modern international telephone joint venture, "Sovintel." SFMT continued to expand through regional partnerships. In 1992, Baltic Communications Ltd. was founded as a joint venture between SFMT, Cable & Wireless, and three state telecommunications companies in St. Petersburg.

At the time of the August 1991 coup attempt, Joel was in Tatarstan signing another joint venture regional telecom agreement. As he called to tell his wife about the success of the business deal, she was much more concerned for his safety. Joel understood that "if the coup leaders had succeeded, people like me would have been very unpopular because the coup leaders were completely opposed to Western communication." If the coup did succeed, Joel had a plan to escape via Turkey disguised as a Russian Orthodox priest. Meanwhile, SovAm Teleport's Moscow employees were working non-stop to communicate news about the coup while all the Soviet news outlets observed a news blackout.

In the post-Soviet Russia other international telecom companies began to explore the market opportunity pioneered by Joel Schatz. His companies were eventually absorbed in a series of mergers and acquisitions to become the Russian telecom company, Golden Telecom, which was then acquired by the Russian mobile telecom company Vimpelcom in 1999.

Gorbachev's opening of the Soviet economy led to several important early joint ventures founded by visionary, adventurous entrepreneurs and by citizen diplomats, like Joel Schatz, migrating into business ventures with Russian partners. These early collaborations were based on close working relationships with Russian partners. The quality and reliability of these partnership relationships determined the ultimate success or failure of the joint ventures.

Dialog – First Important Soviet American Joint Venture

The most important and long-lasting Soviet American joint venture was called "Dialog."

Shortly after Gorbachev became the general secretary of the Communist Party, a very successful Chicago commodities trader, Joe Ritchie went to Moscow to explore opportunities there. He became acquainted with Pyotr Zrelov, designer and manager of the management information systems at Kamaz, one of Russia's largest truck manufacturers. The two men liked each other and decided to explore creating a joint venture. The initial purpose was to specialize in computers and information technology to create a Russian version of IBM. As someone who was embedded in the heart of Soviet industry, Zrelov knew how badly they needed digital technology and modernized systems. For purposes of his investment in Russia, Ritchie formed Management Partners International through which he ultimately invested $5 million in the new joint venture (JV). The Russian side was headed by Zrelov and included Kamaz as the lead partner, Moscow State University, the Central Institute of Economics and Applied Mathematics, the Space Research Institute, and the Soviet Experimental Computer Center at the National Exhibition of Economic Achievements. The Soviet side invested 15 million rubles.

The new JV was called Dialog to evoke the warming relations between the United States and the Soviet Union. It was registered as a JV at the end of 1987.[18] As part of the startup process for Dialog, Joe Ritchie recruited Peter Derby, a young investment banker in the New York area with a Russian émigré family background to assist in preparing a business plan for the new JV. Peter Derby recounted that "Joe Richie sent over $5 million in starting capital. Now they needed to figure out how they were going to spend it. How are they going to actually make money? So, I came to Moscow to look at their business plans. … I realized that the JV was heavily oriented towards technology, software, hardware. My brother worked at Bell Labs, and he was on the team that created the UNIX operating system. … So, I had him come over to Moscow for a few weeks to help me figure out the business plan. He really was the one that drove the original pieces of that business plan. By the way, the Russians did a pretty good job on it and then he helped them with it. … The Russians really developed the plan and Joe Richie's team approved it, with our strong input."

Dialog was officially the second Soviet American JV. Astro Pizza is listed as the first American Soviet JV, but Dialog assisted in its formation. Peter Derby described how this happened. "There was an American guy from New Jersey, who wanted to bring a pizza truck to Russia, like those outdoor food trucks in New York City that have Mexican food and other fried food. He also wanted there to be love between America and the Russians, so he painted Soviet and American flags on the side of this pizza truck. He shipped over the truck through Finland and brought it to Moscow. He thought he was just going to pull up on the street corner or some parking lot off of Red Square and sell pizza with a American flag and a Soviet flag. His problem was that he needed an official Russian partner. Somehow, he connected with Joe Ritchie and got help from Ritchie's partner, Pyotr Zrelov, to start that little pizza truck venture as the official first joint venture, but the real first joint venture was Dialog."

After completing his stint in Moscow working with Zrelov to complete the business plan, Peter Derby left Moscow with the intent of rejoining the investment banking world in New York. He had become friends with all the Russian partners, and they asked him, "why don't you stay and work. I said 'no' I'm into banking, investment banking and stock exchanges, so I left."

DialogBank – First Non-State Bank

Pyotr Zrelov and his team oversaw managing Dialog. The company initially focused on digital technology and was the original exclusive sales agent for Microsoft in Russia. As the JV succeeded and expanded, Zrelov made a new pitch to Peter Derby to return to Russia. Derby invited Zrelov and his wife to attend his wedding in New York City. At the wedding reception, "Zrelov tells me, listen Peter, we did a great job, the $5 million investment turned into $30 million. The sad news is that it is all in hard currency, and it's being held in Vnesheconom Bank [Soviet bank for international transactions] and the Bank now is asking us for a five-year business plan to have access to our own money."

Peter replied, "well, that's not going fly. You're not going to be a successful joint venture if you can't have access to the money earned to reinvest and grow the business."

Zrelov said, "Exactly. You said you weren't going to stay with us because it's a technology business, but you would if it was banking, investment, banking stock exchanges, so on, so now we need a bank."

Peter said, "Okay, but there's only five state banks there's no private bank there you know I mean you want to try to do a joint venture or something."

Zrelov again, "Well, the only structure we're allowed to have now under perestroika is a cooperative. The only thing we have is the law that just recently passed for cooperatives, so I don't know. I don't know how to do this."

Peter said, "Cooperative, really, well we have something in the US called a credit union and a credit union is a cooperative but it's a banking cooperative."

Zrelov responded, "Really, let me go back to Russia and let me give it a try. Maybe we could set up a cooperative bank."

Peter remembered his response as, "Okay, let me know what happens, but it's literally my wedding reception. I just got married. I'm thinking if we start a bank, what am I going to tell my wife. We just got married and now we are moving to Moscow. I told Zrelov, please just give me a little time here. It was July 16, 1989, so he called me at the end of August or the beginning of September. He said we can do it. I think we can form a cooperative credit union bank. Can you get rules on how that works and everything from the US, so we could try to set this up? I said 'okay.' So that's how DialogBank started."

Over the next 5 years, the Dialog JV expanded rapidly opening offices in 34 cities. Within those 5 years, Dialog sold and serviced more than half of the personal computers in the former Soviet Union. It grew to employ over 3,500 people and began to expand into a wide range of other types of business.[19] Dialog became a consortium of more than 100 companies employing more than 4,000 people in fields ranging from software to tourism to construction.[20]

Derby returned to Russia to form DialogBank as the Soviet Union's first non-state bank as an outgrowth of the success of the Dialog JV. DialogBank became the first private Russian international bank with a currency license and rapidly expanded as the bank of choice serving international business in Russia. It became the only bank in the world to service both the archrivals Pepsi and Coke due to the lack of alternatives in Russia. Peter Derby became an influential advisor to Soviet state officials, assisting in writing Central Bank rules and Soviet corporate legislation. This role of DialogBank in the emerging Russian market economy will be explored in more detail in Chapter 3.

Perestroika Joint Venture – First Real Estate Developer

The first real estate joint venture was formed during the Gorbachev era and was accordingly named Perestroika Joint Venture. As a trail blazing real estate development company, it had a significant impact in the Moscow real estate sector that will be described in more detail in Chapter 4. The joint venture was formed in 1988 and has some parallels with the Dialog joint venture. The initiative in formation of the joint venture in both cases came from powerful Soviet enterprise directors seeking access to foreign expertise and convertible currency.

In the case of the Perestroika Joint Venture, the Russian partner was Andrei Stroyev, head of the Moscow State Construction Enterprise (Mosinzhstroi). Mosinzhstroi was in charge of all of the urban infrastructure in Moscow, including office and housing construction, road maintenance, heating lines, and water pipes. The original partner on the US side was a consulting company, Delphi International. However, they did not know anything about real estate development and Stroyev's goal for the joint venture was to gain access to Western expertise in real estate development. So, Delphi International was replaced by an Atlanta-based real estate developer, Earl Worsham. The story will continue in Chapter 4 with the next stages of development of Perestroika and the creation of the private real estate sector in post-Soviet Russia.

TrenMos – American Dining in Moscow

TrenMos is an example of the confluence of a sister city relationship with entrepreneurship in creating one of the first American style restaurants in Moscow. It was the brainchild of New Jersey immigrant businessman and holocaust survivor, Shelley Zeiger and was implemented by his son, Jeff Zeiger. Shelley Zeiger owned a liquor distributorship and hotel in New Jersey. In 1973, during the Nixon-era Détente thaw in US–Soviet relations, Shelley Zeiger went to Russia to try to get the rights to distribute Russian vodka in the United States. Unfortunately for him, Pepsi got there first. Pepsi got a monopoly on US rights to distribute Russian Stolichnaya vodka as part of a barter deal that allowed Pepsi to produce its soft drink in the Soviet Union. Zeiger did obtain rights to distribute Soviet perfume and then Soviet handicrafts in the United States, including the iconic matryoshka nesting dolls.

As the Soviet Union began to open up under Gorbachev, Shelley Zeiger began to search for new business opportunities. In 1987, Zeiger took a delegation from Trenton, New Jersey, including the Mayor to Moscow to try to set up a sister city relationship. The sheer size of Moscow dwarfed that of Trenton, so the Soviet side suggested a sister city relationship between Trenton and the Lenin District of Moscow, which was one of the administrative districts that included much of the center of the city. After an official signing ceremony in Trenton, this became of the first Soviet–American sister city agreements.

Initially, the sister city program focused on cultural exchange with newspaper editors traveling between the two countries and performances in the United States by the Bolshoi ballet and Kirov ballet. Shelley Zeiger wanted to expand the relationship to include small businesses in Moscow, including a dry cleaner, gas station, nail salon, and a restaurant. The restaurant was the only project that came to fruition as a joint venture between the Public Catering Trust of the Lenin District of Moscow, headed at that time by Sergey Goryachev and the Zeiger family company. The Public Catering Trust was a very large organization that acted as the supplier for all the cafeterias and cafes in the Lenin District. The new joint venture was named TrenMos to represent the partnership of the two cities and was the first Soviet American joint venture restaurant.

To run the restaurant, Shelley Zeiger turned to his 21-year-old son, Jeff, who was managing a restaurant in Princeton, New Jersey, in the Hyatt. His father asked him to go to Moscow to open and manage TrenMos. Jeff initially turned down the idea but eventually decided to embrace the adventure with an assurance from Hyatt that he could always return and have a position with them. In May 1989, Jeff got on a plane for Moscow, not knowing any Russian and never having been to the Soviet Union.

As soon as he got off the plane and before he even saw the space proposed for the new restaurant, Jeff and his translator were ushered into a meeting with Sergey Goryachev and his staff of 30 people to begin planning for the restaurant. The vast differences in culture, experience, and age, amplified by language, became apparent immediately in that first meeting. It was clear to Jeff from that meeting that the Soviet side thought that he could not possibly know enough to run this restaurant because he was so young. It was a complete anomaly in the Soviet Union to have a young person in charge. The first question put to Jeff was how much meat do you need for a year? So began the evolution of the TrenMos restaurant business in Moscow.

Jeff persevered and opened TrenMos in October 1989 as one of a handful of restaurants that catered to the expat community and then ultimately exposed Soviet citizens to American style restaurants, serving a menu ranging from T-bone steaks to southwestern chili. TrenMos was the forerunner of the revolution in the restaurant sector that will be described in Chapter 4.

Science Solutions, Inc. – Technology Scouting

On the West Coast of the United States, James Sauer, CEO of Science Solutions, saw the potential for prospecting for advanced technologies from the Soviet Union. Sauer was a plasma physicist who had worked in the fusion program at General Atomics in San Diego. Through the world of fusion and plasma physics, he was familiar with the capabilities of Soviet technology and had entre to significant figures in the space sector and important Institutes of the Academy of Sciences. The company engaged in talks with Roald Sagdeev, director of the Soviet space program and science advisor to Gorbachev, and explored the potential for working with the Leningrad Institute of Fine Mechanics and Optics, specifically with their Department of Optical Glass Technologies.

David Edick joined the company as business development director in 1990. He recounted, "… they asked me to come on board and be the director of development and the purpose of that company was to bring high technology processes and products out from the Soviet Union to the West, particularly the United States. … But it was a long road to figure out. You know, academics in the United States and in the Soviet Union had negligible commercial experience. It's a real learning curve to climb."

The August 1991 coup attempt crushed this endeavor. Soon after the coup took place, David Edick saw that everything that they had been building was going to fall apart. "That was the end of the Union. And it was the end of all these Union structures that we had been dealing with, all these Soviet Union level scientific institutes and relationship structures, whatever funding, there was part of it, but it was mostly the institutional connections."

In September 1991, David left Science Solutions because of the impact he foresaw as the consequence of the August coup and to pursue opportunities he saw emerging in a post-Soviet Far East and Vladivostok. Ironically, right before he left the company, there was a large trade show in San Diego that was part of the signing of the San Diego – Vladivostok sister city agreement that was to solidify his commitment to further business in Russia. "Science Solutions had a display table at this trade fair, which I staffed. I witnessed the signing of the sister city agreement and was deeply impressed by the energy and clarity of purpose displayed by the delegation from Vladivostok, which included several executives from leading enterprises. It changed my life." As with TrenMos, sister city agreements provided a platform for new interactions between formerly separated Americans and Russians who had a profound impact on both sides. Science Solutions was not the last American company that trawled the murky waters of Soviet science for innovations with commercial value.

Late Soviet-Era Partnerships – Dancing in the Dark

Americans typically see events through the prism of their own activities and put themselves in the center of the story as the moving force. What is clear from our survey of this period is that the Soviet side had its own reasons for collaborating with these seemingly American-initiated citizen diplomacy activities and early joint ventures. The success of the American citizen diplomats came from the fact that they were attempting something that the Russian side also wanted. In this sense, the citizen diplomats were fulfilling broader overall objectives as self-selected but somewhat random enablers of broader social forces of change. The success of space bridges, citizen exchanges, digital connections, and early joint ventures lies in the fact that they were also fulfilling Soviet intentions. The Soviets recognized that working through these American individuals who somehow showed up in the Soviet Union was a route to realizing their mutual goals. While we do not know enough about the intentions of the Soviet side, powerful Russian institutions and individuals supported the citizen diplomacy activities of the time for their own reasons.

The primary goal of citizen diplomacy was to bring peace through mutual understanding. Pursuit of these goals led to networks of Americans and Russians who became friends and colleagues. It is a truism that is appreciated by anyone who has ever done anything in Russia that Russians prefer to do business with people they know, family, school friends, or in some cases, foreigners who they have gotten to know. Without intending to do so, these early networks became a human platform for the explosion of American–Russian interaction that was to come.

The early joint ventures in the perestroika period played out much the same processes and foreshadowed the business interactions to come in post-Soviet Russia. One of the things that the successful companies had in common was that there was a powerful Russian partner who needed foreign expertise to understand how to operate in a market economy. This is a pattern that repeats itself beginning with the Gorbachev era joint ventures and continuing up until at least through the 1998 financial crisis and perhaps a bit beyond.

Suddenly, the world began to change with the August coup attempt against Gorbachev, leading to dramatically changed conditions that expanded the scope and depth of American–Russian interactions. The collapse and dissolution of the Soviet Union on December 25, 1991, was one of the key historical nodal points of the late 20th century and the background for what was to come for our story of American–Russian interaction.

Notes

1 Michael Shuman, Gail Warner, and Lila Forest, "Citizen Diplomacy – What It Is, How It Began and Where It Is Going," *Context Institute* (Winter 1987), www.context.org/iclib/ic15/shuman/. Accessed November 14, 2022.

2 A. V. Sazikov, "Global Theater of Joseph Goldin," *Live Journal*, February 12, 2016, Accessed November 30, 2021, https://sazikov.livejournal.com/564.html

3 Sazikov, "Global Theater of Joseph Goldin," Translated by the author.

4 Sazikov, "Global Theater of Joseph Goldin," Translated by the author.

5 V. Saxena, "Soviet Leader Abandoned Communism After Walking into a US Grocery Store," *The Western Journal*, January 18, 2018, Accessed November 11, 2022, www.westernjournal.com/soviet-leader-grocery-store/
6 Sazikov, "Global Theater of Joseph Goldin," Translated by the author.
7 "First Space Bridge: Firsthand History," *RIA Novosti*, October 29, 2007, Accessed August 21, 2021, Translated by the author, https://ria.ru/20071029/85788741.html
8 Helene Keyssar, "Space Bridges: The U.S. – Soviet Space Bridge Resource Center," *PS: Political Science & Politics* (Cambridge University Press, June 1994), 249, Accessed September 9, 2021, www.cambridge.org/core/services/aop-cambridge-core/content/view/5ECF687D9D6C0A2D2A03CC0A2B33BBF7/S1049096500040518a.pdf/space_bridges_the_ussoviet_space_bridge_resource_center.pdf
9 Keyssar, *PS: Political Science & Politics,* 250.
10 Keyssar, *PS: Political Science & Politics,* 250–251
11 "Spotlight: U.S.-Russia Sister Cities," *Sister Cities International* website, Accessed September 28, 2021, https://sistercities.org/2013/08/20/spotlight-u-s-russia-sister-cities/
12 "History," *CCI* website, Accessed September 28, 2021, https://ccisf.org/brief-history/
13 "History," *Rotary Club St. Petersburg* website, Accessed October 2, 2022, www.rotary-spb.ru/index.php?option=com_jumi&view=application&fileid=11&Itemid=197&lang=en
14 "History," *Rotary Club St. Petersburg* website, Accessed October 2, 2022.
15 Connie Zweig, "S.F.-Moscow Teleport – Electronic Détente," *LA Times*, December 9, 1987, Accessed September 9, 2021, www.latimes.com/archives/la-xpm-1987-12-09-vw-18480-story.html
16 Zweig, "S.F.-Moscow Teleport – Electronic Détente."
17 Zweig, "S.F.-Moscow Teleport – Electronic Détente."
18 Paul R. Lawrence and Charalambos Vlachoutsicos, "Joint Ventures in Russia: Put the Locals in Charge," *Harvard Business Review*, January–February, 1993, Accessed October 6, 2021, https://hbr.org/1993/01/joint-ventures-in-russia-put-the-locals-in-charge
19 Lawrence and Vlachoutsicos, "Joint Ventures in Russia: Put the Locals in Charge."
20 "Good Ideas, Idealism Not Nearly Enough in Russia," *Chicago Tribune*, November 27, 1998, Accessed October 6, 2021, www.chicagotribune.com/news/ct-xpm-1998-11-27-9811270238-story.html

2 US Government Aid Programs

Supporting Transition to a Market Economy and Promoting Civil Society

> I learned more about the United States in that whole experience than I did about Russia. I don't think Americans fully understand how powerful and influential this country is.
>
> (Adam Blanco, Peace Corps volunteer in Russia)

> You can't transform a society into what you want it to be, so that it's just like in the US. It doesn't work. It's a different culture, a different history. … We were better able to do that with Germany and Japan after the war because it was a complete rebuild. That was a very different situation than in Russia where we didn't have full control.
>
> (Denis Boyle, Peace Corps volunteer in Russia)

The dissolution of the Soviet Union initiated an historic period of change in Russia, with many open questions about the direction that this change would take. The US government responded with political and economic support for Boris Yeltsin that led to almost a decade of intense involvement of Americans in shaping the contours of the "New Russia." The relatively small number of personal contacts from the civil diplomacy period were replaced by a virtual torrent of Americans and other foreigners entering Russia and directly engaging with Russians in historic numbers. This chapter will tell the story of those times through the eyes of Americans involved with US government-funded aid programs and private institutions that shared the objectives of supporting Russian market reforms and promoting new civil society organizations.

The Brzezinski formulation of American victory and Russian receivership was a dominant narrative of the times. The collapse of the Soviet Union was perceived as proof of the superiority of the American economic and social system as the aspirational goal for all. It was the time of the height of American soft power in the world. The motivations and world view of the Americans interviewed for this chapter varied greatly, as will be true throughout this book. The vast majority assumed that Russia would inevitably become a Western-style society, after some period of transition. In various ways, all the Americans

DOI: 10.4324/9781003182153-3

included in this chapter contributed to this vision of transition. Some of them conformed to the prevailing narrative, but several of them began to question the viability of the receivership model in the real conditions they encountered in Russia.

US Support of the Yeltsin Agenda

As is well-known, Boris Yeltsin led the resistance and ultimate defeat of the coup attempt against Gorbachev in August 1991. In the wake of this victory, Yeltsin seized de facto political control and marginalized Gorbachev, leading to the dissolution of the Soviet Union on December 25, 1991.

Much of the demise of the Soviet Union can be linked to popular, nationalist demonstrations and uprisings in the former Republics of the Soviet Union. There was no similar popular demand for economic reform in Russia at the time of the August 1991 coup attempt. The victorious Yeltsin team wanted to modernize Russia by rapidly creating a system based on private property with new owners as a base of support for a market economy. This dramatic seismic event was primarily a top-down reform with unreformed political institutions from Soviet times still in place.

Yeltsin and his team, led by Yegor Gaidar, Alfred Kokh, Anatoly Chubais, and others, were determined to destroy the economic foundations of the Soviet Union as quickly and as completely as possible. In late 1991 and 1992, the Yeltsin reform team dismantled the centrally planned economy and eliminated the planning bureaucracy's role in coordinating the economy, with the goal of having new market mechanisms govern the economy. Their efforts were obstructed by the Supreme Soviet, the hold-over legislature in which there was deep resistance to the Yeltsin program. This came to a head with the 1993 assault on the Supreme Soviet and the subsequent passing of a new constitution for Russia, strengthening the power of the President and his ability to continue with economic market reforms.

In the realm of Russian popular culture, there was a romantic aspirational attachment to the image of the United States, symbolized best by the popularity in post-Soviet Russia TV of the American nighttime soap opera series, Santa Barbara, and its portrayal of American life and standard of living. These years were the height of US soft power as the aspirational lifestyle and political and economic model for many Russians. During these years, many Russians would express their desire for Russia to become a "normal" country, imitating in lifestyle its European Union (EU) neighbors or the United States.

As will be explored in more detail in Chapter 3, the Russian reformers recognized that they had a narrow window of time to accomplish the destruction of the previous system of state ownership and state planning. To accomplish this goal, they had to transform state property into private property as quickly as possible. The basis for their plans was an historically unprecedented mass privatization as the first step in developing new market mechanisms and institutions to guide the economy in place of Soviet central planning.

In both privatization and institution building, the Yeltsin team relied heavily on foreign experts, including Americans, for technical assistance. The reliance on foreign experts to modernize Russia differed in detail from the previous modernizations of Russia under Peter the Great and Stalin but is consistent with the historical pattern of these past modernizations as described in the Introduction.

The Russian reformers looked to their former Cold War enemies in North America, Europe, and Asia for support and expertise. In response, the United States, Canada, Europe, South Korea, and Japan initiated a chaotic, uncoordinated, and massive set of aid programs that brought a relative flood of foreign experts, consultants, and businesspeople to Russia to assist in transforming the Soviet system to a Russian market system. Russian reformers were thus able to find needed experts, resources, and expertise from foreign sources until such time as Russians mastered the knowledge needed to run their market economy without foreigners.

Russian motives and objectives are often left out of the picture of this period as commonly understood, then and now. Foreigners assumed that they were setting the agenda for Russia and were often frustrated by Russians' determination to set that agenda themselves. Foreigners often simply did not know or understand what was driving their Russian counterparts politically, economically, or culturally. Virtually no one saw the historical parallels with past periods of Russian modernization and saw the period as historically unique. There was little doubt among foreign experts that Russia needed to be raised up to Western standards of business and cultural behavior over some long period of time.

The American aid programs arose out of commitments made at summit meetings between American Presidents George H. W. Bush and Bill Clinton, first with Mikhail Gorbachev and then with Boris Yeltsin.

There was no clear or coordinated plan among foreign governments and experts beyond the general goal of creating a market economy in Russia and integrating it into the global economic and political order. No one really knew how to accomplish this completely unprecedented transformation, but everyone involved had opinions about the correctness of their own approach. The result was a sometimes-conflicting set of programs and policy advice by different agencies of the US government, European governments, Asian governments, and international organizations.

On the critical social level, foreigners provided material aid to blunt popular discontent and economic hardship that accompanied the destruction of the planned economy. The most emblematic material aid enshrined in Russian popular culture were the frozen chicken legs sent to Russia as food aid, popularly known as "Bush legs."

The ranks of the small, existing expat and diplomatic community in Russia that was formed during the years of Perestroika was now joined by thousands of newcomers with wildly different reasons for being in Russia, ranging from adventure to economic opportunity to idealistic visions of transforming Russia into some semblance of the United States.

Transition to a Russian Market Economy

As the Soviet bloc crumbled and countries like Poland and Hungary detached from the Council for Mutual Economic Assistance (CMEA), the Soviet competitor to the EU, the United States, the EU, and multilateral aid agencies pivoted a good portion of their aid and assistance programs from the so-called "Third World" to the developed "Second World" of former Soviet Eastern European states. These agencies developed approaches and funding mechanisms that were then expanded and redeployed to the former Soviet Union in the aftermath of the dissolution of that country at the end of 1991. The United States had already begun to provide some economic aid to the USSR in the waning years of perestroika and that aid turned into a massive wave of spending and programs beginning in 1992.

A US Government Accounting Office study of US aid to Russia states that "From fiscal year 1990 through December 31, 1994, U.S. departments and agencies obligated $5.4 billion and expended $3.5 billion for grant technical assistance, exchange programs, training, food and commodity donations, mutually beneficial science and technology projects, and support of joint space efforts. The U.S. government also provided about $10 billion in credit for bilateral loans, loan guarantees, and insurance." In addition to this government-funded activity, there was also important programs supported by private foundations like the Soros Foundation, Ford Foundation, MacArthur Foundation, Rockefeller's Brothers Fund, and the Kennan Institute.

"During this same period, 23 departments and independent agencies implemented 215 programs in the FSU. However, three agencies, the US Agency for International Development (USAID), the Department of Agriculture (USDA), and DOD implemented the large majority of noncredit programs. USDA also funded the largest portion of credit/insurance programs."[1]

Professor Janine Wedel, who conducted one of the most detailed non-governmental reviews of Western aid to Eastern Europe, constructed a table of "U.S. Assistance to the Former Soviet Union," showing that the United States provided $2,216,820,000 from FY 1992 to 1997 in Freedom Support Act funds. This does not include non-Freedom Support Act funds of $2,643,680,000 for those same years that came through the US Departments of Defense (including Cooperative Threat Reduction programs), State, Agriculture, Energy and Commerce, US Export–Import Bank, US Trade and Development Agency, US Information Agency and Peace Corps.[2]

This influx of spending was implemented through a set of subcontracts with large international consulting companies, universities, non-profit organizations, former citizen diplomacy activists and their organizations, and a range of private individuals. More than two-thirds of USAID expenditures up to March 31, 1996, went to Western consultants.[3] In addition to government-funded programs, a growing community of lawyers representing international companies in Russia assumed informal and sometimes formal advisory roles with Russian government officials, as will be discussed in Chapter 4.

The extensive reach of American-led programs into Russian society is evident from Fact Sheet on People-to-People Cooperation issued on May 24, 2002, in advance of President George W. Bush's trip to Europe and Russia. The Fact Sheet highlights partnerships, citizen, business and scientific exchanges, Peace Corps, Open World Russian Leadership Program, support for independent media, public internet access, and non-governmental organizations (NGOs)to support democratic institutions and practices and health cooperation.[4] In the area of partnerships alone, the Fact Sheet mentions 8 hospital partnerships, 37 university partnerships, 94 Russian–American sister cities and more than 100 partnerships between local governments, judges, businesses, professional associations, and other NGOs.[5] Under the category of exchanges, the Fact Sheet states that more than 50,000 Russians had visited the United States under US government-funded exchanges by 2002.

With this complexity in mind, the chapter will focus on a limited number of the key aid programs and agencies to illustrate the flavor and tenor of the times. While the US government-funded programs in Moscow and to a lesser extent St. Petersburg focused primarily on policy, law, and institution building for the infrastructure of the new Russian market economy, regional business and economic development programs reached deep into the Russian regions. This geographically diverse intervention in Russian life vastly expanded the scope of interaction, collaboration, understanding, and misunderstanding between Americans and Russians.

It is virtually impossible to completely capture the full range of such a large and diverse intervention in Russian life in this period. The attempt to adequately cover in one book this huge and diverse number of aid programs calls to mind an image of a suitcase stuffed to the gills in anticipation of a long journey. Suddenly, something else is discovered that must be stuffed into the suitcase somehow. Following on this analogy, some interesting and important programs were unfortunately left out due to page limitations, while focusing on those major ones that illustrate the times.

Peace Corps – First Shock Troops of Capitalism in Russian Regions

One of the most visible components of the initial US support program was the introduction of the Peace Corps into the provinces of Russia, outside the traditional power centers of Moscow and St. Petersburg.

Between 1992 and 2003, more than 700 Peace Corps volunteers served in Russia, primarily teaching English, business education, and development.[6] For this book, five of the original 100 volunteers who came to Russia in November 1992 were interviewed, Bill Frazer, Kendrick White, Adam Blanco, Jack Horowitz, and Denis Boyle.

Bill Frazer provided a brief history of how the Peace Corps came to Russia. "US Secretary of State James Baker came to Russia in December 1991 and promised Russian officials that he would have 100 American businesspeople there to assist the Russian transition to capitalism within a year."

"This is a bit hearsay, but when he came back, he went to the Commerce Department first. He told them that we must get 100 businesspeople over to Russia and asked how are we going to do this? The Commerce Department said that they don't do that kind of thing and did not have a clue how that works. That's how it ended up in the Peace Corps, as the agency with experience sending Americans abroad."

The Peace Corps, then headed by Elaine Chao, swung into action. An ad was placed in the *Wall Street Journal* asking for 100 volunteers. According to Kendrick White, who became one of those volunteers, there were 25,000 replies to the ad, making for very stiff competition. In distinction to the young Americans who were typical Peace Corps volunteers, this group was supposed to be composed of older, more experienced businesspeople. The motivation for each of the volunteers was different, ranging from a commitment to bring capitalism to Russia, to bringing evangelical Christianity, to seeking adventure in a time of historical change. The initial group of 100 was split into two parts. Half went to the city of Saratov in the lower Volga Region of Russia to be scattered around the nearby Volga-area locations after training and orientation. The other half went to Vladivostok in the Russian Far East to be similarly spread in neighboring cities and towns after training and orientation.

Denis Boyle was one of that first group in November 1992 and stayed for 27 months in Vladivostok. He was visiting his brother, who was working for the US Defense Department in Germany, for Christmas 1991 and watched the lowering of the Soviet flag and Gorbachev leaving office. At the same time, he saw a small article in "Stars and Stripes," the American military's newspaper, stating that there were plans to send Peace Corps volunteers to the former Soviet Union. He had recently completed an MBA. When asked his reason for wanting to go, he answered, "I guess I had a kind of midlife crisis; I was 38 years old at the time and had been working at a community college for years, where some people would say to me 'What are you doing here? You should be somewhere else.' So yeah, it was just an historic opportunity for me to be able to fulfill a life dream. To be able to go somewhere else, and to be part of history. I mean the things that were happening there were unprecedented and incredibly interesting – to be part of that transition of going from Communism and a command economy to democracy. … It wasn't a matter of going to change the world or accomplish something specific. It was more just at a personal level, that I wanted to be friends with people."

Adam Blanco also saw the Peace Corps in personal terms. "It was an adventure. It was an opportunity, not only an economic opportunity, but a chance to be part of history. At that age, you've got your whole life in front of you, and you take the risk, grab the bull by the horns and have some fun. … My goal was to really learn the language and the culture. I knew from my own experience that I needed to be away from other expats. Spanish was my first language and I learned English when I was six. The reason I learned English was because I had no choice. I saw it as huge educational opportunity to do the same with Russian."

Jack Horowitz also had very personal reasons for wanting to take part. His parents were Russian Jews who emigrated to the United States in 1959 when he was 4. He explained, "My parents were deeply rooted in the American culture, but still all their friends were Eastern Europeans. Their culture was instilled in me, and I guess, I was just always curious to learn more about where this culture came from. Then one morning on the way to work, I was watching Good Morning America and Elaine Chao, the head of the Peace Corps, was on the show. She was there to announce that soon the first group of Peace Corps volunteers we're going to go to Russia. So, I said wow that that would be exciting. As soon as I got to work, I called up the Peace Corps and said how do I apply to go to Russia. They said no, that's not how Peace Corps works. You join the Peace Corps, and we'll send you where there is space. I said no, I don't want to go where you're going to send me. Send me to Russia." He got his wish and became part of the first group in Saratov and was then assigned to Togliatti, a heavy industrial center in the Nizhny Novgorod region.

Denis Boyle described the process of becoming part of the Peace Corps program. "They were gung-ho on this whole thing with the businesspeople, so they were actually recruiting through *The Wall Street Journal.* It was really an unusual group. Your typical Peace Corps volunteer is usually in their 20s. In this group, there were several MBAs and lawyers and retired executives, corporate executives. The average age was in the 40s. I was 38 and turned 39 within two weeks of arrival. So, it was an unusual group, and I was proud to be part of it. When you put in the application, they didn't guarantee anything about where you might go, but I made it clear that I wanted to go to Vladivostok."

Bill Frazer went to the Soviet Union with a delegation from Campus Crusade for Christ in 1991 and was overwhelmed with level of interest in their message and interest in the Bible. He came back to his job as Senior Sales Rep for IBM and then was bought out. He saw the ad in the *Wall Street Journal* looking for volunteers for the Peace Corps to go to Russia and saw this as an opportunity to go back to Russia and pursue his religious objectives as well. So, in November 1992, he was one of the first 100 Peace Corps volunteers.

Kendrick White took a leave of absence from ABN Amro to join the Peace Corps. He had written a master's thesis that predicted the Soviet Union was going to become bankrupt by the year 2000 and now saw his predictions coming true much in advance of this projection. He had read a 1991 book by the Harvard Academic Graham Allison and the Russian reformer Grigory Yavlinsky called *Window of Opportunity: The Grand Bargain for Democracy in the Soviet Union.* Boris Nemtsov, a physicist and reform politician who was appointed as Governor of the Nizhny Novgorod Region in 1991 by Boris Yeltsin, was carrying out the programs outlined in *Window of Opportunity* and creating a new institute for transition to a market economy. Nizhny Novgorod became a magnet for reformers and their Western supports, and Kendrick was determined to join them. As Kendrick expressed it, "We were seen as the shock troops from America to bring capitalism to Russia."

As the volunteer applicants were being screened and selected, the Peace Corps was under pressure to put the program in place to meet Secretary Baker's promised deadline. The result was an uncertain support structure in place in Russia. Bill Frazer explained, "The Peace Corps normally spends about two and a half years prepping a site before they bring in volunteers. They meet with local officials, line up housing, all that stuff and then they bring in some volunteers. In this case they had to get some people there before December 1992. So, everything got put on rush, and you know bureaucracies don't move very fast. ... Usually with the Peace Corps you had a 12-week training period in the US before departing to your assigned country. We had a pre-departure orientation of two or three days."

When the volunteers arrived in Russia, one group went to Saratov and one group to Vladivostok to go through a 12-week program of Russian language, along with business and cultural orientation. Jack Horowitz spoke about the limitations of the training program, "the people who are instructing us, they had Peace Corps experience that didn't relate very well to what we were doing there in Russia. There weren't any real Russian experts who could tell us what we were in for." Adam Blanco also stated that there were no real Russia experts involved. "And when I say Russian experts, I don't mean State Department Russia that just speaks the language. I mean Russian experts that understand the culture, the history of Russian that show me that they really understand Russia. This program could have been much different if there had been those kinds of experts." For the volunteers being trained in Russian, there were all kinds of stresses. Beyond the rigors of language study, there were big adjustments in food, housing, and lifestyle that also made life difficult for them as they prepared for their assignments.

Denis Boyle had a particularly difficult adjustment in the early days in Vladivostok. "Getting up every morning to go into language class, then to the lecture hall and going through all these different trainings was not easy. ... There was a Russian woman who was one of the teachers or counselors or administrative assistants. She spoke English and ran into me in a hallway or stairwell one morning. I was obviously not happy, so she just asked me, 'How's it going?' I was like 'all right...' And she said, 'you know, I really don't think you guys are going to make it here. I think Russia is too tough for Americans. You guys are just not tough enough for life here.' I was thinking, 'Oh yeah – well I'll show you!' That was the turning point for me or the critical point, I guess. It made me determined not to quit. That lady has since emigrated to Canada, and I'm still here."

Bill Frazer was part of the group assigned to Saratov. They lived in a dormitory and had intensive language lessons, 6 hours a day, 6 days per week. "After the three month of language training, an Assistant Ambassador or some equivalent came down from Moscow to our graduation ceremony. He said something that was very poignant. At the time I didn't realize it, but I certainly do now. He said, you know you came here with hopes of changing Russia.

I don't know how much you're going to change Russia, but I know Russia is going to change you. … And you know, that was so on the money."

Even at the training stage, the American volunteers began to interact socially with Russians. For Russians in the provinces, the Americans were exotic representatives of the former enemy, now turned aspirational model for the new Russia. They were the objects of curiosity, potential economic opportunity and maybe emigration to the good live in the United States through marriage. Jack Horowitz describes some of this early social interaction. "Oh yeah, I think those first two years I was in Russia was probably the most exciting two years of my life. I have so many amazing stories and experiences from that time. … From the time we came to Russia, we were all celebrities. All the cities we went to had been closed to foreigners until then. So, most of the people we met had never met a foreigner before, never seen a foreign up close. I remember coming to Saratov, where our pre-service training was, and it was like girls were throwing themselves at me. I mean I wasn't used to this. You know, mothers were introducing their daughters, to me, inviting me over for dinner. Everyone wanted to meet us. We'd be walking down the street and we stuck out like sore thumbs. It gave us away with the outfits we were wearing. And you know I thought we were treated very well for the most part."

Denis Boyle found that there was a period of cultural adjustment that ultimately led him to fit into Russian social life. "I just love Russian people now. You know they have the reputation of being rather unwelcoming, especially to foreigners. But if you go inside their homes and get invited into their lives, they could not be more hospitable, warm, and generous. … Life got a lot easier when I sat down and started drinking vodka with people. They were much friendlier, much more accepting, and I was more one of them. By reputation, it's a complex society, with a complex character. I think that they have sort of this duality, a combination of superiority and inferiority complexes going on at the same time. I've always said that there's a big difference between the outside Russian and the inside Russian. When you first come here and you see people on the street, they seem like they couldn't be colder, or ruder and more uncaring. It is like they're telling you 'Get away from me; I'm not interested.' It was more an attitude of mistrust. But once you got beyond that, regular people were incredibly interested in the United States and in meeting Americans. They were really fascinated by us, and most people wanted to get to know us. They also wanted to show us that they were very friendly, generous, and hospitable."

After the training was completed, the volunteers were dispersed to their assigned cities where they were supposed to work with local government officials to support small and medium-size businesses. The Peace Corps provided them with a monthly stipend to purchase food and the government officials were supposed to provide housing. The stipend in the Volga Region was around $200 per month and in the Far East, it was $55. Getting food and housing on the local economy with this level of stipend proved difficult. The actual scope of their activities supporting business was a bit vague with the volunteers tasked with filling in the details based on local conditions.

After graduation, the volunteers who trained in Saratov were dispersed to cities up and down the Volga River. Bill Frazer ended up Nizhny Novgorod. "We were more or less on our own, trying to make something happen. There was a local Russian guy who was assigned to us by the local city administration to try and help us." At that time, there were 10 Peace Corps volunteers in the Nizhny Novgorod region.

Bill Frazer elaborated, "My comment about the Peace Corps is that it is the most screwed up organization that I've ever had anything to do with. However, after saying that, it was the best program on the ground in Russia, compared to everything else that the Federal Government was doing. We were by far the most effective at getting something done and that's because of the initiative of the Peace Corps volunteers, not the organization."

He ended up in Nizhny Novgorod after his initial assignment proved untenable. "I got assigned to this place called Balakhna. I didn't stay there long, it didn't last. It was right near a major factory, not a big factory, but a MiG testing Center, where there were the Russian MiG military aircraft. Everyone thought I was CIA. You know that was the Russian mantra. We were all considered CIA agents. You know it's classic Russian."

"Even after three months of intensive language training, I did not have the level of Russian to really do much. They had only one translator in the town. She worked at a big paper mill there. That's why they assigned me there to try and help their paper mill market their stuff. They put me in the local administration building and then she came to that office every other night, and I'd have a list of things to ask. I kind of figured out they didn't know what to do with me and they weren't sure they even wanted me."

"The Russians were supposed to provide housing and the Peace Corps would provide us with a stipend to pay for our food and other needs. It was a small stipend. I think it was like $200 a month. And the place I was placed to live was like two to three miles outside of town. In the middle of February. They figured that was a safe place to stick the CIA agent because there's no way I could get to anything from out there."

Ultimately, Bill moved to Nizhny Novgorod to work with other volunteers there but did not have an apartment for more than 6 months. "Housing was a big problem. And Peace Corps said that's not in our budget, we're not doing that. You're supposed to be working with the Russians at your assigned place and they are supposed to provide housing."

Denis Boyle also spoke about the hardships of daily living in those early days in Vladivostok. "There was no continued support in terms of eating in the cafeteria and all that. We had to go out and find our own food. It was kind of a really bad time. There was hardly any food on the shelves. In addition, it was interesting going out to buy food. You really need to learn how to shop in a different country. They do things completely differently. For example, you could only buy a whole fish. I don't know what to do with a whole fish. I am used to buying fish in a pretty package and all filleted. And then we might have had a kitchen and a refrigerator, but no plates and frying pans and that kind of stuff. So, there was hardly any food on the shelves anyway and restaurants were not service oriented. Some of them closed for lunch for God's sake. It was like they were saying, 'We have to eat too, you know.'"

As the volunteers were adjusting to life in Russia, they were also expected to develop their own projects and service offerings using the same approach as the Peace Corps used elsewhere in the world. Bill Frazer described the approach. "The Peace Corps does the same anywhere they send in volunteers, Africa or wherever else. They just say here's your place, make something happen. Don't create a crisis, an international affair, or a scandal. And it's really the initiative of each volunteer that really makes something happen. That was that was really the case in Russia for sure because we had nothing to start with."

The Peace Corps volunteers began to interact with local businesspeople in their assigned cities as they developed their projects and programs. In many cases, they found that the objectives set by the high-level agreements between US Secretary of State Baker and the government of Boris Yeltsin did not correspond with the understanding and objectives of regional governments and the developing regional business community.

Denis Boyle described how they began their work in the Far East. "Everybody was supposed to be setting up small business consulting centers where we would work in groups of five, like functional specialists. These consulting centers didn't work out at all. ... They never worked out because the model just didn't fit. It wasn't appropriate. ... Coming in and trying to act like we were going to give advice and tell Russians how to properly do business was completely unreasonable. I mean, Russian business is for Russians. Their circumstances were unprecedented, and they were still figuring it out for themselves. They were going to do it their own way, no matter what. They were not going to listen to somebody else, and we didn't really understand what we were dealing with."

Complicating the situation was misunderstanding in the fledgling Russian business sector about the Peace Corps mission. Denis continued, "The businesspeople would say to us, 'We just need your money to get something started. We don't need your advice. We need money to get business rolling.' It was well known that the US government had committed something like $900 million to assist projects in Russia through USAID. The problem was that Russians thought that we Peace Corps volunteers were the ones that were going to distribute that money. I didn't realize that at the time, but it came to me later that they would call us to try to impress us with their projects and proposals and try to get our interest because they thought that we were making the decisions about who would get that money. ... That was a real confusion that was difficult to overcome."

Denis shared his perception of the motivations of Russians he was dealing within the local economy. "This whole economic development and capitalism thing is all about self-interest. Adam Smith even says that everybody's after their own self-interest. I think that's what happened in Russia. People took advantage of whatever they could to promote their own self-interest, given the situation that they were presented with. It was a completely different process and different circumstances than what created development in the United States. So, I think it would be unreasonable to expect things to develop as they did in the US. ... The idea of needing technical assistance or expertise is one thing. They are fast learners. You don't have to hang around and tell them in detail what to do. ... Whatever worked in other situations, they're going to adapt it to their situation, but with their way of doing things and their way of looking at things."

Bill Frazer described the range of activities they carried out in Nizhny Novgorod. "We put on consulting seminars and whatever we could do to foster partnerships between Russian businesses and the European Bank for Reconstruction and Development (EBRD) and USAID. We promoted other help that was out there to try and connect with it, like exchange programs. We did a lot of sending people back to the States for training sessions. There was some English teaching going on. I taught a course at the university on marketing."

After some period of struggle with the Peace Corps central administration over financing, the local Peace Corps volunteers were funded to open a fully functioning business center in Nizhny Novgorod that was largely self-supporting by the time their term ended in January 1995. Asked about the biggest obstacle to working with local business, Bill responded, "I'd say the biggest point was they really weren't interested in my marketing expertise or organizational expertise or putting together a business plan. All they wanted was money. They were like give me the money. I know what to do with it once you give me the money. I'll make it work. We would say, well, you need to put together a business plan, some idea of where you're going and what you are going to do with the money. They didn't want anything to do with that idea. ... We used to have a saying in Russia that there aren't really any Russian businessmen, there's Russian business-like men."

Jack Horowitz shared his impressions of Togliatti, the industrial city where he was assigned, and his business center there. "Togliatti, let me tell you, it is like a thug city. Organized crime was very much connected with the auto manufacturing business. Everyone who drove off with a car from the manufacturing facility there would have to give something to the mafia."

"I remember, I used to go drinking at the big hotel in the city. They were always there. They just looked like your typical New York hoods. You know, wearing their leather jackets, dressed in black. Young guys with short hair."

"I was from Chicago, and they always called me Chicago because they thought of Chicago as a mafia city. I remember the first time that I met one of these guys in the bar. He was sitting next to me and started this conversation. And then, he was in the corner sitting with his group. He was the head of this little clan, and he introduced me to them. I not kidding when I say this, he said 'Chicago, I want you to meet my friends. This is Igor. He breaks people's legs. This is Ivan and Dimitri. They steal cars. This is Elena and Irina. They are our girls, but they can be yours if you want them.'"

Quite aside from his social interaction with the local mafia businesspeople, Jack was in contact with the small businesspeople coming into his business center in Togliatti. He recounted that "A lot of people were coming into our so-called business center because they thought that we were going to just throw some money at them so that they can start a business. We did help with seed money for small business. We told them that they had to have a business plan. Of course, they had no idea what a business plan was. They didn't really have any idea what their business was either. They had these pie in the sky, totally unrealistic dreams of revolutionizing the world type of businesses. And they had never done anything. They had never accomplished anything in their lives, but they're going to create a spaceship. ... It took a little while to realize that I wasn't going to make a difference with those kinds of things. After I talked with all these businesses, I decided to change direction and look to see if I could do anything from a humanitarian standpoint."

Adam Blanco was assigned to a small city called Stova. He requested an assignment to an isolated location away from other foreigners so that he could immerse himself in the Russian language. He immersed himself in the language and culture of post-Soviet Russia and became embedded in the Russian society around him. This process of integration is typical of most of the successful expats interviewed. As Adam explained, "Learning the culture, living the culture is what allowed me to do what I did." He continued, "Learning the language is not a mechanical process. All languages are tied to the culture. It doesn't matter that your grammar is perfect or even good. What matters is that you're able to communicate and communicate in a way that relates to the culture. You must absorb the culture to really learn the language." His mastery of the language and culture coupled with his American business background enabled his relatively long career in Russia starting with the 2-year Peace Corps assignment.

Adam secured a special status among the Nizhny Novgorod business community as a result of identifying and securing a production and distribution center for Coca Cola in Nizhny Novgorod. "I identified the site for a giant Coca Cola bottling and distribution center. ... It was located on a huge 49-hectare factory that was a solid part of an industrial complex where they machine tooled blades and related manufactured equipment, including for the Russian Space Agency." The plant had been privatized by a local mafia group. "As a result, I had a great relationship with the mafia guys at the industrial complex. They wouldn't bother me. They wouldn't touch me. I was protected because I was bringing in jobs. I was bringing in investment into the factory that they had taken over."

Several years later, Adam was hired by Price Waterhouse to assist them in negotiations for restructuring the industrial complex in which he had helped locate the Coca Cola plant and which was still controlled by the same mafia group. He recounted one episode in the middle of these negotiations that illustrates both the tenor of the times and the value of the ability of people like Adam to cross cultural divides. "There was a director from Price Waterhouse that came in to work with me on the restructuring of the plant. And we're in a meeting with the representative of the mafia group that had taken over the plant. He's got long hair and looks kind of like John Travolta in the movie Pulp Fiction. He had that look and that demeanor. He was high as a kite in the meeting. He spoke good English, but he used a translator intentionally. The mafia guy said to his translator, who was also high, ask him if he has ever seen a man dipped in boiling oil. The translator knew that I heard and understood it. The translator looked at the mafia guy and said you really want to ask him that? And the mafia guy loved it. He said yes. So, the translator asked the question to the Price Waterhouse guy. After the meeting, the Price Waterhouse guy said to me, he threatened us. Do you think we should call Moscow; do you think we should call Price Waterhouse security? He's threatened us. I looked at him and I said no. Don't worry about it. He didn't threaten us, he's just playing with us. I said you know what, even if you call Moscow, it's not going to help us. He didn't like that last part. While that whole conversation was going on, I was looking at the mafia guy's bodyguard in the back of the room, standing by the door. I turned around and I looked at him as we're walking out. He was just smiling, and I was just smiling back at him. He knew the game. By smiling, he was basically saying to me, Adam don't worry. You're one of us." This process of Peace Corps volunteers becoming "one of us" was a life changing experience for them and likely had a similar impact on their Russian friends and colleagues. The exact way that each of them became part of Russian life was quite different, as illustrated by the difference between the experience of Adam Blanco and that of Bill Frazer.

When asked about his greatest success, Bill Frazer opened a window on missionary work in post-Soviet Russia. Missionary work in Russia in the early 1990s was quite extensive and had an important impact on the Russian population as another face of American life and culture. This is a topic about which little has been written but is one that deserves more research and attention. Bill lifted the veil on this world in his interview. He explained that "I don't know if much has been written about it but there was a lot that was going on. The call went out amongst the evangelical community to send missionaries to Russia." This call was what initiated his interest in going to Russia with Campus Crusade for Christ group and then motivated him to return through the Peace Corps. "The Peace Corps has a rule against proselytizing. You're not supposed to go over there and start converting people to some religion. But I looked at it this way, Monday to Friday, nine to five, I worked in the business center for the Peace Corps, to try and do the capitalism consulting, and whatever else we're supposed to do with the Peace Corps. But evenings and weekends, I felt like that's my time. I'm going to do what I want to do. So, I managed to connect with a couple of missionary teams that were over there, trying to start some churches. So, on my own time, I was working to help start to churches over there."

Bill went on to describe his activity on behalf of the two new churches. "One was a Calvary Chapel and the other one was a complete startup that was being done by some missionaries from Louisiana, an independent church. That was probably the most successful thing I did when I was over there. I was leading a Bible study. I was doing some preaching. I basically was the assistant pastor at one of the churches. The church model that we were using over there is something called a cell group model, which meets in homes. We would have small groups in certain regions that would meet. Maybe six or eight families would meet on a Wednesday night in somebody's apartment. And we had like 24 of those groups around the city. … These small groups were really like mini churches in and of themselves. Then we'd meet as a large group on Sunday. We'd rent a hall. We would have the worship team and music. We would have a sermon of some sort and fellowship afterwards. That's what we did. … We started those two churches. Those are still going, and I go back every couple of years to visit. I visit those churches and I get a chance to do some preaching there and visit friends. I just stay in people's homes. I don't go to hotels, or anything. … People have become co-religionists and good friends. I mean real relationships, real friendships. That was my goal in learning the language, to be able to have a real relationship. You can't have a relationship with anybody if there's a translator there with you." What the conversation with Bill revealed was the extent of the interaction between American missionaries and ordinary Russian people that was enormously significant for each side. It also reveals a more general theme that is common to many of the people interviewed regarding the value of the relationships and the deep friendships developed with individual Russians.

After the transformational experience of the Peace Corps, many of the volunteers remained in Russia. Price Waterhouse, which was a co-administrator of the Peace Corps, hired many of them for their ongoing consulting contracts in Russia, including Kendrick White. This led Kendrick to a long and continuing career in Russia in promoting startups and commercialization of Russian scientific inventions. Jack Horowitz was hired by KPMG for their Russian capital markets reform project before leaving Russia permanently. After a brief sojourn in the United States after the Peace Corps, Denis Boyle returned to Vladivostok where he worked for American Councils for International Education and was living there at the time of the interview. Adam Blanco started his own consulting company and engaged in a string of economic development and business positions over the years. His last position in Moscow was as Director of the Roth Holding Group, owned by a syndicate headed by Sergei Petrov, a mini oligarch who was a supporter and financial backer of the later assassinated Boris Nemtsov. Petrov is now in exile in London. Abruptly at the same time, Adam was told by the Russian government to leave the country and is now resident in Naples, Florida.

Even at this early stage of the reform process in Russia, the Peace Corps volunteers encountered an already existing private business sector in the Russian provinces that had its own ideas and approaches to business that did not conform to the Western practices that informed the Peace Corps model. There were some points of convergence, particularly through the entry of multinationals like Coke into the regions. However, the way business was conducted was determined by Russians. The impact of the Peace Corps volunteers seems to have depended upon their ability to integrate themselves into Russian business and find their niche, but they can hardly be said to have been driving the process.

Food System Restructuring Program in Vladivostok – Turning a Grand Failure into Unexpected Success

In contrast to the more highly visible Peace Corps program, other American aid programs produced unexpected impacts that fly under the radar of public notice. An example is a fundamental transformation of agriculture in the Russian Far East that is a by-product of a failed project to build supermarkets in the region.

In 1991 or 1992, TPC, a US consulting company, received a $30 million USAID contract for a food system restructuring program in the Russian Far East. This program was designed to set up a US-style supermarket, working with Giant Foods, a grocery chain in the Washington DC, Maryland, Virginia, area. Part of the project was an attempt to set up an efficient supply chain and to develop branded merchandise for sale in the supermarket. At the time, Soviet consumers purchased their groceries at specialized and separate stores for produce, bread, meat, staples, etc. As was already described by Denis Boyle, this was a time of constant shortages in this complex distribution system. Few Russians owned cars. They were limited in what they could purchase at any one time to what they could carry home with them by hand or by shopping cart. There were no supermarkets in existence at that time.

While supermarkets did emerge in Russia later, this project was way too early in the development of the Russian market economy and ultimately failed. Two supermarkets were constructed, but they had the same problems with reliable supply as the smaller Russian stores. They were plagued by empty shelves and lack of merchandise. In 1995, the US Congress, led by Newt Gingrich, pulled back drastically on aid to Russia, and without aid subsidies, the supermarket project collapsed.

However, there were unintended consequences from the effort to create a supply chain that had a huge impact on farming in the Russian Far East. As part of the effort to improve the supply chain, the project brought Mike Cooper to the Russian Far East to see if introducing new seed varieties could help. Cooper's background was in seed technology, and he had been conducting trials and testing for various hybrid seeds his whole professional life. The supermarket project organizers assigned Mike to work with the Primorsk State Agricultural Institute in the city of Ussuriysk, an agricultural hub of the Russian Far East located in a fertile river valley about 60 miles north of Vladivostok.

Mike's task was to identify varieties of corn and soybeans that would flourish in the climate of the region and that would increase the efficiency of the agriculture of the region. At that time, the variety of corn and soybeans being planted in Siberia required drying in silos, sometimes for years, before the product could be ground into animal feed. Mike identified varieties already in use in the United States that dried in the field and could be ground into feed without waiting for years in silos. "This is going to sound conceited, but I created the concept of corn and soybeans for grain in Far East Russia. The advantage of the genetics of the seed that we could bring had a tremendous yield advantage and dry down so that they could be harvested without mechanical drying. They could be used as a cash crop and as feed forage, rather than limited to use after silage." This innovation was transformative for agriculture in the Russian Far East.

Operating with a license from the US rights holder, he and the Institute created a test plot for the new varieties of corn and soybeans. As Mike explained, "We had done some crossbreeding of Russian and American varieties trying to improve Russian varieties, because it was more plentiful than importing expensive parent stock from the US." Choosing the right seed with the right genetics was not a simple matter. "One of the guys from TPC Giant, noting the success of the first year of test plots, said what we did was the equivalent of shooting a bottle rocket to the moon."

The local farmers were quite aware of this experimental project. "For the next four or five years we grew corn and everybody in the region knew about it. … All the farmers in the region would drive by on the roads watching us harvest and watching the trucks go straight from the fields to the elevator for sale."

This new capability to rapidly produce animal feed led to expansion of animal food production. Mike recounted that "Right after we began, other companies made investments in local food production. A Danish company invested in a chicken broiler operation with a Russian partner, and they now do 1 million birds, a year. There are two or three egg laying operations, because decent quality feed sorts were now available." There was a similar impact in allowing for expansion of dairy farming as well. Over time, the new seed varieties created the conditions for a broader expansion of agriculture and food production and Mike estimated that "today there are over 800,000 hectares of commercial agriculture in corn and soy."

As Mike explained, "everything we produced during the first full year was sold before it was harvested. … Our downfall, if you want to call it that, was the lack of funding caused by the Congressional cutback of aid funding. … There was no funding to follow through and the Agricultural Institute didn't have any funding. Giant got booted with the rest of the programs." But this setback was not the end of the story of Mike's influence on Far Eastern agriculture.

The utility of these new seed varieties overcame the difficulties caused by the aid cutback. Use continued to grow through both front door and back door sourcing of seed. When asked what happened after the funding was cut and he left Russia, Mike said that "the varieties that I brought over are still being planted. The chain of ownership and rights has long been negated by the backdoor stuff." But there were also substantial legal sales of seed, and the US seed company Pioneer became the leading seed supplier in the Russian Far East.

In the long term, Mike stated that "You won't find anybody in Primorski Krai [Russian Far East] that doesn't think there's been a positive result from what the TPC Giant project did. I would say that the effect was very limited directly from the NGO. The real effect happened afterward from the people who were involved in the NGO."

As much as Mike impacted the agricultural economy of the Russian Far East, the experience also impacted him personally in many ways. "My goal when I went there was to experience some of Russia and to see if my ability to select genetics and crop production techniques would work. That was number one, and the other things became extensions of that. Curiosity would be right up there as a motivation, along with a little bit of ego about being able to accomplish something." Asked how experience impacted him, he replied, "you can't be even partially immersed in another culture without some sort of expansion of thought, recognition of humanity in general. … It leads to an understanding that friendship and common caring for each other is not a cultural thing. It's an interpersonal thing. It doesn't matter who you are, where you're from or what you do. If you're a true friend to somebody, you're a true friend. And that's why I've got people in Russia who I consider as much as family."

Pressed as to whether there are differences in Russian and American notions of friendship, Mike responded in a bit of detail about the cultural nuances of this term. "Americans talk about friendship with somebody they know, and they can call. Russians look at friendship more like a, I don't know, like a godfather relationship, a baptismal sponsor type relationship, although it has nothing to do with religion. If you're a friend to somebody and you call them for help, they help you, no questions asked. If your friend calls you, you help them no questions asked. And that's a piece of culture that the United States does not have, and probably will never have. Friendship is so much stronger than it is in the United States."

Mike Cooper made a lasting impact on Siberian agricultural through the seed varieties he introduced, and Siberia made a lasting impact on him through the relationships he formed there. The impact that he made had nothing much to do with grand narratives about receivership of Russia but was the result of bringing a practical solution to Siberian agriculture that had long-lasting impact.

Business Information Service for the Newly Independent States (BISNIS) – Bringing American Business to Russian Regional Markets

On a much grander scale, the Business Information Service for the Newly Independent States (BISNIS) was an ambitious business support organization that proved much more successful than the Peace Corp. BISNIS was set up to provide business matching and support services for American businesses entering the Russian market. As privatization took hold throughout Russia, regional business communities developed that were looking for foreign connections but without the opportunities to meet foreigners that existed in Moscow and St. Petersburg. At the same time, American businesspeople, ranging from multinationals to individual entrepreneurs, were anxious to explore what these regional markets could offer. There was an information void on each side that was filled to a certain extent by BISNIS. Administered through the State Department and the Commerce Department, BISNIS grew from an information service office of the Commerce Department in Washington, DC to a network of regional offices throughout Russia, staffed by Russian nationals and providing business information services to promote American business activity throughout Russia and the other countries of the former Soviet Union.

As explained by Dr. Trevor Gunn, who was first trade specialist and then Director of the BISNIS program from 1992 to 2004, "I think it was more celebrated by the Russian Government, which obviously welcomed the potential to encourage American investment." BISNIS had an investment and trade promotion mission that followed the model of similar organizations funded by the SEED Act for Eastern Europe. The program in Russia was funded by USAID under the Freedom Support Act of 1992.

Before the creation of BISNIS, American business became interested in the potential of the emerging Russian market and the Commerce Department began receiving inquiries about business opportunities and practices in Russia. These inquiries came to one small office that became overrun with these requests. As the conditions in Russia continued to change, it was decided that it was important to support the Russian economic transformation as a part of overall US national security, trade, and investment policy to cement democratization. BISNIS, like the Peace Corps, was one of the earliest US aid and economic development programs focused on business development. In 1992, Petr Aven, then Minister of Foreign Economic Relations of the Russian Federation (1991–1992) and Barbara Hackman Franklin, US Commerce Secretary under George H. W. Bush (1992–1993), opened the BISNIS program as part of an agreement between this Russian Government and the US Government.

An office at the State Department was created to coordinate business assistance programs like BISNIS and other related programs of the US Trade Development Agency. The US Foreign Commercial Service was also expanding in Russia, offering OPIC and EXIM Bank services to US companies. Trevor explained that "our mission was to support US businesses in the Former Soviet Union. Our office was created alongside the work of the State Department, so they could focus on the policy work." The BISNIS office was based in Washington, DC, and lived within the infrastructure of the embassies and consulates (later in BISNIS employees' homes) established in the new countries of the former Soviet Union.

Trevor dug deeper into the mission of BISNIS. "You know the Commerce Department's mission is not to promote outbound US direct investment in foreign countries. Their mission is to promote foreign direct investment in the US.

In this case, because it was working with the State Department and because it was Russia, which is always the exception, Commerce was allowed to promote trade and investment outside of the US."

Trevor had high school and college Russian language training. He wrote his PhD thesis on the Soviet–Russian economy and relations with Scandinavia, and he had experience in business in the United States before applying for the job with BISNIS. As he explained, the mission of BISNIS was "we were mainly there to inform and help guide business, particularly in faraway places. You know the typical foreign commercial service was confined to the embassies and consulates. … The diplomatic protocol was that you can't have people working for the US government outside of the embassy or consulate walls. Given that potential business was outside of where US officialdom decided to establish itself, BISNIS took a more entrepreneurial approach to support US business in the regions."

"We created a whole different network of people working for us. It was legal but controversial. We did some crazy entrepreneurial things, again in support of American business. … We were in places where the commercial service was not even represented, places like Novoşibirsk, Tomsk, Yuzhno-Sakhalinsk, places that we thought represented the real future of business. We also put our people in embassies where Commerce Department was not present, at least initially, places like Baku, Tbilisi, Dushanbe, Almaty, and Yerevan. At our high point, we hired people in all these places, and they ultimately reported into our office. There were 34 people working for us in that whole BISNIS network."

"We hired smart people in Russia, sent them computers and set them up to operate out of their home offices. … We hired people all different kinds of ways. … When we opened in Yuzhno-Sakhalinsk, I remember calling up all the oil and gas companies. I told them that we were opening something new and interesting. I asked if they knew anybody that speaks English, can write reasonably well, understands a little bit about business and knows their local business environment. We ended up hiring a woman there through this process. … In Khabarovsk, I hired a cardiologist. He had been to the US on a Rotary program. He knew a little bit about business, but the main thing was that he could talk to American companies. … We took whatever we could get. There were returnees that came to us after a three-week technical assistance program in the US. That was a big deal at the time."

"As we were expanding our network outside of the embassies and consulates, there began to be more and more Russian returnees from American assistance programs. They knew a little bit about America that could have come from being in an IREX program or any of a lot of programs taking Russians to America for short and long-term stays. There started to be a number of Russian-speaking MBAs, Russians who had applied to Western programs. At that time, they formed this organization called CLUMBA, club of MBAs."

The main purpose of this network and the local BISNIS representatives was to gather information that would be useful for American businesses about a particular region. As Dr. Gunn explained, "the primary functions were gathering information and reporting what they saw, including sector specific reports, for example the automotive sector. … With the Soviet Union breaking apart, all these Soviet type organizations were suddenly in a market economy. Nobody knew what was going on out there, even in Moscow." BISNIS used the information gathered by its network to create what they called International Market Insights. Occasionally, they also produced longer Industry Sector Analyses that were very detailed.

Trevor elaborated, "on the concrete side, it was also about finding trade opportunities. You know, X wants to buy something. Finding out the terms and getting those opportunities out to American businesses. It was also about finding investment opportunities. … The BISNIS representatives had to know their community, their districts. … They were very smart people that had unique talents. If there were opportunities to do other things, I always told them that they should take them. Of course, there were not as many opportunities in the regions."

Once the representative found what they thought was an opportunity they would send that to the BISNIS office in Washington, DC. Dr. Gunn again, "you must understand that in the beginning, everything that we did was controlled by diplomatic protocol and diplomatic cable. No matter where our representative was located, if they wanted to submit a report that's how it would be submitted. It would go through diplomatic channels of communication. These were reviewed and once it was declassified, we would disseminate it. … I remember the day that we opened the office, and we had five clients. When I left, we had 67,000 clients." Gunn added that "We also had specific publications targeted at Russian and Ukrainian businesspeople and government officials and had a Russian language website, and two handbook-like publications 'Business with America' in both Ukrainian and Russian language," said Gunn.

"The Internet was starting to come up and networking started to be available. People started to get Internet addresses, so I would literally type parts of those cables and send it out to a group of people. First, maybe it was three and then there were many. … Honestly, I was the guy that put this whole information distillation and information distribution thing together. … We had confidential information coming to us in these diplomatic cables. We had to make sure that they were marking those cables very specifically. There could be a paragraph that is confidential, but the next paragraph would be unclassified. … We had the first website in the Department of Commerce, before the Department of Commerce, itself had a website. … We were out in front of a lot of this stuff. We also had a publication called Search for Partners."

"When we had our expansion, it meant that we had a lot more information coming in. I launched a big Oracle database across the entire network. Our representatives had to enter their clients in the database, and they had to follow up monthly on these leads. Databases work. It meant that there was local ownership of these leads, and this local ownership of the relationship was really critical."

Asked about memorable success stories, Trevor remembered work with Andrews Corporation on fiber optics and satellite deals, US West on cellular service and Weyerhauser in the Russian Far East. He also remembered the work they did to assist companies who got themselves into bad deals. In telecom, there were "a lot of bad things that happened in that sector for American companies as well. Yeah, we had to pull one investor out of a particular deal in Russia that had all the bad characteristics of a bad Russian deal, threats of physical harm and all sorts of crazy stuff."

In terms of overall impact, Trevor stated, "I remember writing a report and this number sticks with me. I can't remember exactly what the period was, but I remember saying that we contributed about $2.4 billion in trade and investment transactions." Considering that the operating budget for BISNIS was anywhere between $1.9 million and $2.3 million, there was a substantial multiple to the US funds invested in BISNIS.

There was constant debate and shifts of emphasis and funding in the aid programs throughout the 1990s. By the early 2000s, this debate became much more serious and consequential. Dr. Gunn explained, "Russia has graduated, these countries have graduated. They made the transition to market economies; the job is done. You know, these programs should be scaled back or just simply eliminated, they were never meant to be permanent programs."

BISNIS was operational during a time of tremendous change and was directly charged with supporting the integration of Russian regional business with the United States. All indications are that it succeeded in that mission until such time as the Russian market economy no longer needed this kind of support. It is important to emphasize how deep into Russia and Russian regional business circles BISNIS penetrated. There are some foreign government-funded business development activities in the United States, but they are not comparable to the scale and reach of the BISNIS program in its heyday.

Part of the economic integration and reform process was Russians gaining business experience in the United States and in Europe. The numbers of them who had this experience grew exponentially as indicated by Trevor's references to Russians who had been participating in exchange programs and who had begun to obtain MBAs from Western institutions. The story of these exchanges is another part of the American effort to impact Russian reform through training and education in Western practices.

Business for Russia and Community Connections – Bringing Russians to America

For roughly a decade, between 1995 and 2005, the Business for Russia and Community Connections programs brought delegations of Russians, mainly from the regions to the United States for short stays to expose them to the American way of life and business or community practices. The programs were funded by the US Information Agency, later merged into the State Department, and were administered by the International Research and Exchanges Board (IREX). IREX was a non-profit organization that prior to the breakup of the

Soviet Union administered scholarly exchanges between the United States and the Soviet Union. After the breakup of the Soviet Union, it became involved in administering a variety of programs focused on development of civil society and independent media, including the Business for Russia and Community Connections programs. Those two programs sent approximately 800 Russians per year to the United States each year of the decade of its operation, somewhere around 8,000 in total.

The IREX program staff traveled throughout Russia recruiting candidates for the program who went through a screening and selection process before receiving the benefit of a free group excursion to the United States. For the Business for Russia program, the IREX staff recruited young Russian entrepreneurs who had enough English to allow them to manage a home stay and short internship in the United States. They would stay with an American family for 4–5 weeks and have an internship at an American company that was roughly equivalent to what they were doing in Russia. The Community Connections program was a similar exchange program that targeted local government people or citizen activists who were thematically focused, like development of local NGOs, criminal justice reform, or business development support. The programs goals included for the Russians in a delegation to bond as a group through the shared experience and learn from the American way of doing things, with the hope that they would apply this experience when they returned home to Russia.

Steve Mackey was an early staff member working in Russia for IREX selecting candidates for the program. Later, he became the director of Business for Russia and Community Connections. In many ways, he typifies Americans who came to Russia in those years and who ended up staffing NGO offices there. He was strongly attracted to the Russian language in high school and then continued the focus on the language and literature in university. He spent his last semester of university studying Russia in Moscow State University in the spring of 1993 and decided to stay in Russia after graduating as an adventure. As he told it, "Just the lawlessness of it was kind of exciting and really it was just an adventure, a whole big adventure. Of course, at the same time I was still very much drawn to the language and the history of the country."

Steve went home to the United States for a brief stay and returned to Russia in October 1993 on the eve of the Yeltsin government's assault on the Russian Parliament building. "My father came up right before I was going to go back to Russia. He said, 'you know you're going back at a tough time. Are you really following what's going on here?' I landed in Moscow for that return none other than October 2, 1993, which was right before the attack on White House [Russian Parliament building]."

"We were crazy enough to walk down there. … I mean we were in the middle of a civil war. … I'm talking like bullet shots from different directions, that kind of stuff. We were insane to do that, of course. The point is that I didn't really know that was going on. I'm sure that I knew that there were some political difficulties, but I wasn't as drawn to the daily political developments in Russia as much as I was to the interest in daily life."

After a period of unsuccessful job hunting, Steve saw an ad in the *Moscow Times* newspaper for security guards for the US Embassy. He applied and got the job. He spent a year in that position enjoying having a salary of $22,000 per year that made him relatively rich in the Moscow of those years and allowed him to indulge in his first taste of truly independent living, which included frequenting some of the few bars operating at the time, as well as an underground casino in the basement of an apartment building. The lawless tenor of the times made an impression on him, as it did for most Americans who were living there at the time. "Like gangsters were all over the place, I mean it was really like Chicago in the 1920s. … The real thing that stuck out in terms of history in the making was the lawlessness that reminded you of the stories of the American West."

One small incident that he cited in the interview that illustrated the atmosphere of those days was the kind of small everyday occurrence that captures a feeling of the times. "I remember watching some gangster get out of his car and pick up one of those wooden traffic barricades. He just started wailing on this car behind him because the driver did something that pissed him off. In the car was this poor old man, probably some hero of the Soviet Union, just sitting there, too scared to do anything. This young gangster had no problem attacking a senior citizen in broad daylight if it suited him. Clearly, he did not care about any rules and was going to do just what he wanted. It was kind of nuts." Everyday life in Moscow in those days was filled with similar incidents.

After a year in Moscow as an Embassy security guard, he returned to the United States and got a graduate degree at George Washington University. He was then hired to work at the IREX office in Washington, DC. When he started at IREX, he was 27 and had very little work experience. By coincidence, almost immediately after he arrived, IREX was facing an organizational crisis. Their Vladivostok office had just lost its director. It was an important hub for them to recruit participants in the Business for Russia program. It was in their grant proposal that they had to deliver the required number of participants, and the US Consulate in Vladivostok was concerned about the lack of leadership in the office. "The Vice President of IREX came to me and had no choice but to send me. Essentially everyone else had wives or girlfriends or some other reason to stay in America. They did not want to leave. I felt like 'get me the hell out of here.' I was ready to go back to Russia in a second." So off he went to Vladivostok with little formal organizational experience, but with the support of the IREX office in Vladivostok. "There was an office there, so I had the support of the talented local staff who basically told me what to do, rather than looking to me for guidance. There were Russian staff that could train me up and there was email by then, so we made it work."

Steve's job was to travel around the Russian Far East to recruit people to participate in Business for Russia or Community Connections. Every 2 months, he would relocate to a new region of Russia, whether the Volga Region or the Urals, before becoming the director of the program and managing others for this work.

He described his life in the Far East after arriving there in the beginning of the recruitment cycle. "I was living in Yuzhno-Sakhalinsk, Khabarovsk and Vladivostok, cycling around between all of them by train. I would rent an apartment or a hotel room and try to interview local businessmen and government officials. By now I had pretty good Russian, at least for a young guy." Steve remembered landing at the airport in Sakhalin in a small Yak-24 propeller airplane, where he was met on the tarmac by a gentleman who was clearly KGB. "Immediately upon settling in my hotel room, I got a call from a 'journalist' asking questions about my purpose for being in Sakhalin. The US programs and people representing them were clearly on the radar of the security services, as similar incidents transpired in nearly every city I visited."

Living in Russia's regions exposed Steve to a closer view of how society and government was functioning during these troubled times of transition. For example, in the city of Izhevsk, Steve became sociable with a group of local government officials who took him to the countryside for a day of camping, shooting, drinking vodka, and relaxation in the banya [steam bath]. One of the individuals accompanying them was a former Chechen fighter in the first Russian war, who did nothing to hide his affiliation with the mafia, regaling Steve with tales of shaking down a local outdoor market among other things. "The idea that that these Russian civil servants would be associating so freely with a mobster (who had fought against them only a few years before) kind of summed up the lawlessness of the period."

The Business for Russia program would send someone to America for 2 weeks to a month. In Steve's opinion, the programs were designed to spread the funding to impact as many people as possible, so the internships were for short term to maximize the number of participants. Steve described the main criteria as looking for "entrepreneurs who spoke English well enough to live in America for about four to five weeks with a host family and intern with a business that was what they were interested in. … We had to recruit 20 to 30 finalists for this program within two months of my arrival and then departure from that particular city. It started with me knowing nothing about the city and them knowing nothing about the program. I would advertise in local newspapers, try to get on local news, develop contacts with the local government, do press conferences, generally spread the word. We would culminate with applications and interviews. By the time I left two months later, hopefully I would have 20–30 candidates that I could forward to IREX in DC for final selection. Then I would go to the next city and start over again."

The Community Connections program was a bit different in that there were delegations of about ten people selected who were interested in a particular topic, for instance NGO development. These were not businessmen. They were government officials or local leaders who were interested and working on the theme of the delegation's visit to the United States. "We'd send these groups of 10 or so. Public health was one, for which I'd send government public health officials and hospital directors. Everyone in the delegation was more or less of the bigwig category. The idea was to make it a somewhat cohesive group of 10 that went from one community in Russia to another community in the US, let's say Cincinnati, to be given a two-week tour of a local hospital, the local public health administration and so on. Or it could be the theme of education and they would go to schools. ... The model was for the Russians to learn something that presumably could be applied in their own locality with the ancillary goal of developing a cohort of Russians that could potentially work more closely together upon their return to Russia."

The programs were designed to make an impact on the lives of the participants. Steve explained, "You know if your life is generally monotonous for the most part, and then, somehow you experience a week that is just totally different from the other weeks that you've ever had, it sears itself into your memory banks. So, independent of how influential the program was, it still is the experience itself, the very fact that it transpired that makes the impression. Those Business for Russia alumni are out there and remember those times."

These programs were another link in the chain of US government-funded programs to promote US-style business and to prepare the human cadre necessary to transform the Russian economy. Closely related to the business-oriented programs were other forms of exchange and education that targeted promoting the development of Russian civil society.

Promoting Civil Society

American Councils – From Language Study to Citizen-to-Citizen Exchanges

One of the most important interactions between Americans and Russians took place through the exchange and educational training programs that grew dramatically after the dissolution of the Soviet Union. American Councils was the principal administrator of US government-funded exchange and education programs. In the 1990s, American Councils oversaw the Future Leaders Exchange (FLEX) program for high school exchanges, the Muskie Program for graduate student study in the United States, and the Russian Leadership Program, which later became Open World Program. American Councils was founded in 1974, originally as the American Council of Teachers of Russian. By the late 1980s, the organization was sending regular groups of American students to the Soviet Union to study Russian in relatively large numbers. As such, American Councils had the experience and infrastructure in place to administer the new American aid programs that came rapidly online after the dissolution of the Soviet Union to promote citizen and educational exchanges.

Ann Domorad, who was a part of all these programs, provided valuable insight into the nuts and bolts of American–Russian interaction in this sphere. Ann became interested in Russia through high school Russia lessons and through the Peace Child program that paired US and Soviet high school children in a play promoting communication and peace that toured both the Soviet Union and the United States. The Peace Child traveling troupe stayed in her home, and she was part of the local choir for their performance in 1986. This inspired her to major in Russian at Swarthmore College, including participating in one of the American Council's language programs in Moscow. After graduation while visiting a theater friend in Moscow in 1992, she fell into a job at a Moscow private business club and casino as a manager at age 22. After some 4–6 months, she began to look for a new position and got reconnected to American Councils through a friend. This was a period in which American Councils was becoming a major government contractor in Russia and needed to staff up as quickly as possible. She was interviewed and hired almost immediately to begin a promotional tour of 17 Russian cities to drum up interest in the Flex program.

Ann explained the origins of the FLEX program that was her first position at American Councils. New Jersey Senator Bill Bradley visited Russia around the time the Berlin Wall fell and felt strongly that there needed to be people-to-people exchange programs. This was at the time the Freedom Support Act was passed and Bradley got funds for high school student exchanges included. Ann recounted that "this program was funded by the State Department, and it was initially not called the FLEX program. It was called the Freedom Support Act Secondary School Program." There had been earlier high school level exchange programs, but they were relatively small. FLEX rapidly expanded exchanges based on the new funding, "The funding was made available for the beginning of that fiscal year, which started October 1. The design of the program was very quickly figured out between October and December. I came on to American Councils in January and we were traveling around Russia recruiting in February. We really had to work fast because the Russian kids needed to be selected as soon as possible, so they could be placed and brought to the US the following September. So, we were in a big hurry."

Ultimately, the FLEX program remained in operation in Russia until 2014, when it was terminated, along with all other USAID-funded programs. Ann estimated that over the course of its operation some 40,000 Russian students came to the United States through FLEX and attributed its success to the fact that it did not have a specific agenda other than arranging exchanges.

"The Ministry of Education picked the schools. The Director of each school picked 20 kids for us to interview and test. When I was hired, I got my list of schools, the directors, their phone numbers and started calling them up saying I'm coming and asking if their list of students was ready. In the morning I would arrive by train and go right to the school. Sometimes it was a big disappointment to them because I was a woman. The director of the school was expecting a man so they'd have vodka ready, and then I would show up. … The tests were in English. The interview and the screening really focused on whether the student was the kind of person who could be successful in an intercultural experience."

Ann explained her motivation for leaving her previous job at the Moscow business club and joining American Councils. "I felt like that it was part of my responsibility as someone who had an inkling of how Russians thought and who knew that you really could have extremely satisfying human relationships with them. Relationships that maybe you couldn't even have with other Americans because of the Russian soul thing. So, I wanted those kinds of exchanges to happen because I understood that Russian culture is not better or worse, it's just different. There are certain things about Russians and the way they operate that is beautiful and so human. I felt like they had some qualities that were lacking in my own American culture, which is a little more sort of polished and transactional. So, getting these people together was as much me wanting to improve my own country as it was to help the Russians."

After several cycles of the FLEX program, Ann became the Coordinator of the Muskie Program, officially the Edmund S. Muskie Graduate Fellowship Program. This program also began in 1992 as part of the Freedom Support Act and supported graduate students and professionals for 1-year non-degree programs in the United States or 1-to-2-year degree programs. It was jointly administered by the International Research & Exchange Board (IREX), the Soros Foundation, and American Councils.

After several years in this position, she returned to the United States for graduate school and began to focus her research on the growing world of non-profit organizations in Russia and whether US aid programs were really giving them what they needed. What she found was a disconnect between how Westerners saw non-profits and how many Russians saw them. "There was this distrust and dislike of NGOs. I think that they were seen as being somehow Westernized organizations that were going to bring this lurid corruption. … What I found when researching my master's thesis in 1998 was that USAID assistance to the civil society sector was pulling from a limited pool of people who could speak English and who could get through the selection process that required a person to be a Western style manager. There was a selection process in which we culled out the American types [Russians sympathetic to the US] within Russia into a separate class, an insular group of people who were neo-Westernizers. This logically led to opposition by neo-Slavophiles." Ann's concern was that Americans were speaking only with Russians who agreed with them because these were the people who could speak English. The non-English-speaking Russians who were not selected for exchanges but represented much of the Russian population began to resent the imposition of Western models of how society should be organized. The English language selection criteria skewed the dialogue of exchange and limited the impact of exchange programs. The language barrier and particularly the use of language as a selection criterion for exchange programs prevented the kind of interaction that had motivated Ann and people like her who wanted to promote real cultural interchange.

If we look at these educational programs from the point of view of Russian modernization in the pattern of Peter the Great, then they were a great success in developing Russian managerial and business staff who began to replace foreigners working in Russia. As opposition to Western hubris and attitudes of superiority began to grow in Russia, they were able to increasingly replace Western expats. The language bias in the exchange programs masked the depth of the opposition to Western incursions and to Western notions of civil society. At the same time, these programs facilitated the growing independent capabilities of Russian business.

Open World Leadership Program of the Library of Congress – New Generation of Russian Leaders

By the end of the 1990s, Ann's insight was beginning to be shared by others. In conversations between Dan Davidson of American Councils and James Billington, Director of the Library of Congress and a Russia scholar, the idea emerged to start a new Russian Leadership Program that would abandon the English language selection criteria and would target younger professionals and future Russian leaders. In April 1999, this program was formalized, and by September 2, 1999, 500 Russians had been selected and completed a program in the United States. By 2002, the program was bringing over 2,600 young Russian leaders.[7]

As Ann described it, the target participants were "heads of education departments, head of public safety, hospitals, some NGO's, some businesspeople, and local government leaders. The mayor of a small town was sort of the prototypical participant." The program was only for 10 days. Most importantly, it included home stays with American families, even if neither side spoke the other's language. "In those 10 days, it was not like they got an in-depth understanding of anything. … But for those who really had never experienced America and didn't quite understand the US civil society model, it exposed them to learning what is worth being afraid of from the US model and what is not worth being afraid of."

"More important was creating the opportunity for some 'aha' moments from their host family stay. For instance, they went to a barbecue, threw back some shots and made real contact with some Americans."

The Russian Leadership Program was changed to the Open World Program, administrated by the Open World Leadership Center and financed by the US Congress. Since its founding in 1999, it has had a substantial number of participants. According to the website of the Open World Leadership Center, it "has hosted more than 29,000 emerging leaders from Russia, Ukraine, and other post-Soviet states since 1999. By 2020, Open World will have hosted its 20,000th Russian delegate."[8] Despite the current level of political conflict between the United States and Russia, the impact of this program on those who participated could be of assistance in reconstituting US–Russia relations.

Internews – Training the New Private Independent Media

Internews appeared in Chapter 1 because of its founding members' role in the space bridges. The connections in Russia developed through the space bridges led Internews to become involved with the emerging Russian private media sector, primarily TV and ultimately led to large grant funding from USAID and other sources that made them a key influence shaping the independent private media.

In 1990, during the Gorbachev period, a new Law on the Press was passed that allowed for private ownership of press and TV media outlets. It did not privatize or allow for privatization of existing state-owned media, but it allowed new opportunities. As first mentioned in Chapter 1, shortly after passage of the Soviet Law on the Press, San Francisco attorney Liz Hasse and Russian attorney Viktor Manakhov organized a conference of fledgling independent media outlets that led to the birth of Internews Russia.

Liz Hasse described the genesis of the conference, "The conference was in the gorgeous city of Novgorod, near St. Petersburg, sometimes referred to as Veliky Novgorod as distinguished from Nizhny Novgorod which is on the Volga River. We choose Novgorod because the lawyer I was working with, Victor Monakhov, had a contact with the mayor. It was a special city for this conference because it was proud of its democratic and independent traditions having been the seat of the Novgorod republic for several hundred years starting back in the 1100's or so. It has incredible white monasteries, a cathedral, and an old kremlin. ..."

"For the conference I applied for media funding from the McArthur Foundation, which gave a grant of about $400. I raised the rest independently from some supportive lawyers and a restaurant in Berkeley, as well as self-funded support from my own law firm. We also had a French contingent because in organizing a media conference, I did not want it to just be American-Soviet. Olivier Allais, a filmmaker who I knew from an Uzbek/Afghanistan USSR/UN project put together a contingent of French media professionals who led some of the workshops. Olivier raised money from French sources to cover the French group. Manana Aslamazyan was recommended to me to serve as the supportive Russian organizer person. She was working with Alexei Semenov at Glasnost Defense Foundation then."

Evelyn Messenger also attended the conference. She remembers it as a seminal event where she brainstormed with Wade Greene of the Rockefeller Foundation and with Manana about training Russian TV journalists. This sparked the foundation of Internews Russia.

David Hoffman also a key member of Internews explained how Russians throughout the country took advantage of this new legal opportunity under the Soviet law before the collapse of the Soviet Union, utilizing a hack of the popular VCR technology of the time. The giant Soviet apartment blocks were hard-wired for state TV and "for $8 you could get a little thing that you plug into the back of your VCR and could turn it into a transmitter over the hard-wired apartment networks. Russians would go to East Berlin and buy videotapes, mostly pornography and stuff. Then they would turn their VCR into an alternative transmitter in their apartment complex. That is how things started."

Hoffman described how Internews followed up on the initial Novgorod conference, "We had learned that there were these independent stations scattered around Russia. We got a grant through Wade Green, one of the important funders at that time, working for the Rockefeller family to see if we could locate whatever independent stations there might be. Internews sent out six people over Russia and we discovered 200 independent stations." It is important to keep in mind that this was still during Soviet times. "Internews invited them to a conference in Moscow. All these guys thought they were unique. They all thought they were the only ones. Suddenly they're together in a conference room with 200 people all doing the same thing and a movement started."

Around the same time, David Hoffman hired Manana Aslamazyan to be the administrator, later head, of the new Internews Russia office. Internews became the mentor for this new private TV sector providing training on journalism, management, advertising, and all the business aspects of running a local independent TV station. Evelyn Messenger, another of the founders of Internews and the space bridges from Chapter 1, was an advisor to George Soros' Open Society Foundation, which provided initial funding for the project. By 1992, Internews had received a substantial grant from USAID that became their principal funding source. Hoffman remembered that "then we had money pouring in to support the training of journalists and the development of these stations. … It's a huge story, almost entirely untold."

Paul Greenberg was hired in 1992 to head seminar training programs for Internews. "I did a number of seminars based on Alexei Semenov's concept that the centers of power in Moscow were always going to reassert dominance over the provinces unless you empower the provinces. To contest that you needed to develop an exterior network of communication that did not go through Moscow. … He was a real Russian democrat of that era. And, unlike a lot of us, he could see the brewing reactionary trend that was coming. … The meta overview of the program was to strengthen regional TV so that it wasn't subsumed by Moscow."

"These different stations developed quite differently. Some of them started as little cable operations in apartment complexes. Russians are very technically minded. They figured out a way to allow or disallow subscribers on to their apartment complex networks. The first truly independent television stations that I saw started as these kind of micro cable operations. Then they got enough money to go on to the next level. … Everyone was claiming to be independent and democratic. Sometimes there would be a truly independently minded cable operation or maybe somebody just cobbled together enough money to buy frequency. Then, there were these regional parts of the State broadcasting network that were trying to break away, not necessarily for ideological purposes.

Everything was being privatized and everyone was reaching out for their slice of the pie. The fragments of the Soviet system were seeing chaos and anarchy and trying to shore up what they had. They really didn't have any strong desire for any kind of political thing. They just wanted to survive but survive by living well."

"There were two flavors of training seminars. One was more journalistic to really train them in the quality and the fundamentals of objective reporting. … The management seminars were completely different. We started to elaborate the management seminars into advertising seminars and different things like that."

David Hoffman and Manana described the process of providing content for these fledgling stations through organizing them into a network. David explained that "Ted Turner started the first Russian TV network, TV 6. We started the second one, Ren TV." Manana elaborated, "We helped form networks to provide content and move away from piracy and to sell advertising. We organized a system of independent broadcasters of about 60 channels in 50 cities."

Manana described their foray into content creation for the new network, "We came at exactly the right time. We found that the TV station owners would like to start to produce their own local news." David explained the significance of developing local news, "In the Soviet Union, you had no local news. If you were in Smolensk, you don't know what's happening in any other town. There might be a story about what was happening in your town, but you would know about it only if it's on the national news. Local news changed that. … Once we began to connect those dots, we developed a common content management system. Every day a local TV editor would receive a printout of local news stories from all the cities in Russia. They could cover each other's stories and share the video. Suddenly, you have this interlocking network of TV stations. … We had a program called Local Time. Internet Russia took a couple minutes from each city and we would show 20 different local news programs. That was the first time that Russians could find out what was happening in other places." Paul Greenberg emphasized the importance of these efforts, "the goal was to try and get an independent network going, and the news exchange was sort of the first baby steps towards that end. Eventually, there were moves towards making the network a real network."

Over the course of the 1990s, the number of independent media outlets in Russia continued to grow and Internews Russia was at the center of this growing sector. Manana explained that by 1998 Internews Russia had a catalogue of about 2,500 independent Russian TV stations. "There were 2,500 in our catalog I remember that, but it was even more. If we also count newspapers and all independent media, it was probably about 15,000. … By the beginning of the 2000's, we were the biggest, richest Russian NGO, run by a Russian citizen."

But Internews Russia did not survive the crackdown on independent media that was part of the Putin-era rollback of Western-influenced civil society organizations as the 2000s developed. There is no question that the intention of Internews, as confirmed by Paul Greenberg, was to promote Western style political democracy. "First and foremost, it was part of a democratization initiative. David Hoffman pushed the idea in the halls of Congress that the engine of democracy is independent media, in particular local news. ... People doing investigative reporting on a local level, bringing people the truth on the local level. But what we quickly learned, as people regularly in contact with these local TV stations, was that it's all well and good to want to do news, but if you can't afford to run your station, it will not work. It required trying to balance financial infrastructure with news infrastructure. The idea that there could be objective news without regard to politics never fully took root. Russians always asked who's really paying for this, why are you doing this, etc. You couldn't just put this exoskeleton of capitalism on this very wounded place and expect things to fall in line."

Paul Greenberg shared his thoughts about Internews and its distinctive approach to its work in Russia. "What I will say about Internews, is that I think that we made a good faith effort to meet the Russians with respect. We tried to understand their culture and their particular local challenges. We always worked with local partners. In that sense, I think that we were amongst the better of the programs out there. ... I think the ideology that most Americans carried around in their heads about Russians was always condescension towards them. Americans coming to Russia saw the pathetic infrastructure that was there in those dark times. ... And they just sort of laughed and said these are the people that we were afraid of for so many years. They acted as if the Russians were a bunch of yokels and quacks who don't really know what's going on. This grated tremendously against the Russians even though publicly in their interactions they were very polite. ... Generally speaking, there was just too much assuming going on. ... I think overall what was lacking was a sense of urgency. People didn't realize what a small window we had. It seemed like things were going to go on endlessly."

"If you were watching, the only continuous institution that lasted from the Soviet period to the post-Soviet period was the intelligence service, which contained and maintained a super high degree of organization and discipline. Meanwhile, the democrats were diverse and diffused. Looking back retrospectively, they were sitting ducks for the most powerful intelligence service in the world. Unless the democrats were ready to take on the intelligence service, the service was going to win. ... Maybe it's just the idealist in me that is disappointed with the Russia that we ended up with."

Project Harmony – Citizen Diplomacy to Citizen Exchange

As described in Chapter 1, Project Harmony created and implemented an expanding number of direct school exchanges during the late 1980s. The range of their citizen exchange activities continued to expand. They included a disabled children's program, urologists performing laparoscopic gallbladder removals in Karelia and close collaboration with the Ben and Jerry's ice cream company in establishing a joint venture ice cream factory in Petrozavodsk, the capital of Karelia. By the mid-1990s, the amount of government funding for Project Harmony grew. Accordingly, the number of staff expanded, and they acquired an office building in Vermont. In Russia, they purchased coop apartments in Petrozavodsk and Saint Petersburg and opened an office in Moscow. They also continued to expand to other newly independent former Soviet countries, particularly Georgia, Latvia, and Lithuania.

One of the most unusual and interesting exchange programs that Project Harmony developed was around law enforcement. Charlie Hosford recalled how this program began, "In 1992 or 1993, we got a call from Fitchburg, Massachusetts from a couple of police officers who had heard that we were doing exchanges in the former Soviet Union. They were from Fitchburg, Medford, and Leominster, all relatively small cities in Central Massachusetts. We had some contacts with police in Petrozavodsk through our school exchange program, so we began working with these guys to develop an exchange program for them. We formulated a concept of a group that would focus on various community policing elements, drug and alcohol, rape investigations and domestic violence. Everyone who participated would have to be able to present something on one of these topics. We put together a group that was like 30 people. The chief of police organizations funded the various participants, and we even had some Massachusetts State Police. We also convinced CBS to embed a correspondent in the delegation."

"Off we went to Petrozavodsk with this police delegation, and we were loaded with gifts, everything from armored vests to special PR 24 batons. We took a drug dog with us as gift. It was unbelievable because the Ministry of Internal Affairs is slightly military anyway. As a result of all of this, we became very friendly with the Chief of Police in Petrozavodsk."

"Then, we organized a return trip for the Chief and his group. By that time, the State Department somehow got wind of this program and invited us to meet with them to discuss it. They basically just asked us how much money we wanted and how many exchanges did we want to do. The money was more than we had ever dreamed of having."

"When we brought this delegation to the States, we were focused on Central Massachusetts, with programs in Worcester, then in Boston and even in Cambridge. Earlier when I went to Washington to visit the State Department, Louis Freeh, who was head of the FBI at that time, invited us to come to Washington DC and stay at the FBI Academy as part of our program for the delegation. The FBI Academy is a facility in Quantico where selected police officers go for special training. So here we were bringing Russian police officers from Petrozavodsk to take part in seminars at the FBI Academy in Quantico. These high-class officers from all over the country were interacting with these Russian guys from a provincial part of Russia. They were asking the Russian guys about the Russian mafia and such, but there was very little the Russians knew to share."

"Anyway, this law enforcement program exploded in popularity. We developed a program for domestic violence coalition building in Odessa, Lvov, Petrozavodsk, Volgograd, among others. We had police delegations coming from all over the US to Russia, from New Orleans, from Michigan, from all over. We put together these groups around the domestic violence program to go in and build coalitions of community groups that would intervene where there were instances of abuse. When we began uncovering what the data on domestic violence was in these cities, it was just staggering. We brought in a superior court judge from Essex County, Massachusetts to teach them about restraining orders. This was something about which they had no concept and did not even have an equivalent word in Russian. What we found was that often Russians were not open to this kind of policing. … This was particularly a problem when we started a program in Tbilisi, Georgia. The Georgian men said to us that they know how to take care of their women and don't be telling them anything. Despite this, we started up these women support groups, but not sure if they are still active."

No matter what the long-term impact of these police exchanges might be, the fact that there was a period in which police from small towns in New England and later across the United States were interacting with their colleagues across Russia in something that is unknown and inconceivable under current conditions.

Internet Comes to Siberia

Sarah Lindemann-Komarova is an American who was active in Novosibirsk before she became a USAID subcontractor. Her view of aid programs was decidedly ambiguous. She describes how the USAID push into Russian Regions looked from the perspective of Novosibirsk. "There had already started to be all these projects showing up in Novosibirsk. … The Deloitte business support project had come out. We had KPMG doing a banker training program. We had someone who was going to revolutionize the healthcare system. So, there would be these Americans come out with these ridiculous projects. They would just show up in Novosibirsk thinking that they could tell people what to do. The local government was furious. It was like, 'who are you and what are you doing here?'"

Sarah applied for and was awarded a grant from the Eurasia Foundation to establish the first Internet public access site in Siberia, located in the Akademgorodok suburb of Novosibirsk. It was opened in an information center located in the same building as the Sun Microsystems office. Then, she formed her own non-profit and paired with the Fund for Democracy and Development in a grant application to USAID. The purpose of her grant was to expand her project into a network of 11 Internet access points across Siberia. "There was this big push at that time, around 1994, to build civil society and get out into the regions. It was being done through this thing called the Civic Initiative Project and it was huge. It was a $60 million project through Save the Children at the top and including John Hopkins University and EDU in Boston."

When she received the grant, she moved to be as compliant as possible with Russian law. "We registered as fast as we could as a Russian organization. We were so vulnerable. We were so noticeable because our first grant was $2 million. It was a huge amount of money. ... This was 1995. Nobody had any money. We were the only people in all of Siberia who had any money. ... We went and we looked for existing NGOs in Siberia and asked whether they would be interested in expanding their mission. ... We created opportunities for people to meet and work together. We ended up giving $600,000 of that $2 million in grants to NGOs. ... But the mandate was not about giving these people money. I was focusing on what worked."

Sara later became more critical of USAID programs as they became more and more focused on funding civil society organizations that had increasingly political objectives, rather than social service objectives.

Foundations and Institutes – Knowledge Transfer, Democracy Promotion, and Education Reform

Alongside the myriad government-funded programs, US private foundations were actively involved in Russia in the 1990s. The key foundations active in Russia were the Soros Open Society Foundation, Ford Foundation, MacArthur Foundation, and Rockefeller Brothers Fund. Several of these foundations have already been referenced in Chapter 1 and in this chapter for the critical early financial support that they provided for SovAm Teleport and for Internews. Much later, in 2008, the Russian American Foundation was formed out of the legacy funds from the US Russia Investment Fund, as will be described in Chapter 3, with the mission of supporting long-term Russian economic growth and the strengthening of the Russian market economy.

Along with the seed funding already mentioned, the private foundations focused on knowledge transfer based on their firm belief that the American models of politics, economics, and academia needed to be adopted by Russia. This part of their activities focused on facilitating Russians accumulating sufficient understanding of how those models work to apply them to their own society. The longer the private foundations operated in Russia, the more their focus shifted to support of pro-democracy civil society organizations and to reform of the Russian university system.

While not a private foundation, the Kennan Institute of the Woodrow Wilson Center played a complementary role, alongside the foundations. For insight into this world, the main interview was with Blair Ruble, former Director of the Kennan Institute of the Woodrow Wilson Center.

Blair became Director of the Kennan Institute in 1989. The Kennan Institute was established to help Americans understand Russia and Blair became Director in 1989, still in the Gorbachev era. At that moment, the possibilities for mutual understanding through academic exchange programs was blossoming. The

Kennan Institute provided grants for Russian mid-career academics to come to the United States to study for a year of unfettered research. As Blair explained, "It was 1989 and you couldn't have a better moment for exchanges. My goal was to create meaningful professional experiences on both sides. This experience was more than an exchange. It was an opportunity to integrate Soviets and then Russians and Ukrainians into the life and academic studies of the Kennan Institute, and to support those Americans who would be involved in studying Russia … The purpose of these exchanges was also to explore how Russians can help Americans to understand Russia. We sponsored a massive speaker series and drew on the more academic side literally to create Russian colleagues. … My greatest legacy is a network of 500–600 Russians who came through our programs."

Blair went on to describe the impact of these early academic fellowship programs on the Russian academics. "Particularly in the earlier 90s, Russia was just opening to the world. For Russians living in Washington and seeing how things work or how things didn't work was eye opening. … For most of the Soviet scholars, the initial reaction was, oh my God, this is wonderful. Then three or four months into the residency, they would become much more critical about what they were seeing on the US. This helped them form their own views about how the world works, so I think that was very valuable."

When asked what the general approach was to Russia among the private foundations, Blair responded with an anecdote that illustrated his experience. "I think it varies from foundation to foundation. The Stanley Foundation used to hold convocations on different subjects. I chaired one for them about engaging Russia. This would have been in 1993, I think. I invited representatives from several foundations, a couple of USAID people and some scholars. It was about 15–20 people, who were well-placed and from several American institutions. One of the questions I asked people was why are you doing this? What excites you about it? Almost to a person, they responded because this is an opportunity to change a culture. … Obviously that didn't work out so well. In general, a lot of the philanthropic institutions were about taking the US model of the good society and getting it in place in Russia. It was because we think it's a really good model and if only Russia did X, Y and Z in economics or educational reform, pick your field, they'd be so much better off. We really believed in these models. I think that that was a big part of the Foundations' perspective."

When asked about his personal perspective, he responded, "I felt in a way, and I still do, that the only Russian future is a future integrated into international systems. I really felt that, and I still believe that. What with the changes in China and the changes brought by Putin in his return to the Presidency, changes elsewhere in the world, that's not the dominant paradigm these days. But I think Russia is a country full of remarkably talented people who could swim effortlessly in the international environment and know Russians who do."

Blair made a very conscious effort to bring his exchange programs to Russia's regions and his experience traveling around the country began to show him very early on that the idea of imposing an American model on Russian reality without learning to listen to Russian voices was going to falter. "I hung out a little bit with the journalists, but the expats in Moscow did not want to hear what I had to say. I was going out and about the country and coming back and saying, you know something is not going all that well. ... There are warning bells going off that people did not like being lectured. ... One incident I really remember was probably in 1992 because the Soviet Union had already collapsed. I walked into an interview with a factory manager, I don't remember which one. He said that he had just had an American, a 20-year-old, who was probably 30, but anyway he said a 20-year-old American in here telling me how I'm supposed to run a factory. Who do you people think you are?"

Continuing to describe the process of souring of the romance between Russians and Americans, he said, "I would say, by time you got into the mid 1990s, 1994, 1995, 1996, it was pretty clear relations were going badly. The war in the Balkans really seemed to be a disjuncture. ... I think that people who are willing to respect and listen to Russians did manage to connect rather well. I think that for people for whom Russia was just another assignment, they never connected."

Blair believes that the 2008 economic crisis, precipitated in the United States, was the final stage of unconditional belief in the United States as a model. He described his attendance at a symposium in 2008 in Tatarstan. The Tatar Republic is one of constituent territorial regions of the Russian Federation and relatively prosperous as an oil-producing region. The symposium brought together top-notch foreign experts and mid-level officials from Russian regions. He recounted a lunch conversation that illustrates the importance of this turning point moment in time. "We came to lunch, and they put me at a table with economic officials of the Tatar Republic. I am wondering what we're going to talk to about. What they wanted to talk about was the US financial crisis. It turns out that the Tatar Republic had not wanted to turn their oil revenues over to Moscow. So, they had invested their money in Fannie Mae and Freddie Mac bonds. They wanted to know why they had lost 10's of millions of dollars. What the hell are you Americans doing? Are you becoming like us, are you becoming Russians? ... It was at this moment when the curtain was pulled back in August 2008 and there wasn't anything there." The attractiveness of the American model of the market economy was significantly undermined by the 2008 financial crisis at the same time as there was a more general backlash against Western attitudes of superiority.

As the rejection of Western tutelage began to take hold in the Putin era of the 2000s, private foundations were squeezed out of Russia by regulations and political hostility. At the time of the interview with Blair Ruble, only the Carnegie Moscow Center was still operating. Rockefeller Brothers was active in Russia until 2004. Ford Foundation closed its office in 2008. The MacArthur Foundation closed in 2015. The Open Society Foundation was ordered out of Russia in 2015 as a threat to Russian state security. Also in 2015, the US Russia

Fund was declared to be undesirable by the Russian government and forced to leave the country.

These private foundations have been excluded from active participation in Russian life but now play a role in funding and supporting American public institutions and supply research and analysis for those trying to understand Russia. As such, their institutional memory and conclusions from their history in Russia continue to color current views on Russia among scholars, experts, and students.

There are themes that emerge from the interviews and experience highlighted in this chapter that will appear again and again in this book. The principal one on the American side was the conviction that Russia was to be integrated into the world political and economic order by remolding itself in the model of liberal democracy. While there was an initial acceptance of this proposition by the liberal Russian reformers around President Yeltsin, within other sections of the elite and the Russian public, there was a gradual disillusionment with the American model. American experts misread Russia over time mainly through relying primarily on the perceptions and opinions of English-speaking Russians. Meanwhile, throughout this decade, Russians acquired an increasing level of sophistication as they gained experience in the globalized world and came to consider that they had the capacity to run most aspects of the Russian market economy without needing the assistance of foreigners. This is the theme of Russian modernization that appears throughout this book.

Hopefully, the reader has not been lost in the details presented in this chapter and its bulging suitcase. The purpose of this level of detail was to prove the extent of American influence in post-Soviet Russia. Whether one considers this level of intervention, good, bad, or undetermined, the scope of these activities is not well known or appreciated among the American or European public. The programs described here are the heart of the effort to mold post-Soviet Russia into some version of the United States that is a central part of the story. What has been described in this chapter is only part of that story. In the chapters to come, we will examine the impact of private individuals and companies in the newly formed private sector of post-Soviet Russia, which only deepens this chronicle of American–Russian interaction at all levels.

Notes

1 US Government Accounting Office, *Former Soviet Union – An Update on Coordination of U.S. Assistance and Economic Cooperation Programs* (Washington, D.C., 1995), 2.
2 Janine R. Waddell, *Collision and Collusion – The Strange Case of Western Aid to Eastern Europe 2989 – 1998* (New York: St. Martin's Press, 1998), 203.
3 Waddell, *Collision and Collusion*, 24, footnote 3.
4 "The President's Trip to Europe and Russia," *George W. Bush White House Archives*, May 24, 2002, Accessed January 26, 2022, https://georgewbush-whitehouse.archives.gov/news/releases/2002/05/print/20020524-9.html
5 "The President's Trip to Europe and Russia," *George W. Bush White House Archives.*

6 "Peace Corps Completes Service in Russia," *Peace Corps* website, Peace Corps press release, February 19, 2003, Accessed November 12, 2021, www.peacecorps.gov/news/library/peace-corps-completes-service-in-russia/
7 "Fact Sheet: People to People Cooperation," *The White House George W. Bush, Office of the Press Secretary*, May 24, 2002, Accessed January 26, 2022, https://georgewbush-whitehouse.archives.gov/news/releases/2002/05/print/20020524-9.html
8 Message from the Executive Director, *Open World Leadership Center* website, Accessed December 21, 2021, www.openworld.gov/about-us/message-executive-director

3 Privatization and Capital Markets with an American Twist

Stephen [Jennings] and I set up this war room in the Metropol Hotel and brought in a bunch of young guys, trained economists and bankers from Credit Suisse and got to work. I would say we just slept maybe two to three hours per night for three months as we worked through the plan for privatization. We had beds in the office there and we would take turns sleeping. … As we were writing and rewriting what was to be implemented, I must give massive credit to Chubais for giving us political cover for what we were doing. … We made every mistake an American makes in a foreign country. We were arrogant. We'd walk in a room and tell everybody how it's supposed to done. Everybody would be looking at us as if to say who the … are you? And why do you think you know everything when we're a country with 1000-year history, etc., etc. Chubais gave us cover, he believed in us.

(Boris Jordan, Renaissance Capital, Interview on April 6, 2021)

I joined Troika with a hundred-dollar salary, and everybody looked me like a crazy person. I already had a good position in a commercial bank. … I did it with a purpose in mind, because I wanted to learn how to work in financial markets in Western style. When I met Peter [Derby], I understood that Troika Dialog would be a unique combination. We were a Russian company, but we worked by international standards, which was quite an unusual model.

I said to myself that the period we were entering into was going from a government planning system to a market economy. What mechanism will be replacing the government planning system? It will be the securities market and commercial relations.

(Ruben Vardanyan, Troika Dialog, Interview on April 21, 2021)

As already introduced in Chapter 2, the principal goal of the Yeltsin reform team was to dismantle the basis of the Soviet economy as quickly as possible to prevent any possible restoration of the socialist planned economy. The foundations of this project were to replace socialist state ownership with private property and to replace state planning with market mechanisms. There was probably no other sector of the emerging Russian economy that was more influenced by Americans than the support and implementation of these two pillars of the new Russian economy. This chapter will focus on the experience

DOI: 10.4324/9781003182153-4

of Americans in assisting with the technical implementation of privatization of state property and with the creation of a new financial system resting upon privatization as a market mechanism to replace state planning. It is also the sector that most dramatically shows both the impact of looking to the West for modernization following historical patterns and the limits that Russia put on American or foreign control of their economy.

During the Yeltsin period, Americans were instrumental in providing technical expertise for the new architecture of a Russian market economy, including facilitating privatization, creating institutions for trading in company shares, attracting foreign investment, and restructuring Russian enterprises to comply with international accounting standards and management practices. As an important qualifying note, it should be emphasized that there are many European and multinational organizations, like Technical Assistance to the Commonwealth of Independent States(TACIS), the World Bank, the Organization for Economic Cooperation and Development (OECD), the International Monetary Fund (IMF), European Bank for Reconstruction and Development (EBRD), and others, that played equally important roles in this process but are beyond the scope and limits of this book.

The creation of the post-Soviet Russian financial sector is worthy of a separate book, perhaps two or three. Within the limitations of space for a book as broad as this one, the chapter will focus on key institutional developments mainly in the Yeltsin period and the role and experience of Americans. In this period, Russia allowed Americans and other foreigners to come into their country, set up very profitable investment companies, and essentially teach Russians how to set up and operate financial institutions in a market economy. What is remarkable about this period is the degree to which that much sovereignty and foreign autonomy was ceded to another country to shape Russia's institutions. To state the obvious, it is inconceivable that the United States would allow anything analogous on its own soil. After the new institutions were created and after Russians assimilated the skills required, they began to take back the sovereignty and autonomy that they had previously allowed.

Like many aspects of the Yeltsin period, there were a lot of moving pieces and simultaneous processes at play that are difficult to describe in a linear fashion. The period was defined by the interrelationship of the Yeltsin Russian government reformers, remaining Soviet structures, state enterprise directors, regional political leaders, foreign advisors, and private entrepreneurs. With this complexity in mind, the chapter will focus on the broad overview of the American impact on privatization and on formation of the new Russian financial sector.

Kamikaze Reform, War on State Property, and Voucher Privatization – Destroying the Basis for a Return of Socialism

The group of academic reformers who assumed leading government positions around President Boris Yeltsin were absolutely convinced that they had to privatize Soviet state property as quickly as possible to prevent the restoration of Communist Party control of the Russian government and continuation of the socialist system. They often described themselves as kamikaze reformers, borrowing the term used for Japanese pilots near the end of World War II who undertook suicide missions flying their planes directly into US naval warships. The Russian reformers were led by Yegor Gaidar and included Anatoly Chubais, Alfred Kokh, Dmitri Vasiliev, Sergei Ignatov, Sergey Vasilyev, Alexander Shokhin, and others. They all knew that they had a limited time in government to push through the dramatic legal, social, and institutional changes that were necessary to restore private property, create a class of owners to support the new order, and establish the institutions of a market economy. In the words of Alexander Shokhin, "We convinced ourselves but also [Gennady] Burbulis and Yeltsin that our mission was to clean the Augean Stables and do unpopular dirty work. … no one would be patted on the head for doing it, and we would be kicked out of the government in a year at best …"[1] While they had very clear priorities and a definite sense of urgency, none of them had any practical experience in how to accomplish these priorities. For this, like their historical predecessors, they turned to the West.

Having already sidelined two of the institutional pillars of Soviet society, the Communist Party and the KGB, in the aftermath of the August 1991 coup attempt, Yeltsin and his team wanted to completely undermine any possible restoration of the Soviet system by putting as much state property as possible into private hands as quickly as possible. The quality of ownership was not important to them. It was only important that private property as the basis of the economic system was established. According to Alfred Kokh, who was Deputy Prime Minister of the Russian Federation in the 1990s and a chief architect of Russia's privatization as Chairman of the State Property Committee, enterprises representing about half of the economy were privatized between 1992 and 1994.[2]

The Russian reformers adopted the general "shock therapy" model from Eastern Europe and moved rapidly to create a new class of property owners through voucher privatization of state enterprises and privatization of apartments.

As this transition was taking place, the system of the planned economy collapsed and the real economy along with it. In the process, the reformers created tremendous hardship for much of the Russian population while promoting opportunity for those willing and able to thrive in the new system. In 1992, foreign trade declined by 27 percent and industrial production dropped by 14 percent. As a result of removing price controls, overall inflation in 1992 reached 2,508 percent.[3] For most of the Russian population, this was a time of extreme hardship as the reformers raced to create a Russian market economy before their political opponents could recover their strength.

Voucher Privatization – Creating a New Class of Owners

The policy and practice of privatization was the context for the creation of new financial institutions that were supposed to replace state planning mechanisms. As opposed to the reconstruction of Germany and Japan post-World War II, Russians still maintained control of their own country and the Yeltsin team were the drivers of the reforms, as they looked to foreign expertise to help them implement their plans. It is important to recognize how much Russians set the reform and privatization agenda, with American and foreign experts providing technical expertise and business skills to implement that agenda.

The Russian description of this period leans heavily on the initiatives and policies of the reformers in Yeltsin's government, Alfred Kokh, Anatoly Chubais, Dimitry Vassilyev, and Yegor Gaidar. According to Kokh, the original idea for voucher privatization came out of discussions he had in 1991 with the Russian academic Vitaly Naishul when Kokh was head of privatization in Leningrad [now St. Petersburg]. Kokh brought the idea with him when he joined the Chubais team in Moscow. At the time when Chubais was Chairman of the State Committee for Privatization and Chubais was the person mainly responsible for implementing the idea.

In Kokh's book about the privatization process, *The Selling of the Soviet Empire – Politics & Economics of Russia's Privatization-Revelations of the Principal Insider*, there is no mention of foreign advisors for this process at all, a revealing omission. According to other sources, including interviews conducted for this book, the voucher plan was borrowed from the Czech privatization plan and modified for use in Russia. Others link it to Poland and the shock therapy used there.

The plan was for every person in Russia, roughly 147 million people, to receive one voucher, dated September 2, 1992, that had a face value of 10,000 rubles, equivalent to about US$100.

In October 1992, the Russian government began the first stage of privatization of state enterprises that had been re-registered as private companies. Managers and workers in companies being privatized could exchange their vouchers for shares in their newly private company through a private subscription prior to public auction. Voucher holders could either participate directly in privatization auctions, entrust their voucher to an investment fund, or sell them on the open market. Then, as the government put firms up for auction, these vouchers could be used to bid on and purchase shares in the new private enterprises.[4] According to a study conducted in 1994, 18 percent were exchanged for shares by employees, 28 percent were exchanged for shares in voucher funds, and 30 percent were sold for cash on the open market.[5]

A significant number of state-owned enterprises in key sectors like oil and gas, telecom, utilities, and several others that were considered of strategic importance were not included in the voucher privatization process. Many of these companies were privatized in 1995–1996 through the so-called "loans-for-shares" program that will be described in detail below. They later became the most valuable publicly traded Russian equities, sometimes referred to as the Russian "red chips."

As Kokh explains, the reformers were not only pressured by a possible Communist return to power but also faced illegal unilateral privatizations by enterprise managers. This process was a continuation of reforms initiated in the Gorbachev period by the Law on State Enterprises that gave effective control to enterprise managers and worker collectives, who began treating these enterprises as their property. Kokh recounted that "... From late 1988 through July of 1991, thousands of State-owned companies large and small – from two to three percent of all companies that would ultimately be privatized in Russia – were converted in this frightening way en masse into other forms of ownership, lacking any legally established framework. Billions of dollars' worth of State assets were literally stolen in this way by management teams brazen enough to risk the consequences in the hazy legal vacuum of the period. ... More government property was stolen every day; our team was under tremendous pressure to come up quickly with a workable, legal method of privatizing the economy."[6] This extra-legal privatization, coupled with the emergence of mafia-linked control, accounts for the emergence of the new business sectors that the Peace Corps volunteers in Chapter 2 encountered as early as 1992.

The battle for control of state enterprises between the former management, sometimes referred to as the "Red Directors" and new owners who held stock from the privatization process was one of the features of the complex battle among contending individuals and social forces in the evolving Russian market economy.

Implementing Privatization – Harvard University and the American Team from Credit Suisse

The Russian government was determined to carry out privatization to break the back of the planned economy but needed technical help on how to implement this massive economic change. The State Committee of the Russian Federation for the Management of State Property (Goskomimushchestvo, "GKI"), led by Anatoly Chubais, was responsible for privatization. They received technical assistance in developing the framework for voucher privatization from the International Monetary Fund, the World Bank, the US government, and academic advisors, primarily Harvard University and Harvard Institute for International Development (HIID). According to researcher and author Janine Wedel, in the 1991–1992 period when the Soviet Union was disintegrating, "Harvard Professor Jeffrey Sachs and other Western economists participated in meetings at a dacha outside Moscow where young, pro-Yeltsin reformers planned Russia's economic and political future. Sachs teamed up with Yegor Gaidar, Yeltsin's first architect of economic reform, to promote a plan of 'shock therapy' to swiftly eliminate most of the price controls and subsidies that had underpinned life for Soviet citizens for decades."[7]

HIID was awarded $57.7 million from USAID and became one of the primary American agencies supporting Russian economic reform. The primary buzz word used for HIID's approach as indicated above was "shock therapy." This method of economic reform was closely associated with then Harvard Professor, Jeffrey Sachs, who was an advisor to Gaidar from 1992 to 1994. Sachs then served as the Director of HIID from 1995 to 1999. Andrei Shleifer was another key figure from Harvard who served as the head of the Russia project for HIID. Shleifer advised Chubais from 1992 to 1997 and one source claims that voucher privatization was his idea.[8] The importance of Harvard in Russian privatization was driven home in a 1998 article by Janine Wedel in The Nation entitled, "Harvard Boys Do Russia." In that article, she emphasizes the American role in supporting privatization. "Essential to the implementation of Chubais' policies was the enthusiastic support of the Clinton Administration and its key representative for economic assistance in Moscow, the Harvard Institute for International Development."[9]

As the privatization law was being drafted by an amalgam of Gaidar's team and HIID, the GKI put out a tender for additional technical assistance from leading investment banks. This is where Boris Jordan enters the story.

Boris Jordan is an American of Russian descent, whose grandfather had fought with the White Army opposing the Bolshevik Red Army in the Russian Civil War. He graduated from NYU and after a short stint as an investment banker with Kidder Peabody, he went to work for the entrepreneur Tony Ryan, founder of Ryanair. While attending a conference on NAFTA in Los Angeles in 1991, he picked up a newspaper with the famous picture of Boris Yeltsin on a tank in Moscow opposing the coup against Gorbachev. He knew that his calling was in Russia and made plans to head there.

Through contacts in the finance world, he was introduced to Credit Suisse and flew to London for an interview. "I literally found the only guy in Europe that was interested in Russia, Hans-Joerg Rudloff. He was a Swiss German, and he was the chairman of Credit Suisse First Boston in Europe. He had launched an East European banking operation in Prague and Hungary and wanted to launch in Russia. I walked into his office, and I said I want to go to Moscow. He said 'well, nobody else does, so you got a job.' That is the fastest easiest interview ever had my life. It had nothing to do with whether I knew anything, or whether I had any kind of background, I was willing to go."

Jordan went to Moscow and immediately jumped into the privatization process. "I went to Moscow and when I got there the Russian privatization of industry was going on. The GKI had put out a tender to hire a Western advisor on privatization." In order to win the tender for Credit Suisse, Jordan made a bold and aggressive proposal. "I told the GKI that I would do it for free. I got approval from my boss and then I came to New York to speak with the Chairman of the Bank. I said that I think you should let me do this for free, because the education we're going to get on Russia is going to be enormous. Goldman Sachs, Morgan Stanley, and everybody else also submitted their proposals to win this tender, but they all wanted to make money on this advisory. I walked in with the same proposal, but said I'll do it for free. So again, it had nothing to do with some big difference in our proposal. I just said I'll do it for free, so they [the GKI] hired me."

After winning the tender, Boris Jordan set about constructing his team for the project. He was not an academic or an economist so he looked for help from within Credit Suisse to build the capacity he would need. "I recruited a guy by the name of Stephen Jennings who was working as an economist at Credit Suisse and was an advisor on privatization in Hungry and Poland. He was very knowledgeable on the subject. So, I literally walked into his office in London and said, do you want to go to Moscow? He looked at me and said 'absolutely.' He went with me and after that we worked together for many years.

By the time, Boris Jordan and his team began work, the GKI had already drafted a privatization law and the vouchers had been distributed. The open question was how vouchers were to be used to secure equity in newly formed companies. There was little time to work out the implementation because the Yeltsin team was racing against time to begin privatization before a scheduled meeting of the National Congress of People's Deputies, the hold-over legislature from the Soviet Union, scheduled for December 1992. The Yeltsin team felt that there was a danger that the National Congress of People's Deputies would kill privatization if it was not underway before they convened.

Boris Jordan described the impact of this situation on the Credit Suisse team. "They [GKI] called me into a meeting in October and said that the National Congress of People's Deputies is meeting on the eighth of December. If we don't launch privatization by then, we're in trouble. They will shut us down and fire everybody in the Government. ... The Congress was filled with people left over from the Soviet Union, dominated by communists." With this timetable in mind, the principal task was how to implement privatization; however, the authors of the program on both the Harvard side and the Russian side were all theoreticians. Continuing the story, Jordan said, "I walked in, and I said OK, let's take this document and let's put it to work. So, the first thing was to read the law. What we found was that what they had put together with Harvard and with other advisors just would not work in real life in Russia. We had literally two and half months to go from drafting the law to launching privatizations before the Congress could shut us down."

"Stephen and I set up this war room in the Metropol Hotel and brought in a bunch of young guys, trained economists and bankers from Credit Suisse and got to work. I would say we slept maybe two to three hours per night for three months as we worked through the plan for privatization. We had beds in the office there and we would take turns sleeping. ... As we were writing and rewriting what was to be implemented, I must give massive credit to Chubais for giving us political cover for what we were doing. ... We made every mistake an American makes in a foreign country. We were arrogant. We'd walk in a room and tell everybody how it's supposed to done. Everybody would be looking at us as if to say who the … are you? And why do you think you know everything when we're a country with 1,000-year history, etc., etc. Chubais gave us cover, he believed in us."

The biggest issue driving this process was time. "Chubais understood full well that he only had a certain amount of time to break the system of central planning and to get assets into the hands of whomever. It did not matter to him who got the assets. He just had to get these assets out of the hands of the government. The phrase that he would always use is, 'we need to make this process irreversible. We must do it in such a way that the opponents of capitalism cannot reverse the process.' It was 100 percent a question of timing. He understood that if you didn't get this thing launched fast, it was never going to happen. … That is why the privatization process was built the way it was. He didn't care about profiting or having the government profit from the process. He didn't care about whether he was selling these assets to competent people are not. He only cared about one thing, he had to get assets out of the hands of the Government and into private hands, so that people would feel a sense of ownership. That was the most important thing. That was the mandate. Within that mandate, we had to work as fast and as hard as possible. … Chubais' favorite saying was 'I'm a kamikaze. I will not survive in the political world for very long because everyone will hate me for what I did.'" The Credit Suisse team was able to meet this deadline and privatization was underway before the National Congress of People's Deputies met.

As Boris Jordan and his team completed their work, they stayed for the launch of the first two or three privatizations and then their advisory contract was finished. Looking back Jordan said, "At one point in time, I must have had 15 people under my direct report working for free on behalf of the Russian Government. That can get very expensive with hotels and everything like that, so I was very lucky that Credit Suisse supported those expenses. Hans-Joerg Rudloff, Credit Suisse's head of European operations at that time was one of the few who really believed in what was happening in Eastern Europe and Russia. The fact is that he let us do this for free, basically using the capital of the Bank. American banks don't like to do anything for free. The fact that he allowed us to do it this way, I think, was great for Credit Suisse evidenced by the fact that by 1994 the Russian business unit was the most profitable unit for Credit Suisse globally."

As a side note, the role of Harvard and HIID in Russia did not end quite so well. In 1996, the new USAID mission director in Russia, Dr. Janet Ballantyne, discovered irregularities in HIID's program. She contacted the US inspector general's office regarding allegations of HIID staff using insider information for personal gain and buying stocks on their own account. Her whistle blowing caused her problems with both some of reformers in the Russian government and with US Embassy staff supporting these reformers. In her oral history of this period recorded with the Association for Diplomatic Studies & Training, Dr. Ballantyne recounted that "When we found out about it, I called our inspector general's office in a way that caused some issues with the US

Embassy. The so-called Russian reformers were also key to the Embassy's policies and diplomatic goals. They were key interlocutors and the Embassy felt that Russia could not move to the next level without these particular reformers. Well, some of these were the reformers that were very much involved in the issues with HIID."[10] As result of Dr. Ballantyne's actions, in 1997, the US government sued Harvard and individually Jonathan Hay, Elizabeth Hebert, Andrei Schleifer and Nancy Zimmerman.

In 2005, the litigation was settled with Harvard with the Court ruling that "while being paid by USAID, Shleifer and Hay engaged in prohibited investments and businesses in Russia. These actions (which are disputed by the defendants) included: Shleifer and Zimmerman's investment of $200,000 through Renova-Invest, a U.S./Russian investment entity, in various Russian companies and Russian government debt; Shleifer, Zimmerman, and Hay's purchase of several hundred thousand dollars' worth of shares in Russian oil companies (ownership of the shares was placed in the name of Shleifer's father-in-law); and Hay and Shleifer's help in launching and/or financing Russia's first licensed mutual fund, started by Elizabeth Hebert, Hay's then-girlfriend and current wife. They did the same for Russia's first mutual-fund depository, started by Hebert's business partner."[11]

In 2005, Harvard settled the suit by paying the US government $26.5 million, the largest settlement ever received by the US government from a university.[12] Additional sums totaling around $4.5 million were paid by the individual defendants as part of the settlement. All this is against the backdrop of widespread questionable conduct in Russia at that time, a time in which Russia was sometimes referred to as the "Wild East."

Business Environment in the "Wild East"

The pillars of stability in the Soviet system were the domination of the Communist Party backed by the KGB and state ownership of all the means of production in society. During the Gorbachev period, the hegemony of the Communist Party was undermined. Then the failed coup of August 1991 marginalized the power of both the Communist Party and the KGB.

In late 1991, the KGB was reorganized, with its functions distributed into several different agencies, including the Federal Service of Counter-Intelligence (FSB), Foreign Intelligence Service (SVR), Federal Agency for Government Communications (FAPSI), Federal Protective Service, Federal Border Service, and others.[13] In 1993, a new agency the Tax Police was created.[14] The practical impact of this reorganization was the creation of competing centers of power no longer answerable to the ultimate authority of the Communist Party. The resulting rivalries between different security and police organizations contributed to the overall chaos of the times.

State ownership as the other pillar of stability was now in transition under the Yeltsin privatization program. The destruction of the Soviet centers of power and stability led to a period of lawlessness and the rise of new alternate centers of power. Privatization created an environment where Russian regional political elites, factory general directors and underground criminal groups, referred to generally as "mafia" gained control of local economic assets that could generate cash for individual or group enrichment. The use of the word "mafia" in Russia in those times referred to organized criminal groupings, but they were not the commonly understood and capitalized "Mafia" that originated in Italy.

Some of the criminal groups were ethnically based and some were from the criminal underground that had been formed and suppressed in Soviet times. With the dissolution of the unified structure of the KGB and the dysfunctional array of competing law enforcement agencies, these criminal groups were able to seize assets through violence, sometimes in collaboration with the Red Directors.[15] One of the important observations made in *The Vory – Russia's Super Mafia*, Mark Galeotti's study of the Russian criminal world, is that while these mafia groups emerged in the post-Soviet period as important economic actors in many sectors of the economy, by the end of the 1990s mafia-linked business largely disappeared as Putin re-established the power of the Russian state and the FSB, as a reunified successor of the KGB. However, for the chaotic and lawless period, particularly the first half of the 1990s, these criminal "mafia" groups were important economic actors. In this period, many private businesses had to have "krisha," the Russian word for roof, as paid protection from one or another mafia organization. The various criminal mafia groups and the necessity of krisha was a fact of life in this period that reoccurs in several contexts in this book as an important part of the tale of the 1990s.

Alongside the privatization of former state economic assets, there was a tremendous upsurge of entrepreneurship creating new small businesses throughout Russia in retail stores, restaurants, software outsourcing, trading companies, local private TV stations, hairdressers, florists, kiosks selling cigarettes and magazines, and many more. These new businesses created pockets of private wealth among entrepreneurs as an entirely new sector in local and regional economies. These entrepreneurs had to navigate tremendous obstacles, including tax inspectors who carried over Soviet-era antagonism toward private business, government health and safety inspectors looking for a bribe and local mafia groups seeking to become uninvited partners.

Taken together, complex regional business communities developed that were composed of a divergent mix of general directors of giant state-owned or newly privatized state enterprises, mafia business groupings, local government officials looking out for their own personal interest and newly minted small business entrepreneurs. This period was also the time when the first generation of ultra-rich oligarchs arose, usually through marshalling resources to gain control of severely undervalued state enterprises.

Rapid privatization took place with very little or no financial, institutional, or regulatory structure in place. Attention to corporate governance or the quality of ownership of the newly privatized companies was not a part of privatization process. In the words of Cameron Sawyer, an American lawyer and real estate developer featured in Chapter 4, the lack of attention to quality of ownership "was tragically mistaken. It did matter, because huge state enterprises ended up in the hands of the aggressive, criminal, and politically connected people who became a deeply corrupting influence on politics." An entirely different view was expressed by Boris Jordan in the section on loans-for-shares below who argues that the fact of private ownership was more important because most of the state enterprises transferred through that process in 1996 were improved and modernized by their new owners.

Paying for Government – Debt Financing

During this period of privatization and transition in the Russian economic system, the Russian government faced substantial deficits caused in part by a high degree of tax evasion. Nominally, taxes were high, but they were complex and expensive to administer, and no one paid them. Here too, Americans played an important role as advisors and facilitators for new modes of financing government deficits.

To pay the costs of government and cover the deficits from low tax revenues, the Russian Government issued bonds at very high interest rates. These bonds were short term bonds (GKOs) and federal loan bonds (OFZs), which attracted substantial foreign investment due to their high interest rates. According to Peter Derby, the American Director of DialogBank introduced in Chapter 1, the GKO's were the product of collaboration between Boris Yeltsin and E. Gerald (Gerry) Corrigan, President of Bank of New York. After a meeting between the two featuring vodka and a closing bear hug, Corrigan dispatched a team to work with Andrei Kozlov, Vice Chairman of the Russian Central Bank, to implement the Russian government's interest in developing debt financing. The work of the team was facilitated by Peter Derby, utilizing his experience in both Western finance and the emerging Russian finance sector. Derby had already established a working relationship with Kozlov in developing and writing the rules for establishing private banks in Russia. In describing his work with Kozlov and several other young reformers in the Yeltsin administration Derby stated that "it was all their initiative. We were just helping it along in certain ways."

Derby described the significant help that came from the Federal Reserve Bank of New York. "The first GKO markets were created based on Gerry Corrigan's bear hug and his team coming into Russia." The team met with Andrei Kozlov and told him "We're here to inform you and help you in any way we can but it's going to be your decisions, the entire way." Kozlov thus "empowered brought in two of his other staff. The three of them [the team from the New York Federal Reserve] and me, from time to time, really put together the structure and created the GKO market." As the GKO market grew during the 1990s, it became large and controversial. Some saw it as a form of government pyramid lending. It finally collapsed in the 1998 Russian financial crisis, under the pressure of the general world-wide financial crisis at that time.

Stock Markets, Investment Banks, and Private Equity – Replacing Centralized Planning with US-Style Capital Markets

Foreign expertise was required to create a private sector in finance in post-Soviet Russia because there were no market-based financial markets or institutions in the Soviet Union. In the Soviet centrally planned economy, money was simply an input for production, like raw materials and human labor. Money was not capital, playing an independent role in the development of enterprises and in the overall economy. The criteria for the deployment of all inputs were set by the central planning apparatus in accord with economic development goals and priorities set by the Communist Party, not profitability. In short, there was no private financial sector at the end of the Soviet era. It was created almost from scratch and was heavily influence by Americans and other foreigners.

In Soviet times, there were certain institutions in the financial sector that had a nominal equivalent to those in capitalist countries, but with much different functions. This was primarily in the banking sector where there were Soviet banks that served defined functions in conformance with centrally planned operations, i.e., Gosbank (State Bank), Sberbank (Savings Bank), and Vneshtorgbank (Foreign Trade Bank). All these institutions were instruments of the state and played no independent role in determining economic activity or investment decisions.

Since Russian reformers who grew up in the Soviet period had no direct experience with market finance, they leaned heavily on US models, practice, and expertise, which they modified to fit Russian conditions and interests.

Stock Exchanges and Equity Trading

The privatization process, which began with the issuance of one voucher coupon to every Russian citizen as described above, spawned a boom in voucher investment companies trading in those vouchers. From 1992 to 1993, the number of voucher investment funds grew dramatically from 10 small firms to more than 640. In parallel, hundreds of unlicensed investment companies were established. All these companies established a market in voucher coupons trading in the new investment vehicle.

This period was a time of substantial fraud through large pyramid schemes in a poorly regulated market at a time when the general public had no understanding or experience with financial investing. The most famous of these voucher funds was MMM, a company launched in February 1994 that recruited investors through extensive TV advertising, promising returns of 3,000 percent. By July 22, 1994, MMM was revealed as a classic Ponzi scheme. The Russian Ministry of Finance announced that MMM had illegally issued unregistered securities. The company collapsed, owing its investors somewhere between US$50 million and US$1.5 billion.[16] This kind of very public fraud was duplicated by imitators of MMM and led to public disillusionment with the whole notion of investing.

While voucher privatization was primarily a Russian story, foreigners also participated in this early stage through purchasing vouchers to use in the privatization auctions. Some of the active organizations in purchasing vouchers included Credit Suisse, Merrill Lynch through Troika Dialog, Russian Broker House, Rinaco Plus, Grant and Aton.

Later as vouchers were turned into shares in privatized companies, new foreign-linked investment banks dominated the trade in shares linked with foreign buyers. The leading new investment banks were Troika Dialog, Renaissance Capital, and United Financial Group (UFG). Each of them was associated with founding Americans who had powerful Russian partners. All played instrumental roles in the nascent financial system that developed in post-Soviet Russia.

As share ownership through voucher privatization proceeded, there was growing interest and need for formalized infrastructure for trading the new forms of property represented by company shares emerging from the voucher auction privatization process. The first stock exchanges in Russia were set up at the end of 1991, the Moscow International Stock Exchange (MICEX) and Moscow Central Stock Exchange.[17] Peter Derby's DialogBank and the Russian Central Bank were the founders of MICEX. "We were the founders with the Central Bank of the Ruble – Dollar exchange market. There was a set of banks, Russian banks at that time that were licensed. There was about a dozen of us, and we were the founding members of the MICEX." At that time, the ruble was not directly convertible to foreign hard currency, so MICEX was an important step in development of the Russian market economy.

By 1992, there were 120 organizations with stock exchange licenses.[18] From 1991 to 1996, the securities market was regulated by different bodies within the Ministry of Finance with shared responsibility with the Bank of Russia. There was no powerful central regulator, but instead a set of sometimes conflicting regulations. Resolving these conflicts was not addressed until the Russian Securities Market Act in 1996 that set up the Federal Commission on the Securities Market.[19]

In this early period of Russian capitalism, the fundamental infrastructure for conducting stock trading was simply not present and there was no expertise inside Russia to construct it. USAID stepped into this void by funding several initiatives to build the necessary infrastructure, including share registries, professional associations, professional standards and ultimately the first automated stock exchange, the Russian Trading System.

Dan Hill was one of the early American consultants brought in by Price Waterhouse to develop a shareholder registry system. He had a cosmopolitan, unconventional childhood with missionary parents who moved the family around from Korea to Native American reservations. He was already working on international projects for Price Waterhouse when tapped for the new contract in Russia. "I worked for them, for several years, managed the project that they had with the US State Department, installing a financial management system at American embassies around the world. … I didn't know anything about the subject to be honest with you. But they knew I wouldn't come running home to momma after five minutes. Russia was a tough place back then and some people really didn't adjust. Some people loved it; other people couldn't quite make the adjustment."

"I arrived in Moscow on March 31, 1993. My project was to help build a shareholder registry function. They privatized all these companies, some of them were small companies and suddenly, they've got all these shareholders. They did not know how to keep track of who owned the shares and that type of stuff. We worked with a couple of small Russian firms to develop shareholder registry software that was then given for free to a lot of small and midsized businesses."

"One of the first meetings I had was with a director of a kind of food warehouse. I wanted him to test our software, so I went to meet with them. I told them that we had developed this shareholder registry software and asked if he would have his people use if for a week and then give us some feedback about what you like and what you don't like. We were developing a couple of alternatives. If they did not like one, we could give them another one. So, he asked 'when are you coming back?' I told him that I would be back the following Thursday afternoon around three o'clock. I came back the next week and he had organized a party for me."

"It was a typical Russian party with a table full of sliced meats, Olivier salad and all the Russian specialties. There was lots of wine and vodka. I was sitting at the head of the table with him, and I have a guy with me who was translating. After many toasts, the director wanted me to get together with them again for some advice that he wanted from me."

"The advice he wanted was for me to tell him how to get his employees to either give him their shares or to sell them to him for almost nothing. I think that this happened everywhere. I mean the shares very quickly ended up in a few hands."

"He told me that it was hard to manage workers if they think they are owners. I told them that, you want them to be owners so they would work harder. They would feel bought-in, but the truth is that I don't think that I convinced him."

"Even though the idea was to create a country of shareholders, it didn't really happen. … I think I had one or two other conversations with other businesspeople like that one. It became clear to me that whoever oversaw a company was going to do everything they could to get control of all the shares in their organization. … You had people who were used to obeying orders, which was certainly part of the Soviet system. I can't tell you exactly how it all played out, but I don't think there were very many shareholders, at the end of the day."

"Eventually of course that's how the first oligarchs happened. There are some very young, smart people who understood the game and bought up shares for pennies on the dollar of oil giants and everything else."

When his contract with Price Waterhouse ended in November 1993, they wanted to move him to another country location, but he did not want to leave

Russia. "I didn't want to go. I thought this was the most exciting place I've ever been. You would wake up in the morning in Moscow in the 1990s and you did not know what was going to happen that day."

Dan learned that KPMG had gotten a big USAID contract and he contacted them to see if there was a position for him. "I contacted KPMG because they had a bigger funded, shareholder program. I told them that I had six months of experience in Russia and at that time that was a big deal." KPMG hired Hill for their project to launch a Professional Association of Registrars and Transfer Agents (PARTAD).

"We got people together who already knew a little bit about the shareholder registry function and there were people that were starting to provide that service and the software that we had developed [in his previous position at Price Waterhouse] was also being used. ... Basically, we had a group of maybe 20 people. I had a couple of lawyers working for me that helped define the rules and bylaws. Then we got people to come and sign up for PARTAD. Later, there were actual professional ratings that were put out to ensure that these registrars always do a good job."

"We also had a couple of experts from NASDAQ who came out and helped us. ... They were good guys, much smarter than me. They would come on loan for a week at a time. They would work with our team and with the Russians who were becoming registrars. ... I think that it is still a functioning trade association." It may seem obvious that experienced American experts from NASDAQ or other major US financial institutions would be involved in setting up new institutions in Russia if one looks at this only in terms of expertise. However, if the perspective is shifted to consider how Americans would react to British or Chinese experts setting up our American financial institutions then this whole process becomes quite remarkable.

The funding ran out for the KPMG project in the middle of 1995 and Dan Hill then moved into InterComp, a payroll company serving foreign companies. "Some guys from Texas had started a payroll company, like a paychecks company in the US. ... Anyway, I was the managing director of the little payroll company and that's probably my biggest claim to fame and Russia. We ended up turning it into Russia's biggest payroll provider and the company was eventually sold to Sberbank."

As evidenced by Dan Hill's consulting experience, by the year 1994, there was still limited trading of shares on the secondary market due to inadequate trading, clearing and settlement systems.[20] It was a period in which investment funds were fighting for control of privatized enterprises, often opposed by enterprise managers who were gathering up workers' shares to keep control. It was an environment without established rules and institutions and often with little transparency about the actual state of the companies. Within this high-risk environment, there were many drawn by the possibility of profit despite the obstacles.

Boris Jordon remembered those early days of trading. "There were many exchanges at the time, exchanges where vouchers traded and then they became exchanges were shares traded. You know it was a very long process. There were different self-regulating bodies that we all formed. We wrote the laws and the rules. It was a long process to get to where we are now with a very sophisticated fully electronic digital-based exchange. It was a lot of work."

"There were the first self-regulatory bodies, NAUFOR, PAUFOR. There were these different bodies that were set up and we were founding members of all of them. The guys that really worked on all those were a small number of banks. There was Credit Suisse and after I left them, Renaissance Capital. There was Troika Dialog, with Ruben Vardanyan and Peter Derby. Peter wasn't really involved in the day-to-day business of Troika; he was the chairman and an owner. Then there was a firm called Rinaco Plus. There was another firm called Grant and one more called Brunswick. Renaissance and Brunswick were foreign owned, and Troika was 50/50. All the others were Russian owned. So, it was about five groups of young guys. There must have been 10 of us in each one of these banks. We got together and started forming the stock exchange."

During all of the chaos and conflicting systems of the early 1990s, USAID financed another project by KPMG to establish a centralized stock exchange. This exchange was opened in September 1995 as the Russian Trading System ("RTS"). The RTS was a continuation of the work already begun by the existing investment community, but was created somewhat from the outside, requiring persuasion for adoption by the broker community.

A key figure in establishing the RTS was a New Yorker named Fred Berliner, who had been an OTC market maker and independent equity trader for 30 years. In early 1994, he answered a small ad that KPMG had placed in the *Wall Street Journal* looking for staff for their recently won contract to develop a Russian stock exchange. By the time he received a call back in April 1994, he had already forgotten that he had answered the ad. After a call with the Moscow head of the project, he was offered what was supposed to be a 6-to-9-month contract. Fred Berliner had never been to Russia and had no real connections with that country. His wife had been a Russian major in college and they decided this was an adventure too good to pass up, so Fred accepted the offer.

The interview with Fred Berliner for this book largely tracked his written account of his experience in Russia expressed in the book, *In from the Cold – The Rise of Russian Capitalism*, edited by Peter Westin. Quotes repeated here are taken directly from his written essay in that volume as a virtual match for what he said in the interview.

Fred Berliner described the scope of the KPMG project. "I became part of a team assisting the Russian government, Russian security brokers and the financial community in establishing a stock market that would be consistent with international standards. There were several USAID, World Bank and other philanthropic projects underway in Russia at the time, and some operated in conjunction with ours. Our group consisted of men and women with backgrounds in management, telecommunications, logistics, compliance and both American and Russian law, to the extent that there was Russian law."[21]

He continued, "My main role was that of a live trader, one who had been on the equity market firing line and could relate to the needs of market participants. This was a new role for me, because I have always been a player. Now I was the coach, using my experience to try to impart to the trading community some idea of how the arena would evolve. Before this mission I had never once considered what factors characterized a workable stock market. I never questioned what series of events relied on each other for the successful completion of a transaction, or how vital telecommunication was to the structure of the marketplace. A viable equities market was of utmost importance to Russia since the country desperately needed capital to finance the restructuring of industry from state to private ownership."[22]

He describes the market conditions of the time and the chaos that his project was trying to sort out. "Where were we even to begin? The systems in place were barely functional and archaic at best, and every procedure had to be modified. What existed was an extremely elementary bond trading platform totally unusable for equities. The contract agreements between brokers were nightmares. There were so many variables involved in the contractual agreements that it took the patience of Job and Cassandra's vision to sort everything out."[23]

"Moreover, registration was not an easy task since it required someone hopping on a plane, train or mule to stand in line at the company registrar, which might be open only on the third Tuesday of each month between 11 and 11:15AM. A month or more could pass between the verbal agreement to buy or sell a security and actual completion of the transaction – and all the multitudinous variables affected the transaction price to such an extent that it was difficult to quote a firm price for a given stock. The computer technology was there, but there were no systems in place to standardize and track all this information, such as a central clearing organization, and adaptation to Russia's particular way of doing business would be a long and tedious task. …"[24]

"Another huge problem was taxes. Many transactions took place 'offshore' to avoid the authorities. Russian brokers sold to their own offshore accounts for little or no profit and no tax liability, and then, from Cyprus or another agreeable jurisdiction, would sell the stock at a profit to the real buyer. Actual ownership of the said securities was another problem."[25]

"All these complications, unfortunately, were linked to each other and to our project. Giving Russia the infrastructure of a securities market was proving to be very difficult, and the selection of an electronic information and trading system was needlessly delayed for several months by infantile haggling. Two choices were available. One was a Russian-designed system for trading treasury notes that was jury-rigged to accommodate stock trading. As an alternative, we offered the specifications for Portal, a NASDAQ type trading system, and at the end of 1994 that system was chosen by the brokers. Portal was a system designed by NASDAQ to trade restricted securities in the U.S., and basically was a flop gathering moss until it was resurrected by interest from the Russian market. There was no doubt that the system had to be upgraded, modified and customized, but for Russia and its stage of development at the time, the system was ideal. One crucial enhancement was creating a window to negotiate trades in Cyrillic, not easy but doable. There was a spirited debate with Dmitri Vasiliev, the head of the newly formed Russian Securities Commission, regarding symbols using the Latin alphabet and price quotations in dollars. After I patiently explained that the investors came from the States and Europe, and their initial comfort level was the most important factor in the system's success, Vasiliev reluctantly acquiesced. I was later reprimanded for speaking so directly and forcefully to him, but my modus operandi served the project well."[26]

"The problems with telecommunications were mind boggling. Getting through to various brokerage firms in Moscow was frustrating, and the implications for business were obvious. Telephone systems for military use were fine, but in Soviet times the government didn't want to make it easy for the common comrade to exchange ideas, so that part of the country's infrastructure was purposefully neglected. We installed seventeen direct lines, expensive but necessary, to the temporary Portal computer site for the Moscow broker's association. But in two months we needed many more, so the logistics were intricate."[27]

"We formed self-regulatory associations in Moscow, St. Petersburg, Yekaterinburg, and Novosibirsk to write the rules and regulations for the markets. It was our intention to pre-empt government legislation that might be written by bureaucrats with little knowledge or understanding of what a securities market is. A standardized contract with four basic options was blessed by the Moscow and regional broker dealer associations, and it eliminated delays in the actual settlement of transactions and facilitated inter-regional trading. The stage was now set for one national market with a level of transparency that was previously non-existent."[28]

"By the end of July 1995, the trading system was functioning not only in Moscow, but in St. Petersburg, Novosibirsk, and Yekaterinburg as well. In a year's time, a fragmented, indicative priced market had changed to a national market with hundreds of system users displaying real prices, reported transactions, and for many issues, a depth of market makers rare in emerging markets."[29]

"So, what did the triumph of the RTS do for the equities markets in Russia? First and foremost, the RTS has been the key ingredient in the success and spectacular growth in stock trading. Without it, Russia would have been on the fringe of the equity business. The RTS became the basic, required tool."[30]

"The creation of the Russian Trading System was a marquee success story in the annals of USAID projects in Russia, and perhaps worldwide. We achieved huge, concrete, tangible results relative to the money invested. We had a thriving equities market that couldn't have been created without the young, Russian entrepreneurs seeking a higher standard than that which evolved from the voucher days. Their desire to change, to overcome the fear of the unknown and greet an unsettled future with an enthusiastic spirit, was the wellspring of this success."[31]

"What I was engrossed in for eighteen months wasn't work. I was myself, virtually unfettered and unmindful of protocol as the spirit and trading experience behind the crucial part of the project, and its success sits at the pinnacle of my career. The most difficult obstacle we had to overcome was the natural resistance to change, and our great challenge was to make the Russian brokerage community believe that the trading system and the inevitable, structural upheavals it would beget were beneficial. The single, most important achievement in this process was convincing market participants to make firm, real markets–and to honor them."[32]

The Russian Trading System was originally set up as a non-profit, but then converted to a joint stock company. In December 2011, as part of a long-term trend in policy to centralize control of financial markets in the hands of the Central Bank, RTS was merged with the Moscow Interbank Currency Exchange (MICEX) to form the Moscow Exchange.

Investment Banks

Against this backdrop, a whole range of new private financial institutions came into being, often modeled from US analogues and utilizing the operational experience of Americans who came to Russia in these early days of reform. These new investment banks became the bridge between the chaotic and translucent world of Russian share trading and foreign investors seeking to find opportunities in the transition from state ownership to private ownership, with potentially large profits available from mispriced or underpriced Russian company shares. These banks provided the research, linkage and access to shares those foreign investors lacked and were the cutting edge of integration of Russia into world financial markets.

As remarked by Mike Calvey, co-founder of the private equity firm Baring Vostok, "There was a brief period, perhaps just 2 or 3 years (1994–1995), when foreigners had a real advantage looking at equity investments in Russia. This was partly because few Russians had experience valuing companies the way it is typically done internationally. But the bigger reason probably was that Russians were simply more pessimistic than foreigners about Russia's future and especially about equities. They did not believe that holding a piece of paper stating that you owned a share in a company would translate into value. It depended on so many things out of any individual investor's control, like whether management of the company would share the profits with shareholders. During those early years, Russian professional investors preferred investing in bonds, which had a clear coupon and predictable cashflow. Early success stories like Vimpelcom and Chernogorneft showed Russians that owning shares of companies had a much bigger upside potential than bonds. Once that light bulb switched on, smart Russians poured into the equity market. They quickly caught up in terms of valuation skills and had an obvious advantage over foreigners in sourcing opportunities directly."

Troika Dialog

As described in Chapter 1, DialogBank was already established as a private commercial bank before the dissolution of the Soviet Union. Troika Dialog was founded as a joint venture between DialogBank and Peter Derby on January 18, 1991. It was intended to be a Russian investment company operating according to international standards and officially opened on February 1, 1991.

Ruben Vardanyan, a former student at Moscow State University, who had entered the private banking world at age 22, was one of the first four employees. "I joined Troika with a hundred-dollar salary, and everybody looked me like crazy person. I already had a good position in a commercial bank. ... I did it with a purpose in mind, because I wanted to learn how to work in financial markets in Western style. When I met Peter [Derby], I understood that Troika Dialog would be a unique combination. We were a Russian company, but we worked by international standards, which was quite an unusual model."

"I said to myself that the period we were entering into was going from a government planning system to a market economy. What mechanism will be replacing the government planning system? It will be the securities market and commercial relations."

"I made this decision because I thought that is will be very critical for Russia to build internationally. It would be very important to help international clients invest in Russia through building the securities markets. I also understood that it would be easier to build from scratch compared to transforming Russia's old commercial banks."

"I highly appreciate Peter Derby who as a teacher was very consistent. He allowed us to build that Russian brokerage firm but working by international standards, so he was very important."

"The company represented a symbiosis of Russian and world experience. Troika was a Russian company where foreigners came to work, while usually it's the opposite, and they brought with them best international practices. They laid the company's multiplicative foundation, its openness to everything new. Playing a tremendous role in this was managing director Bernard [Bernie] Sucher."[33]

Bernie Sucher's family were immigrants who had fled Europe in both World War I and II and who saw the Russians as the enemy that had forced them to flee to the United States. Completely opposite of the citizen diplomats encountered in Chapter 1, Bernie saw the Soviet Union as the enemy that would have to be fought at some point. This led him to learn Russian and to study the Soviet Union as an adversary. In furtherance of this goal of learning about the enemy, he traveled around the Soviet Union as a tourist in 1980. To his surprise, amidst the shabbiness and disorganization, he found it not very threatening. After graduating from the University of Michigan in 1984, he began a career on Wall Street, eventually ending up at Goldman Sachs, but never lost his fascination with the Soviet Union.

As the Soviet Union began to come apart during the later stages of Perestroika, a university classmate, Robert Langer, who will appear in Chapter 4, convinced the law firm where he was working, Chadbourne & Parke, to open an office in Moscow. Moved by this example, Sucher began to lobby Goldman Sachs to open a Moscow office as well. With no functioning financial markets or stock exchange in the Soviet Union, Goldman Sachs declined.

By the end of 1992, Bernie decided he could wait no longer and quit Goldman Sachs. He took his bonus as a successful trader and his experience in financial markets and went to Russia, where he funded a small venture firm, IM Galt, and seeded the start-up of several Moscow businesses, some of which will be covered in more detail in Chapter 4. His early projects included A/O Practica, a medical and scientific text publisher and Flying Foods, the parent of the Moscow Beach Club, American Standard fitness center, Uncle Guilly's, American style steak house and Starlight Diner, American style diner. He saw his personal mission in Russia to "transfer expertise, capital, good governance and a positive example of how to do business with the goal of constantly raising standards." Simultaneously with his other ventures, he became an advisor and participant in Troika Dialog.

Shortly after arriving in Moscow, Bernie saw an ad for Troika Dialog on the subway. He called Peter Derby to find out more about buying stocks, which resulted in a fateful meeting with Ruben Vardanyan. "On a Thursday morning, a few weeks after my arrival, I was sitting in the lobby of the Radisson Hotel. It was a scene that recalled the famous bar sequence from the original Star Wars. No purple aliens were required, the locals were naturally outlandish. It was 10.30 AM, and I was surrounded by gun-toting Mafiosi, drunken Asian suits, and massive Texas oilmen. Every one of them was with what looked like a teenage supermodel in a cocktail dress or a disco outfit dating from the 1970s. In sharp contrast, opposite me, was an earnest young man, conservatively attired. He was trying to persuade me to join his tiny investment bank. Perhaps conscious of the wackiness about us, Ruben Vardanyan shifted forward and said softly, "I know this is not a normal country. Maybe it never will be. But if we build a normal business, and if other people do, too, maybe that's how Russia will become a normal country. Will you help me build a normal business?"[34] Bernie was hooked and joined Troika Dialog as a volunteer advisor and then later a paid member of the staff.

Sucher began working with Troika Dialog in the chaotic days of voucher privatization and described the process of buying up vouchers to accumulate for privatization auctions. "Every day we shouldered duffel bags of cash, our wares for trade at the bazaar in the old Moscow post office on Myasnitskaya Street [a Moscow Street]. A million US dollars isn't that heavy, but the 50,000 vouchers it typically bought meant 50,000 opportunities to own a forgery and a total of 450,000 digits to enter manually in triplicate into that evening's privatization register with Goskomimushchestvo [government property registration]. At least those transactions were physically settled. But for every moment of every one of those days, and for long months following the end of voucher trading stretching into late 1994, what weighed on my mind like a thousand of those duffel bags was the anxiety that our investors would get nothing for their money. Or worse (much worse!) that other brokers would deliver 100 percent on their promises to their clients and that when the accounting was finally done, we would find that we alone had done it all wrong."[35]

After completing his assignment with RTS, Fred Berliner re-enters the story as the lead manager at Troika Dialog. He described this transition as follows. "In July of 1994, I met Ruben Vardanyan at one of the initial meetings with the Russian brokerage community. He was the 25-year-old President of Troika Dialog, a small brokerage company that he had started a few years earlier. We hit it off immediately and he implored me to join him at Troika. I told him I had a commitment to the USAID project, but when it was successfully completed, I wouldn't go anywhere else. I joined Troika in November of 1995. Now I had another mountain to climb and achieving the goals I established for Troika and myself was a challenge, handicapped as I was by a level of Russian on the fair side of pathetic. During my tenure with USAID, I always had at least one interpreter at my side, and often at important meetings I had an interpreter on each side. My role at Troika was trader, teacher, mentor, and visionary to a fast growing, young Russian brokerage firm of which I was the senior citizen. I was given free rein over equity trading and its small staff, all young enough to be my children."[36]

"Initially the sales force consisted entirely of expats, but the traders were and would remain Russians, some with a rudimentary command of the English language. ... Over the more than three years that I ran the equity desk, my command of the language progressed to learning numbers in Russian and developing the ability to referee squabbles on the trading desk. But my traders learned western adages and became proficient in English as well as much language painful to the politically correct. But most importantly, Troika evolved into the premier market maker for the burgeoning equity community and eventually became the top broker in Russia. I also assumed the role as policeman for ethical standards and fair practice among all Moscow market makers."[37]

"So, an assignment that was supposed to last for less than a year turned into a five-year love affair. I had no expectations in travelling to Moscow and could not even have speculated that I would be making a serious contribution to establishing a Russian securities market, both with USAID and Troika. But the most satisfaction is that I was able to a make a real difference to so many, and I am very proud and honored to have been a part of the community."[38]

Daniel Wolfe joined Troika as Chief Operating Officer in late 1996 after having accumulated experience as an attorney and entrepreneur in a career in Russia that began in 1992. Initially, he was hired by the British law firm

Clifford Chance for their Moscow office. "I started working as a lawyer back in the days when they were just a handful of foreign lawyers here. And after two years, I realized, you know, even though it was great experience for me, as a lawyer, I had my own clients. I was really doing interesting work and it wasn't like the sort of soul crushing associate life that you get in in New York as a young lawyer. But I realized that I was a lawyer in a country which hadn't really gotten around to getting laws in place to make that a worthwhile endeavor, so I became an entrepreneur."

"Basically, I got into this sort of uncomfortable position of seeing that what my corporate clients wanted to do was the right thing to do, and it made sense. The legal risks were minimal. But you know very often legal departments in foreign capitals don't see things that way. So, things would get shut down. After a while, I just decided that as a young person without a family, I could make a bigger impact and have more interesting things to do if I stopped being a lawyer and just became an entrepreneur."

His journey as an entrepreneur led him into a warehouse business that was servicing large international brands, like Duracell, Wrigley's and Johnson and Johnson. This led to the purchase of a privatized Russian plywood mill. He then helped one of the investors in these two ventures set up a financial services company. After that Wolfe moved to Troika Dialog, "and within a couple of years I was chief operating office of one of the leading investment banks in Russia, Troika Dialog, essentially because of Bernie Sucher. … One of the other things that's interesting to me is that this was the first of several jobs that I've had for which really, I had no qualification. … But at that time there was no one else who did in Russia that you could hire at any cost."

"We were lucky at Troika that we had people like Bernie and people like Fred Berliner who were knowledgeable and experienced in international financial markets. They could say, 'I don't know if that's going to work here, but in New York this is how they do it, or in Tokyo, this is how they do it.' So that was one of the sources of knowledge and growth that we had at Troika, these people with amazing experiences, who are able to translate that experience into something that worked in Russia in the 90s, with my help on the operational side and with lawyers and accountants."

James Fenkner became Troika Dialog's chief strategist in its research department in 1998. His career in Russia was varied as he moved from company to company in the financial sector. He originally became involved in the former Soviet Union through a Soros-sponsored program in Lithuania, then he moved to Brno to work in a stock brokerage with Mike Sassarini, a friend from university days at Tufts University. He later became head of research at Robert Fleming and Co., then a broker at the firm Centreinvest and ultimately at Troika.

Fenkner's career in Russia spanned the early post-Soviet when there were countless opportunities for foreigners in Russia until the end of the 1990s when foreign expertise and experts were less and less in demand. "In the beginning, as a foreigner, I walked on water. I mean I got a position that I would have never gotten if I worked at Merrill Lynch or Goldman Sachs. It would be 30 years for me to get to that level and I probably would have burned out before I got there. … For me, career wise, it was fantastic."

"But by the end, it went from where being a foreigner was not neutral, it was negative. … It's just that the sentiment in Russia became very nationalistic under Putin. It was no longer that period where Russians said our system didn't work so let's bring in foreigners, a la Peter the Great, and figure out how to do something better. … It had gone one eighty. I'm a little slow on the uptake so it took me a couple of years to figure that out. You know, I guess that I lost the Russian plot. … It was not going where I wanted to go. I was not fitting in. It wasn't so much language; my language was improving. It was just being a foreigner and having a different view."

"On the other hand, the work at Troika was amazing. I mean that there were Russian locals, people from Georgia, people from Murmansk. The Skolkovo School of Management had been set up and operating. A lot of them had gone off to Harvard, London School of Economics. Bright people were coming back to Russia, and the talent level was very high. I mean bushels full of talented people. I think that in the beginning we foreigners probably got a perch that we did not deserve just because we had experienced a different type of system."

Renaissance Capital

In January of 1995, Boris Jordan left Credit Suisse and formed Renaissance Capital as an investment bank. He described the foundation of the new company, "the original five partners were all working together at Credit Suisse, and we walked out and started Renaissance Capital. … We had all gotten paid very well based on our successful 1994 earnings for Credit Suisse. The money that we got paid was then put into the new bank. We also attracted a $20 million check from a Russian named Vladimir Potanin, who at that time wasn't yet an oligarch. He gave us a $20 million check for 20 percent stake in our bank. Together with the money that the five partners put in which was $5 million total for the rest of us. That was literally everything we had because we had just had one good year bonus and we were very young. So, I would say that all in, we had $25 million dollars and that is what got Renaissance off the ground. Obviously, back then $25 million was a lot of money."

In those early days, relationships were of critical importance in Russian business. Jordan acknowledged that while they benefited from relationships developed through Potanin but emphasized that his team had its own strengths and relationships from having been so intimately involved with voucher privatization. As Jordan stated, "I would say that relationships through Potanin surely helped, but you know we were at that point in time we became very, very plugged in Russia. We ran the privatization process. We got to meet all the powers that be. We had been involved with most of the companies being privatized because we were privatizing them. All the guys that owned the companies basically owed us for helping them be privatized. That advisor assignment was a bit of a stroke of genius to be honest because we got to know everyone in the country."

In the beginning, Renaissance did not focus on natural resource companies because access to most of them was still heavily under government control. "There were different levels of strategic assets. There were some strategic assets, where the government just kept control, but privatized a minority stake. There were those assets where the government was focused on not allowing foreigners to invest at all. To be honest, there was so much to do, outside of those assets that we did not care so much. Generally, our position as a foreign owned bank was to stay out of the political stuff anyway. We felt like we didn't want to go into anything the government was interested in keeping us out of."

Instead, Renaissance focused on the consumer sector. "In the beginning, we really focused on the consumer goods sector. For instance, we sold tobacco factories to Philip Morris and British American Tobacco. We sold breweries to Heineken. So, we were very involved in consumer goods areas."

"The reason we were able to do that is because we were the only guys there that spoke both English and Russian. When these big foreign companies came to Russia, they didn't have anybody to work with because none of the big banks were there yet. It's kind of funny to say today, but Renaissance was the big bank in Russia for investment banking. So, we got to work with these big multinationals and large Russian entities. It wasn't because we were smarter than anybody else, we were just there. ... Foreign direct investment was a big issue at that point in time. The success of Russia at that time wasn't judged as much by its GDP or rate of inflation. It was judged by how much foreign direct investment was coming into the country."

"We tried to stay out of natural resources and heavy industry as much as we could. We dabbled in steel. Then later, we made some investments in oil. But to be honest, every time we got involved in any of the natural resources, it was always very political, and it turned me off. Whereas telecoms, banking, consumer goods, nobody bothered you."

"I took the first Russian company public on the New York Stock Exchange, since the revolution. It was Vimpelcom. That was Russia's first Western IPO. Renaissance Capital led it, together with DLJ."

In 2008, Renaissance Capital entered a strategic partnership with ONEXIM Group, owned by the Russian billionaire Mikhail Prokhorov, which purchased 50 percent minus one share in Renaissance for $500 million. In 2012, ONEXIM acquired full ownership of Renaissance Capital.

United Financial Group

The United Financial Group (UFG) was founded in 1994 by the American banker, Charles (Charlie) Ryan and Boris Federov, a former finance minister under Boris Yeltsin. Ryan, who declined to be interviewed for this book was originally from Philadelphia and educated at Harvard University. He then took a job with Credit Suisse First Boston, before moving to the EBRD. He came to

Russia in 1991 as the EBRD representative soon after the failed August 1991 coup attempt. His responsibility was working in St. Petersburg as an advisor to local government on privatization of local municipal assets. In this capacity he met several young Russians who were part of the St. Petersburg privatization who would later become leading figures in Russia as a whole. They included Alfred Kokh, Anatoly Chubais, Boris Federov and Vladimir Putin, who was a deputy mayor of St. Petersburg at that time.[39]

Ryan and Federov had worked together at the EBRD in London from 1991 to 1994. Ryan moved to Moscow from St. Petersburg in 1994 to set up UFG, in partnership with Federov. Through their business contacts they secured an initial investment of $1 million from the French Banque Paribas for 25 percent of their new investment bank. Their first activity was to focus on researching investment opportunities, but they quickly realized that it was important to get a brokerage license and began stock trading that same year.[40] The partnership of Ryan and Federov combined Western banking expertise with Russian insider contacts and knowledge to form a highly successful and influential investment bank.

Martin Skelly, Ryan's roommate at Harvard became the Chief Operating Officer of UFG in 1997. Skelly described Ryan as "One of the most successful people in Russia in terms of striking the right balance between controlling his ego, controlling his ambitions and actually doing the right thing, making things better." With all the talents and qualities that made Ryan successful, Skelly emphasized the strategic importance of the Russian members of the UFG team. "It was also critically important for the success of UFG to have a Russian as a leader, even if not in an executive capacity." Skelly also praised the analytic ability of the Russian staff of UFG. "There were certainly things the Russians could learn from us. But they were the ones doing the teaching in a lot of ways when it came to analytics. I mean the big joke in the oil industry was that for years and years, everyone said the Russians were lying about their resources, but it just wasn't lies. They knew much better than the Western geologists. … We were dealing with the intellectual top 1 percent or 2 percent of the academic pile."

Along with his respect for his Russian colleagues, Skelly expressed the opinion that their success depended at least partly on the willingness to adapt to Russian conditions. "The analogy that I always use about my job as a manager in Russia was to make sure that we went with the grain. If we found a splinter, we sorted it out and didn't let it become a wound."

Skelly emphasized the positive impact of the adaptation of Western expertise by Russians and its long-term impact. "I think if you're going down the route of why they let the Westerners create the financial neural network or the financial mechanisms, it's a good question. I think what I would say goes back to one of my happiest moments in Moscow. We were having a retreat at the Country Club of Moscow just after we had done an IPO for Sedmoi Kontinent, a Russian convenience store. We looked out at our Russian staff who had done most of the work. We said to them that you guys should be so proud of yourselves. You've created an investment report about Sedmoi Kontinent. You've investigated the founder of the company and made sure they've got the earnings they claimed. You're going on road shows and bringing in all this capital investment that is basically allowing people to get staples more efficiently and more affordably. You have helped ordinary people to enhance their quality of life. I mean the growth of the entire convenience store, grocery store sector in Russia is a huge success story, the modernization that took place in the consumer field. … If you look at the diaspora of people who came out of that experience at UFG, you will find key people throughout the finance industry in Russia. None of those guys have Western bosses anymore. They are the ones now running everything. It is remarkable and it is how things should be."

"One thing I can say that we taught the Russians was how you can do something that will make an investment more valuable. How you package and dress up an investment so it can be showcased and have people bid up the price of it. I think that's one of the things that we did. I would be loath to say we taught them that as much as we gave an example for how it can work. The Russians were intimately involved and, in most cases, leading this process. I mean there were as many Russians on all those companies as there were Westerners."

Michael Sassarini, from Robert Fleming & Co, acknowledged UFG as the leader in bringing new share issues to market. "Everyone wanted a piece of the equity trading. It wasn't very liquid, and the prices were not transparent to foreigners. … The prices of blocks on the market were more than transparent between the five major brokers who were Western or Westernish. Everyone knew what blocks were coming on to the market and everyone was trying to get, let's call it, the primary market. Everyone was trying to get those shares of whatever region or company that its owner was going to sell directly. How do you get those shares? Well, you know, this is not a market where there is going to be a bid with sophisticated Goldman experts coming in to organize a private placement or an IPO on the secondary market. Instead, it was a question of who had the connections and the cash to pay for that deal. UFG was the clear winner most of the time because they had Federov. … People respected him and trusted him. They never lost money, and everyone knew that."

Later in the 2000s, Ryan became known as the most successful foreign banker in Russia after selling his interest in UFG and related entities in a series of tranches to Deutsche Bank.

Private Equity

As visible as the equity markets were, particularly to foreign portfolio investors, some would argue that private equity was much more important in terms of its real impact on modernization of Russian firms and supporting the new private sector. Private equity capital entered the Russian economy through a small number of private equity investors that included Baring Vostok, Robert Fleming & Co., TUSRIF/Delta Capital Private Equity Partners and Russia Partners. Foreign private equity investors were not as public as the investment bankers and were a much smaller group, but they penetrated much deeper into the operational side of the Russian economy than equity traders.

There are different opinions about the importance of private equity financing in the Russian economy, particularly as the Russian market matured over the course of the 1990s. Martin Skelly, the COO of UFG, had experience both in investment banking and in private equity for UFG. "The challenge of doing deals in Moscow after a while was that Russians had so much cash generated from their own businesses that the people who had good opportunities already had access to money, so the ones that you were going to put your money into might not actually need it. On the other hand, they might also be the weakest of the litter that you should not be backing anyways. So, there was a little bit of a problem in that your selection criteria were kind of skewed towards bad deals that maybe should get your investment. ... Who knows where the real truth is, but I would say that private equity had its day, where it was more important than right now [2021]." Nonetheless, private equity did play an important role in the early and mid-1990s.

Michael Sassarini pointed out that equity markets were profitable primarily for investment banks and foreign investors, not for Russian issuers of shares. "You made your money from Western investors. If the valuation of those shares goes up, the brokers would run with it. You cannot take advantage of that rise in value as a Russian company unless you issue more shares. ... There were very few examples of that happening. That is the truth and equities were not really doing much for the Russian economy."

"People were not going into private equity. It was only for the bold and the brave. Even Baring Vostok was very, very slow."

As Mike Calvey of Baring Vostok explained, "private equity is so different than investment banks or brokerage companies. In fact, they are so different in approach, how they make money and time horizon that they can hardly be considered the same industry."

These two contrasting types of investment activity are grouped together in this chapter to illustrate the significant role of Americans and other foreigners in the initial stages of all aspects of private financial market development in post-Soviet Russia.

Baring Vostok Capital Partners

The formation of Baring Vostok Capital Partners (Baring Vostok), one of the leading private equity firms of the period begins with the EBRD and two individuals who worked there in the early 1990s, Richard Sobel and Mike Calvey.

Richard Sobel first visited the Soviet Union as a student at Stanford in 1983. Much later in 1990, he joined a small team of people working with the maverick investor Dean LeBaron of Batterymarch Financial Management on a project for commercial conversion of Soviet military enterprises in collaboration with the Soviet Defense Ministry. At the time of the August 1991 coup against Gorbachev, Richard was in Moscow with high-level American investors following up on a limited number of projects that this team had developed. In the aftermath of the coup, Batterymarch did not have the same warm relations with the new government as previously with the Soviet government. Dean LeBaron was interested in protecting his team and the projects that were being developed. With the new lack of access, he approached Ron Freeman, who was developing the newly organized EBRD Russia program, to suggest that he take on Batterymarch's team and projects. The EBRD brought Richard Sobel to London where he became acquainted with Mike Calvey, who was working at the EBRD. Then in 1994 both were recruited by the British merchant bank Barings to staff their new investment fund in Russia.

Richard Sobel and Mike Calvey recounted two slightly different versions of the same story of the foundation of Baring Vostok. Richard recalled, "in 1994 I was recruited by Barings to be the manager of the first fund for Barings, which later got renamed Baring Vostok, and I worked with Michael Calvey for three and a half years. He was my right-hand guy. We were more like partners. ... We raised $160 million dollars and invested in 17 private companies. We also invested quite adroitly in the public stock market and made a lot of money and that was fun. ... The $160 million investment turned out to be worth $650 million dollars. We invested in Vimpelcom, Borjomi, Volga Tanker, the largest river-sea tanker shipping company, and a bunch of other companies. We got involved in an oil field in Turkmenistan. The company became Buran Energy and that paid for the whole fund. Each of these is a story."

"I have found it oftentimes easier to work with local partners than with foreign partners because local partners understand the necessities on the ground. That doesn't always mean that you must do backhanders and things like that, but they understand that you can't always pin down every single part of the deal or the business. You must live with some uncertainty. You must be able to understand what risks and problems, you can manage and accept and which ones you won't manage and won't accept. You deal with risk through relationships. If you had a bad relationship going in and if you don't have trust, the contract is not going to help you in the Russian legal system. If you have a good relationship and the contract doesn't work out, then you probably are going to have a better chance to work it out. ... Sometimes these big companies don't understand that this is important. So, I decided to go out on my own and set up my own business. I thought that I had the right partner and wanted more of an American style business. I found out that when things changed because of the macro-economic meltdown, they pulled out. I then left Russia for three and a half years until I came back in the 2000s."

Mike Calvey was originally from Oklahoma and after graduating from university began working as an analyst for Solomon Brothers in New York. He was accepted at Harvard Business School but decided to take a year off to gain some international experience before business school. He had no familial, ethnic, or language connection to Russia, but after joining the EBRD in London in 1991, he was assigned to work with financing multinationals in joint ventures with Russian companies. This brought him to Russia where he stayed. "I never went back to Harvard Business School. I could see from my first visit to Russia all the opportunities. First, I loved Russia from the very first days. I loved walking around Moscow. I loved meeting Russian people, making Russian friends. I loved the food, the sense of humor and the culture."

"I could sense that what was going on in Russia was going to be a great opportunity for entrepreneurs and venture investors. When Russia embarked on its mass privatization program that's when it really kind of felt like this transition towards a market economy was going to be irreversible and would also present opportunities for institutional investors. I was recruited to join at one of the first private equity funds that was raised in 1994 to invest in Russia and in the former Soviet Union, which was backed by a part of Barings, an old British merchant bank. ... They hired me to move to Moscow and to help hire a Moscow-based team to raise and invest that fund. At that time, Richard Sobel was hired, and we co-managed the fund together. He left after maybe two years. He decided to pursue other things. At that point, I took over and restructured the team. We created what became Baring Vostok shortly after that. Before that there had been Baring Asset Management and a local company called Sovlink. After Richard left, we consolidated the management into Baring Vostok and then moved forward from there."

"We raised funds really with Barings track record. They had a team with significant experience investing in listed equities and other emerging markets. Obviously with a 400-year-old brand they had a lot of credibility which we didn't have yet at our age. ... Also no one really had a track record in Russia at the time."

With the lack of transparency and basic information about Russian companies at that time, Baring applied a formula to find where to invest that followed an international perspective. "Where did we start? We would work backwards by looking at what succeeded in other markets of similar size and what companies had the most success, either companies valued in public capital markets in other emerging countries or companies that were acquired by strategic investors. So, where there had been the most interest and where there had been exits at attractive rates. Then we worked backwards from that. ... From 1994 to 1998, during the four years when we invested that fund, Russia's GDP declined by almost 40 percent to 50 percent. ... At the same time, Russian consumers needed everything so there were a lot of promising consumer companies. We invested that first fund in mostly in fast moving consumer goods companies, chocolate, beer, mineral water, things like that. We invested in forestry and forest timber processing and in cement. These were all sectors that were successful in Southeast Asia and in Central Europe. There had been several success stories there. ... Several of the investments were failures, 100 percent losses or write-offs, but we also had several big successes. We were one of the first investors in Vimpelcom, which became one of major Russian mobile operators."

Asked about their approach to the Russian companies in which they invested, Calvey stated, "We never tried to play an operational role in the companies. We always partnered with entrepreneurs and managers. We were usually a minority shareholder, but we approached the business the same even when we were a majority shareholder. We always expected the managers to be our partners and to be owners of the business alongside us. We expected them to take responsibility for operational matters and be accountable for it. When the shareholders view themselves as being involved in the operations, then they also have accountability for it. … I think inside Baring Vostok we created and built a fantastic team that was unique in the Russian market overall, with a culture that was focused on building great businesses, rather than doing clever deals. We had a very long-term investment horizon."

"We were focused on investing in companies that they either had or were building killer brands that Russian consumers loved or that had unbeatable service that Russian consumers loved and that created the potential for a sustainable sustainably growing business that could then be sold, either through an IPO and public markets or to a strategic investor. Usually, these were companies created by entrepreneurs who were not successful based on the connections that they had but were successful because of their brains or their innovation or their creativity and hustle."

Like the rest of the Russian financial sector companies, Baring Vostok took a big hit from the financial crisis of 1998, but because of the wisdom and support of Barings and their institutional investors' patience, they were able to withstand it and eventually profit from it. "Obviously what happened in 1998 was a catastrophic economic collapse, with the devaluation and default. What had been the kind of nascent Russian stock market that was generating interest from 1996 and 1997 completely collapsed in 1998? I think if you had a million dollars invested in the Russian stock market in December 1997, it was worth $20,000 by December 1998. The drop in value was almost as bad as it gets. At that point we had had a few exits and returned some funds to investors. … About half of the capital of the Fund, more like 50 percent of the investors' money was returned through some early realizations in 1997, as we sold some of our positions. Fortunately, in hindsight, it was near the high point in the market, so unlike a lot of other Funds, our shareholders did not pull the plug on the Fund. Many other people just said, Russia, it was worth trying but it's over. … Our shareholders believed that since they had already covered some of their exposure, it was worthwhile to stick it out. They even allowed us to reinvest that small amount of capital that we still had in the Fund. The small amount of capital became like a mountain of gold because the follow-on investments that we made in 1999 turned out to be very profitable. … We went on to have several big successes and ultimately returned four times the investors' original investment in dollars, which was way better than what any of the shareholders expected. This allowed us to raise our second fund, which we did in 2000. As far as I know, it was as the only fund raised in Russia from 1999 to 2002."

"August of 1998 was really the low point from a macroeconomic perspective. If you looked at Russia's GDP in dollar terms at that time, it was obviously not a fair reflection of what was really going on in the country. The devaluation dramatically improved the cost competitiveness of all exporters in the country, and they immediately became very profitable. The kind of cash generating engine coming from natural resources then started to get deployed into other parts of the economy. This was the beginning of a 10 year long growth cycle in Russia. I think that what really changed things for us was when for the first time it became interesting to invest in Russian technology companies, especially the emerging Russian Internet."

The story of Mike Calvey and Baring Vostok continued into the 2000s but is beyond the scope of this book. However, this beginning period illustrates the shift among some investors from equities into the heart of the new private sector in Russia in support of Russian and foreign entrepreneurs, some of whom will be highlighted in Chapter 4. It also shows the collaborative partnership approach to the Russian partners that was indicated by several others interviewed and contrasts starkly with the standard tropes of conflict emphasized in accounts of this period.

Robert Fleming & Co.

Robert Fleming & Co. was a Scottish merchant bank with a long history in Asia as part of the United Kingdom's Hong Kong banking establishment. It had an eccentric connection to Russia through Ian Fleming, nephew of the founder and author of the James Bond series of popular fiction. The bank was active in Russia until it was purchased by Citibank and then absorbed into JP Morgan when Morgan acquired Citibank a year later. Strictly speaking, it does not fit within the parameters of this book as a Scottish institution, but two Americans interviewed for this book, James Fenkner and Michael Sassarini, friends who leapfrogged each other in different positions in the financial sector, and who were connected to Robert Fleming & Co, offered insight into the world of private equity, as well as equity trading.

Fenkner and Sassarini knew each other from California. Fenkner convinced Sassarini that the two of them should take part in the Soros-Yale program in the Baltics. Sassarini went to Estonia in 1992, but Fenkner changed his mind and stayed in Boston, working at Fidelity. Then Sassarini convinced him to quit his job and take a similar position in Lithuania. Both moved around in positions in Eastern Europe, but never overlapping. Fenkner came to Russia first, in the spring of 1995. Then Sassarini came to Russia in December of 1995, initially to work for United City Bank, a company set up by Hans-Joerg Rudloff, who had left Credit Suisse.

James Fenkner, initially began his career in Russia as head of research at Fleming, later moving to Troika Dialog as described previously in this chapter. "At the time that I came in 1995, Fleming had the largest foreign investment fund in the country. They basically had some investors from London that wanted to buy vouchers to participate in privatization, and so they set up a fund."

Fenkner worked for Elizabeth Hebert, who was running the Fleming fund at that time. Hebert appeared previously in the section on the role of Harvard and HIID in privatization. She was the girlfriend and then wife of Jonathan Hay. "At the time I joined there was an American woman, Elizabeth Hebert, who was running the fund as the fund manager. She knew Russian, but she did not understand how to value anything. My day job was to get pricing for companies like LUKOIL just as it was coming into the market, to figure out what you should pay for it and what it was worth."

"At that time, it was very rare to go out and see the assets, to go out to the fields. I remember at that time there was a lot of distrust between what the Russians would say in terms of their [oil] reserves and what investors thought that they could have. People couldn't believe that you could buy reserves equal to Kuwait. … It was too good a deal, it was so big. … It was kind of shocking. A lot of people thought that it just couldn't be true that Russia had the number of reserves and assets that were there. … You're always worried about whether you might be off by decimal points. It sometimes looked that way because it's not like Russian assets were 30 percent cheaper, but in some cases, 30,000 times cheaper. That was because everything was given away free in privatization. … I think that what was remarkable is that they privatized in a period when nobody had money. It was pretty much done in a vacuum. … Any of those folks that happened to have export contracts at the time made a killing. Those are the oligarchs of today."

"There was a lot of stuff you could buy, and it all went up and down. There were very few people that actually understood how or why."

The two friends, James Fenkner and Michael Sassarini, never actually overlapped in employment with the company. Michael Sassarini had a very different experience. "My exposure to investing in Russia was so fundamentally different from what James experienced. While he was at Fleming, there was Beth, an analyst Dimitri, and Jonathan Hay taking naps of the office couch. That was kind of it." Sassarini became part of Fleming when it acquired United City Bank, where Sassarini began his career in Russia. This acquisition took place after Fenkner had already departed for another company.

United City Bank was founded by Hans-Jeorg Rudloff after he left Credit Suisse and included in its investors, Mark Garber, who was deeply involved in rail transportation and commodity trading in Russia. The managing director of United City Bank was Alex Rodzianko, a member of a Russian aristocratic émigré family that had fought against the Bolsheviks, like the families of Peter Derby and Boris Jordan. Rodzianko's grandfather was the last president of the pre-Revolutionary Russian Duma, which gave him cache in the anti-communist Yeltsin period. Taken together, the leadership of the United City Bank had unique access and understanding of the emerging Russian economy outside of Moscow. Rodzianko told Sassarini when he joined United City Bank that he needed a greater understanding of the country. Rodzianko engaged Sassarini in a lengthy process of studying the language, getting to know Russia by traveling throughout the country and developing contacts with enterprise managers in Siberia.

Sassarini described how the process of hunting for opportunities in the Russian Far East pushed United City Bank away from equities trading and into private equity investment. "It's just that things became so illiquid sometimes there was nothing to buy. We didn't want to lose business. There were ideas and they were risky, but at the time everything was going up. So, it was like can I get something."

"There were not a lot of us active in the region. Along with other investment groups, I led my first investment in Sakhalin in the timber industry. The forestry industry in that neighborhood was always corrupt. … We knew that, and it was simply a matter of trying to put it to the general director that he should not steal more than X. You know, in a $20 million business, you can skim off three or four million, okay. But nothing above that or else we were all going to get in trouble. And the guy just couldn't stop."

"It got to the point where we just could not negotiate our way through it, and he needed to be removed. He didn't understand and thought it can't be that way because we had always been his friend and made him a lot of money. There was a shareholder meeting called where he was in a very good mood, and I couldn't understand why. Then we broke it to him that we must vote as our investor clients instructed us. Then he realized that he was about to lose his job."

"There was nothing hostile about it, but it was just he had already taken too much. He refused to go, and he shut down the shareholders meeting. Lawyers come in, we tried to reschedule the meeting. We were sitting in a cinema in Yuzhny-Sakhalinsk and he tried to freeze us out. It was in the middle of February, and he turned out the lights and electricity. He had every single worker come up to complain, you know filibuster. Then the car of our management person was firebombed. And ultimately, the general director lost. He blamed me personally for him losing his job."

The struggle for control of this timber concern illustrates the nature of the struggle between outside investors and the Red Directors of former state enterprises during this period. It also shows how much more deeply private equity investment penetrated Russian economic life and practices. It was not easy money and therefore had many fewer investors than those involved in equity trading.

Ultimately, Fleming bought United City Bank. "Fleming bought us because to that point they had gone through all this crap. James left and they didn't know what to do. They had positions to fill, and they started hiring. Then, they decided just to acquire us, because we had all the staff they needed in every single department, corporate finance, equity, debt, research, and development. It was just a plug in."

With the acquisition of United City Bank, Fleming became a major player in Russian investment.

Asked about the size of Fleming's investments in Russia, Fenkner replied, "Well, you know numbers no longer mean what they used to, but Fleming's Russia fund, I think, was a quarter of a billion dollars, and it was one of the biggest funds in Russia at that time. ... We traded maybe a million dollars a day. something like that. The market probably did $10 million, something like that as I remember. Then with the 1998 crisis, everything ground to a halt." Others interviewed disputed the assertion that they were the biggest fund in Russia at that time, but all agree that they were one of the largest funds along with Baring Vostok, Russia Partners, and TUSRIF/Delta Capital Private Equity Partners.

Michael Sassarini filled in more details on the size of their holdings and the impact of the 1998 crisis, which differed from the account of Fenkner, who had left Fleming before the acquisition of United City Bank. According to him, "As we entered 1998, we had positions, including client positions, that were closer to $700 million dollars. Fortunately, we had Christopher Granville, who later went to UFG. Granville got the call right on the political situation, and we started to sell-off slowly, month by month. When the crisis hit, we were down to probably $150 million. We had gotten almost all our clients out of the market, and this is how we were able to survive."

TUSRIF/Delta Capital Private Equity Partners

The US Russia Investment Fund (TUSRIF) was funded by the US Government in 1995 to promote the development of the private sector in Russia through direct investment and technical assistance to private Russian enterprises.[41] The US Congress pledged $440 million for TUSRIF and ultimately allocated approximately $329 million for both investment and fund development activities. An experienced venture capitalist, Patricia Cloherty was recruited by the White House to manage TUSRIF. The allocation of government funds was for 2 years only. Cloherty fully invested those funds and then raised an additional $500 million from private sources and became Delta Private Equity Partners ("DPEP").

In 2008 in an interview in ECVJ European Venture Capital and Private Equity Journal, Ms. Cloherty gave a brief overview of her career with TUSRIF and DPEP. "In 1995, when I was a president of Apax Partners US, a $10 billion private equity company, President Clinton appointed me to the Board of Directors of the U.S. Russia Investment Fund. At that time, there were neither private equity business in Russia nor people to run such companies. The US government promised to invest $440 million. But do you know any government to fulfill its promises? We got $329 million. We successfully invested this fund and are returning all money we got down till the last penny. This fund stopped investing on the 16th of June 2004, having invested in 44 companies and sold all of them but the last four. In 2003 a successor private fund, the Delta Russia Fund (DRF), was formed. I returned to Russia to become a CEO of the new management company to manage both funds. DRF already has made 11 investments. Five of them have been sold, with a healthy internal rate of return."[42]

In our exchanges for this book, she provided a bit more information about her relationship with Russia and how she became the unpaid manager of TUSRIF. "I got involved with Russia at the end of 1994, and that was totally by accident. I was involved in extremely high risk investing for almost four decades in five countries – the US, UK, France, Israel, Japan – all to secure higher than average returns for investors to adjust for the risk."

"Russia as a target? Never thought of it. I had read a Kissinger book in the early 90's; the chapter on Russia said the country is '*sui generis.*' Given its' unique history and geography, it will define itself, post-Soviet Union. I never saw myself as an actor in this evolution."

"However, at the end of 1994, the White House Personnel Office called to see if I would go on a mission with President Clinton, to see President Yeltsin, to discuss 'deliverables' from the US to the struggling country. ... I agreed to this challenge against a background of ignorance and joined the mission."

"I told the White House group to dump me after the mission, as I had full responsibilities with my firm and our industry. But they did not 'do the dump.' I stayed on and got immersed in Russia for years after my retirement."

"Previously I had little interaction with Russians, except for one scientist we backed out of IBM, making semiconductor chip packages pursuant to patents purchased from IBM. In Russia, of course, it was different. My staff of 33 was Russian, except for two or three, and virtually all were multilingual. The financial professionals were highly educated, many in the US or UK. The support staff, i.e., driver, cooks, administrative personnel, were smart, loyal, hard-working and open to new ideas from me, a strange American. I attended their christenings, weddings, and birthdays with great joy. Mutual trust was the key."

Pat Cloherty was adamantly against the idea that the purpose of the fund was to change or restructure Russian society or the Russian economy. She approached her work with the fund strictly as a business like any other of her prior investment activities. In her words, "We were not reforming a country. It was all we could do to build 55 companies from scratch where no legal, regulatory or entrepreneurial climate had existed since early in the Twentieth Century. If we succeeded, others might emulate (and, hopefully, bring us deals). But our goal was the health and value of our portfolio companies."

"Our impact was substantial. Our firm's first name when the US Government ("USG") was involved was The US Russia Investment Fund ("TUSRIF"). When USG stopped funding after two years, (it's idea of long-term investing), we raised another $500 million privately around the world, and became Delta Private Equity Partners ("DPEP")."

"We launched 55 new companies – the first mortgage bank, the first credit card issuing bank, the first bottled water company, etc., all managed by Russian entrepreneurs. In 2001, we launched The Center for Entrepreneurship, to teach skills like managing cash flow, hiring and rewarding key people, and so on. Fifty-two of the companies were sold for extraordinary returns. Our failures were insignificant, given the business we were in. In addition, all the employees shared in profits from investments, a totally novel concept of 'sharing the wealth' with investors."

Delta Private Equity Partners, like other investment companies in this section was a training ground for Russian staff who later became major players in the Russian financial sector. Kirill Dmitriev, arguably the most important financier in today's Russia as head of the Russian Direct Investment Fund was one of her employees.

Ms. Cloherty emphasized the uniqueness of private equity investment and the relatively small number of foreigners engaged in this type of investment in Russia. "DPEP was in private investment markets, the primary risk of which for investors is profound and often sustained illiquidity. Mike Calvey [Baring Vostok], Drew Guff [Russia Partners], a few other smaller groups were in that hitherto untouched area. Most investors, world-wide, invest in public securities markets where, at least theoretically, you have liquidity. Come a downturn, sell, without the heartburn of living through any broad correction that may or may not, occur. Bill Browder, for example, was a very successful investor in public markets. Though a good friend and always straightforward with me, he wouldn't touch private markets, for that reason."

Asked whether she thought that Russia would continue to follow a Western model of market economy, she responded, "No. Like Kissinger, I do not think Russia is bent on emulating any other system, except at the margin. I was at the entrepreneurial margin, which they loved, because if you do it right, you can support yourself and your family, without resorting to stealing heifers, digging up railroad tracks, or prostitution for a few rubles. Having oligarchs fleece the country is not an acceptable alternative to entrepreneurship for normal people, but they will have to sort that out."

When the fund began to liquidate its assets in 2004, it was agreed that 50 percent of the proceeds would be used to establish a legacy foundation, the US–Russia Foundation for Economic Advancement and the Rule of Law (USRF), and 50 percent would be returned to the US Treasury. USRF was set up with an endowment north of $100 million and registered in the United States as a nonprofit corporation in 2008 and was registered in Russia in 2009.[43] It relocated to Washington, DC, in 2015.

Russia Partners

Russia Partners was another of the small group of influential private equity firms and is closely associated with Drew Guff. He studied Russian in high school and at Harvard before going to work on Wall Street at Paine Webber. "While at Paine Webber, we created one of the very first private equity funds in Russia in 1994. In fact, we closed that first fund the same week, I recall, as Baring Vostok closed their fund. So, we were both off and running in the new Russian economy, sometimes competing, and sometimes investing together, making long term investments in private Russian companies. We also invested in Ukraine and other countries of the former Soviet Union. Before that I'd been working in mergers and acquisitions and later in the merchant banking department at PaineWebber. The then-Chairman and CEO of Paine Webber, Don Marron, took a trip to Russia with Commerce Secretary Mosbacher in 1989 and learned of the Russian Government's plans to privatize most of the old state-owned economy under Russian economist Shatalov's "400 Day Plan." It was absolutely revolutionary and was meant to be a full reform of the Russian economy from the Communist centrally planned economy to one based on supply and demand. With all citizens to receive vouchers and shares in state-owned companies, it was also a political move to ensure that Communism would be stamped out forever, as people would be incentivized to protect and care for their new private property. … Upon Don Marron's return from his trip to Russia, he came into my office and said 'oh my Lord, they're about to privatize the entire place. Drew, you're one of the few people who knows Russia, speaks Russian, and went to school there and you are a real finance guy now.' I was working for the President of Paine Webber, Paul Guenther who gave me the mission go figure it out on behalf of the firm. One of the investors in our fund was Archer Daniels Midland. The then CEO, Duane Andreas was friendly with His Holiness Alexei of the Russian Orthodox Church and ultimately, we created a joint venture with the Russian Orthodox Church."

"At that time, the Russian Orthodox Church was being given back all their church properties that had been taken over or expropriated in Soviet times, most of which were in a destroyed or dilapidated condition. Many of those churches had been turned into state institutions such as prisons, women's mental institutions, etc. I even visited a beautiful church in St. Petersburg that served as a garbage incinerator where the smoke was vented through the dome of that small cathedral. It was absolutely appalling and the most tangible evidence of how Communism completely stamped out religion under Soviet rule. The church had been given back these assets but had little means to pay for its repairs, and so they were looking for ways to earn money for their renovations. We started a joint venture working with their economic division and that joint venture ended up kick starting the private equity fund. At that time, the Church was viewed as a trusted institution, in a country where almost all the old previous institutions had been torn down or were being discredited. Under Yeltsin, in fact, the Communist Party was outlawed, and its private property was nationalized." It is worth pointing out that Paine Webber/Russia Partners followed a pattern of almost all successful Western investment companies entering Russia of partnering with a powerful Russian partner who had political access and the ability to access Russian assets but needed Western capital and expertise.

"We started talking to investors about that first fund in 1991, a time when the friendship between the US and Russian governments was probably at its peak. A special commission was formed called the Gore – Chernomyrdin Commission which created an active working group that met regularly to promote the budding US–Russia relationship. As a result, we had meetings with

Prime Minister Viktor Chernomyrdin who, as an industrialist, understood that long term capital was much more valuable than voucher trading and beneficial for the country. I brought Paul Guenther the president of Paine Webber over to Russia and we sat down in a meeting with Victor Chernomyrdin and his staff to educate them as to what a private equity fund could be. We basically said 'look there's all these vouchers trading, but that doesn't bring in any new capital. You need some real long-term investment.'"

"We asked the prime minister to reduce investors' risk by having the Russia Treasury itself directly invest in the fund. We essentially said 'We want the Russian Government to put its money where its mouth is because investors still feel that Russia is very risky place. If you put in $25 million, then we will go raise a $100 million dollar fund. And that's a great way to leverage your money. We will create this real private equity fund, something you don't have here yet, but, trust us, you need to have this as you develop this new market economy. You need to have long term private capital flow.'"

"Chernomyrdin was a rational, practical person. He had founded Gazprom and before that ran the Oil and Gas Ministry. He saw the wisdom of doing it and the government invested. Instead of $100 million, in the end we raised $150 million and that became Russia Partners I, the first truly private equity fund in Russia. That was September 1994. The fund was announced and initiated at the Gore – Chernomyrdin Commission with all the requisite pictures of Gore and Chernomyrdin shaking hands and smiling over the birth of a bold new venture. It was kind of like the Apollo – Soyuz mission comes to finance."

"Our first investment was the worst investment we ever made. It was a joint venture to run raw logs through a sort of nuclear car wash for logs where the company irradiated the logs before they were put on ships and sent to the US or sent to Japan. You cannot transport logs intercontinentally unless they've been treated so that bugs and pests don't invade the export destination's national forests. It was also a kind of swords to plowshares deals that provided jobs for nuclear engineers from some of the top research institutes. Unfortunately, it just didn't work. It had to be run far off in like the Sakhalin or Amur Regions of the Russian Far East. It was a million miles away and hard to manage and the company couldn't get enough throughput to bring down very high costs."

"That's when we decided that we were not investing in anything that we couldn't physically get to within a two-hour flight from Moscow or Kiev or Minsk. We ended up just writing off that first investment. But after that we were part of early financings and privatizations of some of the oil companies and forest products companies."

"We also started Russian MTV. I was introduced to a great music video empresario who was a creative genius but lacked capital and an asset base of TV stations. At that same time, we were going around the country buying TV stations and TV affiliates in places like Volgograd, Saratov, Samara, and other regional locations, because we knew that those local stations were valuable assets trading at a fraction of Western prices. But we had no idea what kind of network we wanted to eventually become. In privatization, everything was atomized so local people got to own their local channels. We knew that they would come back together in the same way that the hub and spoke network affiliate setup in the US came together. And our bet was that Moscow was going to be the hub of a valuable national TV network based on advertising revenues. … Once we met our entrepreneur, we decided what we wanted to be when we grew up. There were already a bunch of general entertainment channels. But there was no music television. So, we looked at MTV as a model. My partners at Russia Partners also had experience in building strong accounting and operating controls over fast-expanding businesses, so all the pieces were in place. We decided to build Russian MTV."

"We first launched MTV with Viacom as a licensing deal around 1996 and in 1998 Viacom invested directly in the business, which we owned 50–50 together. It was a great business relationship, and we remain friends with many of those media executives from Viacom."

"Russia had a great tradition of music and a great rock scene and underground rock scene. We knew that we were going to run Russian rock on the channel, which was going to be revolutionary. We were going to run international rock as well. That's exactly what we did. At the time we sold MTV Russia in 2007, MTV Russia was Viacom's most successful overseas MTV. We sold the business to a local Russian station owner, and it was the most successful investment in Russia Partners I. Viacom made around 10 times their money from their investment and royalties and kept a licensing fee stream to boot!"

"MTV revolutionized the Russian concept of music. It was highbrow and lowbrow at the same time. … We would throw music video awards ceremonies at the Kremlin in Red Square. We were granted permission to shoot fireworks over the Kremlin. We asked the Russian Space Agency if we could announce the song of the year from the International Space Station one year. They said okay as long as we could get some young people interested in becoming cosmonauts or getting into the space industry. We played old Soviet bands from the 1970's talking about walking on the moon and stuff like that. We brought the Red Hot Chili Peppers to Russia to play a free concert in Red Square. It was a hell of a ride."

"Later we were the first investor in the software engineering company EPAM, which much later went public on the New York Stock Exchange and has a $20 billion market cap today."

"We raised four Russia Partners funds, but none since the invasion of Ukraine and annexation of Crimea. In fact, we stopped all new investments in any Russian companies after the annexation back in 2015. We've been liquidating our small number of legacy investments since then. We made the decision at that time, which was not shared by many others, that Russia had become un-investable. The composition of the Russia government changed dramatically after 2014. The leadership in the government no longer included liberal economists, in-system reformers, or businesspeople. It became the realm of national security, military, and FSB professionals. Add heavy sanctions to that and Russia was no longer the interesting investment destination it had once been."

Asked about Russia Partners' total investment, he estimated, "roughly a billion and a half dollars. From that there is the value that we created, which would be around $10 billion, some of which was company growth after we sold or distributed several the investments, like EPAM. Many of these investments just kept growing."

Investor Perspective – Fidelity Investments

In the early 1990s, Bob von Rekowsky was a sovereign research analyst in the Fixed-Income Research Group for Fidelity Investments, the largest privately held asset manager in the United States at that time. "When I began, I made investment recommendations on specific fixed-income instruments, including Russian defaulted Vneshekonom Bank obligations, Russian MinFin Bonds and, later, stocks of Russia's Red Chip companies like Sberbank, Gazprom, LUKOIL and Norilsk Nickel."

"Due to the nascent nature of the asset class (Emerging Markets Debt and Equity investing), the role of investment analyst included a give and take with policymakers, elected officials, regulators, political personalities, journalists, NGOs, IFIs, that both ascertained policy as well as provided our firm's perspective on what types of legal and market regulatory and policy frameworks were the most suitable, if not minimally necessary, to investing."

Bob's perspective on Russia, as the representative of such a large investor and one that was governed by strict guidelines and regulations, was quite different from the investment bankers on the ground in Russia who were essentially engaged in trying to attract investors like Fidelity into the country. As an analyst, he was a close observer of the development of Russian financial markets and through his periodic visits to Russia from his London office, he witnessed the transformation of those markets and in particular the influence of Americans and other foreigners.

"Fidelity was launching a brand new emerging markets debt fund, which was called the New Markets Income Fund that we started from scratch. … I always tried to explain to people I've met in Russia that the firm didn't necessarily care, one way or the other about Russia. Within our internal groups, if we felt there were investment opportunities, you could allocate your time to it. I always spent an inordinate amount of time because I was interested in Russia and felt there was a good reasonable risk return profile."

"I remember when I was still on the debt side of the investment world, I traveled with a colleague of mine. He looked at equities and we went on an investment trip to St Petersburg. I'm going to forget the name of the engine and tractor works there, but we just did a random meeting. It turned out that the market cap of this company was something like $12 million, and it made no sense. It made no sense at all, given the volume of output and importance of the factory. A lot of those opportunities came up, but we really couldn't do much with them."

"At that time, you could buy these companies, for kopecks on the ruble. We wanted to get them into our funds and wanted to figure out how to do it. Then we'd speak to our legal teams and our compliance and back-office teams. I talked to them, and they'd say 'you are crazy. They are not ready for prime time. You can't really invest in Russia from a compliance point of view.' … Eventually there were some restructured government debts in which we could invest."

Large investors continued to try to find a way to take advantage of Russian opportunities while maintaining their compliance requirements. "There were different investment alliances of investors to pool their efforts and to meet with Russian officials. We all would say the same thing, 'we'd love to invest in your country. Here are the kind of mundane back-office things that we need for settlement clearance and the like.'"

"One of these alliances was the Russell 2020 group in which a lot of firms in Boston, including our's, were members. It was not so much a lobbying group to tell Russian officials what we needed and offer help. Instead, we offered to facilitate conversations with our back-office people. A lot of those conversations went very well. These alliances along with other groups, including the brokers, pushed to have the Russians establish American Deposit Receipts (ADRs) or Global Deposit Receipts (GDRs) because we could purchase those securities. It was much easier once there was a LUKOIL ADR and a Gazprom ADR. Then we're good because we could work through the Bank of New York as the depository receipts holder, and we could purchase them."

Bob provided a lot of insight into how investors were looking at Russia at the time and the atmosphere of foreign-led change in the early to mid-1990s. "It was probably in the Bush Senior administration when everybody was going to Russia. I felt like there was a big wave of people going over to try to open them up after the Berlin Wall fell. It felt like you were part of a private army that was trying to help extend the foreign government embrace of Russia from the private angle. … I felt like we knew it was going to be fits and starts."

"I got to do a lot of things because Russia was not a priority for our senior management. The Russians would ask, can you send the CEO of your company over and that just would never happen. … So, I went in place of senior management. … One time our senior legal counsel in Boston got invited through somebody in Washington to take part in an International Finance Corporation (IFC) trip to Russia for one of their meetings. … Our counsel in Boston could not go so they asked if anyone in the London office could fill in, so I scheduled a trip around it and got to go."

"It was during the Clinton Administration and the guy who led the delegation was Ira Millstein. There was a bunch of institutional investors, maybe one or two US pension funds. I had met all the Russian CEOs from my previous trips, but I don't think anybody on my side had met them before. I immediately felt like our side, the IFC side, was kind of lecturing the Russians about corporate governance almost in an unintentional condescending way. They were saying that you want to do this, you don't understand that, etc. The Russian guys were dealing with the realities of investing in Russia and running a company."

"There was a Georgian guy named Kaha Bendukidze who was running Uralmash, a large industrial concern in the Ural Mountains area. He was a big man physically and extremely smart. He spoke fluent English, as well as Georgian and Russian, but he decided to speak Russian because he was annoyed. He basically said, 'I know you guys would like to come here and teach us heathens how to eat with a fork and knife and just to make sure we brush our teeth, the right way. However, I'm running this company in the Ural Mountains. My Deputy CEO was shot in his car last month. We have mafia guys trying to get control the company. We have all these things going on and a lack of law. I can't find a replacement for this Deputy CEO, wonder why? I have audited quarterly reports. My share price is still pennies on the dollar, from where it should be to reflect the massive amount of output at my company. We have a corporate governance code. We tried to get a foreign investor on the board of directors. We have an independent auditor.' He just laid it on the table. I totally identified with him that they were sick of being lectured by each new wave of people that didn't do their homework to be ready for prime time for the Russians. What disappointed me was that we just had endless waves of newbies from the West coming over and the Russians eventually just tired of it."

He described the interaction between the international organizations and the Russian State Duma and other government officials at that time. Many of the Russian politicians in the Duma had quite a different orientation than the Chubais-led reformers. Less interested in adopting Western advice and practices, they were being subjected to increasing pressure to conform to international standards. Bob remembered "a situation where Duma members were told 'if you don't pass this particular law, then they're not going to get the IMF lending. If they do not get that lending, then the ruble was going to collapse.' … I remember one of these foreign insiders telling me that one particular vote was important. He said at the end of the day, 'what's a few hundred laptops distributed amongst Duma members to get the vote to go the right way.' … It felt extremely cynical. I felt that this was not sustainable. I remember people engaging in special pleading, like 'can't Yeltsin just pass a decree.' … In those early days, we heard the rhetoric at the top level, but did not see it in terms of what was happening on the ground."

"I just felt that a lot of the people who interacted with the Russians were younger Americans who had their own market and political shibboleths about our country, not even appreciating the journey that Russia was going through itself. … It felt like they came and made a bunch of demands. The West always held expectations up and we'd be late to deliver. Then it just felt like a constant wooing of the Russians to get something done. There was always a fire drill, like you have to pass this law to get this money before this happens. It just seemed like a treadmill until Putin came in."

Loans-for-Shares and the Election of 1996 – Consolidating the Power of the Oligarchs

In the early stages of the Russian Presidential election of 1996, Boris Yeltsin trailed Gennady Zyuganov, the Communist Party candidate, by a substantial margin, with Yeltsin polling in the single digits. Zyuganov went to the annual Davos Conference in February 1996 as the presumptive next President of Russia. In response to Zyuganov's star turn at Davos, Chubais who was also in attendance warned the Russian oligarchs in attendance that a Zyuganov victory would mean their time was up. Chubais warned that "If Zyuganov wins the Russian presidency, he will undo several years of privatization and this will lead to bloodshed and civil war."[44] According to the *New York Times* account, the Russian banker oligarchs in attendance, Boris Berezovsky, Vladimir Gusinsky, Mikhail Khodorkovsky, Mikhail Fridman, Pyotr Aven, and Alexander Smolensky and others made a pact with Chubais for him to lead the campaign to reelect Yeltsin that they would finance and support.[45] The same account says that Chubais was compensated with a $3 million fee in the form of an interest free loan.[46]

Simultaneously, these same bankers were collaborating on the so-called loans-for-shares program to prop up the Yeltsin government in return for access to the crown jewels of the state-owned enterprises that had not yet been privatized. The format of the program was for loans to be advanced to the government that were secured by shares in the leading state-owned companies. If the government defaulted, the banks making the loans took ownership of the shares and hence control of the enterprises. Since no one expected the government to repay the loans, this program was a form of second round privatization of major government assets. Given the strategic importance of these assets, foreigners were not allowed to participate in the loans-for-shares program with two notable exceptions. Long-time Chubais supporters George Soros and Harvard University, in the form of the Harvard Management Company, the non-profit subsidiary of Harvard University that manages the Harvard endowment were allowed to participate.

The combination of support from Chubais and the oligarchs, the infusion of cash into the government, support of the Clinton Administration and background campaign advice from experienced American political consultants resuscitated the Yeltsin campaign and resulted in a victory touted by a *Time Magazine* cover celebrating the Yeltsin victory.

This was a controversial program that elicited different opinions from different people interviewed.

James Fenkner opined that "in my opinion, loans-for-shares is what created the Russia we have today, which is not like Germany or Japan. Basically, what they did was to allow a group of insiders to get the sweetest of sweetheart deals that you could ever imagine. ... I remember because we're trying to research this to figure out how we could participate. You could only participate if you had a bank. This is what solidified the oligarchs. ... You could lend to the government, then let the government default and get assets basically for free."

"Seeing how it played out, this is the point in which we lost Russia, if you want to call it that. We didn't really lose it; the Russians made the choice to either give the assets to your friends or have foreigners take it from the market. ... That's the thing about Russia being too big. It was going to do its own thing and it was not going to be a plaything of the rest of the world. It was going to preserve Russia for the Russians, if you will."

Boris Jordan provided the insider view of how the loans-for-shares program developed. "You know that Stephen Jennings and I wrote the loans-for-shares program. Regarding the loans-for-shares program. I'm very open about where we were right and where we were wrong. I still think net-net it was a good program."

"It was written by Stephen Jennings and me in our apartment late at night. For about a week we wrote the concept. The purpose of what we wrote was slightly bastardized once it got out of our hands and into the hands of the politicians and the oligarchs."

"What happened was is that someone in the Russian federal government came to us, Nemtsov, Chubais, Minister of Finance, Fedorov, I forget who. Anyway, they came to us and said we need money. They had no money. This was a regular thing. Once a year, they would come to us and say we need money. One time, we got a big loan from George Soros. Another time, a $1.4 billion loan from George Soros. Then another time we did loans-for-shares."

"The loans-for-shares concept that Stephen and I had was to take the controlling interest in these assets and put them in the hands of entrepreneurs, but not as owners. They would lend money to the government with the asset as security. The entrepreneur would manage and fix the company, all of which were in dire straits and then they would get to sell those assets. Whatever those assets sold for, either as IPOs or to strategic investors, the entrepreneurs who lent money to the government would keep 20 percent of the proceeds as remuneration for the work they did fixing the company."

"Of course, that's not what happened, but that's what we wrote. What happened was that the oligarchs got ahold of this document because we gave it to Chubais. They bastardized it and said it was loans-for-shares, but then they bought the assets themselves. They did not sell the assets to third parties which was our concept."

"In the end, I will tell you that if anyone asked me, I'm going to still turn around say that was good and I'll tell you why. It was good because it created an ownership class that wanted these assets to thrive. And did they get very rich, yes. Did it go exactly as it was supposed to go, no. But all these companies, every one of those companies that were privatized in loans-for-shares are still around today. They are global leaders at what they do. That's, all I can say."

"The guys that were sitting in those companies at that time were all feeding off the company. I mean that you had Soviet-era directors, that all they did was steal the money. They would put nothing back into the business and the businesses were all on their ass, to be honest."

"These guys who loaned the money to the government put in real money. I mean they had hundreds of millions of dollars that they risked on these assets, and they had to make these things work. And they did, and they put their energy and their everything into it. They made these companies work and now these companies are true global players."

One of the important aspects of the loan-for-shares program was that it tilted the economic balance away from equity markets toward banks and the small group of oligarchs who had their own banks. As Boris Jordan explained, "Back then all these guys had banks. Alexander Smolensky had Bank Stolichny. Mikhail Khodorkovsky had Bank Menatep. Vladimir Gusinsky had MOST Bank. Vladimir Potanin had UNEXIMbank. Mikhail Fridman had Alfa-Bank. They all had banks. … The way a bank survived back then when people had no money and there were no deposits was when the government held their funds in those banks. So, the banks got cheap funds from the government and the government let them use those funds to build their businesses. There were not that many banks. There were like eight banks at that time in Moscow. With Moscow being the center of power in the country, those seven or eight guys became very, very powerful."

"Because they had these banks and because they were getting their hands on these assets and consolidating these assets by buying shares on the secondary market and doing all that, they became very powerful. What they did was unite in their efforts to influence the government to get what they needed. So, they were entrepreneurs, but that entrepreneurialism gave them the power that could create an oligarchy."

Asked in this context about the difference between an oligarch and an entrepreneur, Jordan replied "that word came out of the Yeltsin era and then, it was picked up when the conflict with the US started happening. It was picked up by the US in the 2000s. But the fact is that under Yeltsin, there was a bit of an oligarchy. You basically had seven or eight business guys that between them had massive political influence, massive. They would trade money for decisions from the Kremlin. So, in the beginning, there was an oligarchy. But under Putin, there was no oligarchy. I mean Putin massacred the oligarchy overnight. The first guy that tried to challenge him [Mikhail Khodorkovsky] went to jail."

"Gusinsky and Berezovsky, they all challenged Putin. His position was that you are businessmen, we are politicians. You go do your business, but if you try to use your money to influence underpaid politicians, because I can't afford to pay them market wages today, I'm going to throw you in jail. So, the rules were very clear to everyone. Putin was very transparent, and the oligarchy fell apart at that point in time. … It also got dissolved because you had a huge amount of entrepreneurialism in the 2000s and lots of people made money on new, not privatized businesses, but new businesses. New businesses that they started and, in many cases, became wealthier even than the old oligarchy. ... Then you had the whole St Petersburg crowd that was associated with Putin show up in Moscow and they got their piece of the economic pie. So, what happened was that Putin destroyed the concept of an oligarchy as a small group having an influence on politicians and the central government now runs the show."

Financial Crisis of August 1998 – Impact on New Financial Institutions

Before Putin came to power 1999, Russia suffered a severe financial crisis in 1998 related to a general world financial crisis. The impact of the world crisis on Russia signaled the extent to which it had become integrated into the world economic system and now subject to economic forces out of control of Russia. The crisis was the result of a wave of crises that swept through emerging markets worldwide that had a special significance in Russia.

On August 17, 1998, Russia defaulted on its domestic debt, declared a moratorium on foreign debt and devalued the ruble. As summarized by Dmitri Vasiliev, the former head of the Federal Commission on the Stock Market, "The August 1998 crisis, on one hand, seriously undermined the development of the securities market in general, but, on the other put an end to the pyramid of GKOs, the overvalued ruble, the strong power of the banks and created conditions for the economic growth in 1999-2000." It was a turning point for the Russian economy in its transition from its Soviet past in the 1990s to the expansion of the reformed economy, buoyed by rising energy prices that took place in the early 2000s. The 1998 crisis led to the end of the Yeltsin period and the appointment of Vladimir Putin in 1999.

When the crisis reached its pinnacle on August 17, there was little indication that Russia was going to experience renewed economic growth. On the contrary, the financial institutions and the people working in them were counting their losses and trying to find ways to mitigate them. With the resulting economic downturn, large numbers of foreign expats who came to Russia in the 1990s were forced out. While there was another influx of expats in the 2000s, 1998 was a nodal point in the replacement of foreign experts with Russian managers and professionals.

Expat Americans were of declining importance particularly after the 1998 financial crisis as oligarchs and their related banks became more important drivers of the Russian economy than stock markets and foreign investment. By that time, Russians had increasingly mastered the skills of business so that high salaried expats were less necessary and as nascent Russian nationalism began to develop and emerge.

Rob von Rekowsky put the 1998 crisis in its global context, "Russia got caught up in the crisis that began in Asia with the Thai baht collapse. In global emerging markets there were waves of default that stemmed from US monetary policy being very tight, draining global dollar liquidity. All the regimes that had pegged their currency against the US dollar saw their liquidity and access to finance draining away. They had to abandon their currency pegs. It started in Asia with Thailand, then Indonesia got hit. It moved to Eastern Europe. As the Czech krona came under pressure, Russia devalued the ruble that set off an acrimonious set of relationships from the West to Russia."

The 1998 financial crisis called into question the whole course of Russian reform. The Atlantic ran a cover with the title, "Russia is Finished." The financial sector suffered huge losses and many expats left the country. It turns out that The Atlantic's prediction of Russia's economic demise was proven false in the economic expansion of the 2000s, but that was not something anticipated by many.

James Fenkner discussed the impact of the 1998 crisis on him and his situation in Russia. In response to the question of whether he considered leaving Russia in 1998, he summarized his situation at that moment. "Up to that point, it was a huge party. There were so many foreigners. Then when the crisis hit, I basically lost all my money. I lost my job. I did not have money for a flight out. ... I knocked on the door of Troika Dialog. They decided that they were going to give me a shot, so I decided to stay. ... I remember sitting in my apartment reading *Master and Margarita*, not knowing what reality really was. ... But it turned out to be a great decision not to go. If I had left then, it would have been at the bottom. I just didn't feel I had my full of it. I didn't want to leave with such a bad taste in my mouth."

"There were so many going away parties after that devaluation. It was just like everyone was leaving. I think at the time we referred to Russia as the land of broken toys. ... The only people that stayed were either Russophiles or maybe had some other connection. ... Or like me, they just had not had enough punishment."

Boris Jordan also reflected on the impact of 1998 on Renaissance Capital. "Renaissance was hit incredibly hard because we were the largest intermediary between the West and Russia for capital. And what happened was that we were borrowing money in the West and on-lending in Russia through something called repos, billions and billions of dollars. The West was happy to lend to us because we ran our business in a way that they understood, right on our balance sheet. And we then would on-lend in Russia. We would take a cut between the two. So, we borrowed at 5 percent, then lent that money out at 8 percent. We took that cut. And what happened was that when the Russian ruble was devalued, all the Russian banks lobbied through the government for this moratorium, where they didn't have to pay back their debts."

"And, of course, you know, I didn't accept that as a way to do business. Maybe it was my mistake, but I kind of feel like if you borrow money from somebody you have to return it. So, I took it upon myself to return the money that I borrowed in the West, but I got nothing here in Russia from anybody."

"Basically, within about five days, I went through all my capital. I was minus, I think, 100 million dollars of capital. I went through $400 million of capital and I was minus $100 million, basically bankrupt."

"I had done it in such a way that I made sure I had one creditor, Barclays. The chairman of bank at the time was the guy that had been my boss at Credit Suisse, Hans-Jeorg Rudloff. And although he wasn't happy with me, I went to him, and I negotiated a three-year deferral. And I put up a bunch of illiquid assets as collateral. Then I repaid them in full."

"At that point in time, once we paid them in 2000, I decided I no longer wanted to be in the banking business. I sold my shares in Renaissance and went off on my own to be an entrepreneur investor."

Martin Skelley looked back at the impact of the 1998 crisis on UFG. "We had a very tough route initially because we weren't that well capitalized. We were founded with a million dollars from Bank Paribas in 1995–96 and bought out Paribas in 1998. We did that go it alone thing and almost blew ourselves up in the financial crisis of 1998. We spent the time after the financial crisis building up our balance sheet and profits to the point where Deutsche Bank would buy 40 percent of us. After that Fidelity and Pioneer and these other groups that weren't going to trade with us as an independent broker were willing to do business with us."

Rob von Renkowsky and Fidelity had a similar experience of difficult times after the crisis. "That was crazy. That was a really tough time. We owned Russian debt in our funds that caused some serious underperformance. My boss spent a good 18 months restructuring the portfolio and getting back to outperforming. It took a lot of our time, as with other competitors in the emerging markets debt crisis."

He went on to summarize the lessons he felt that Russians learned from that experience. "I think that the Russians realized that the ship maybe had not already sailed but that it is elusive. They just better be prepared for whatever wind is blowing out of the US at any particular time and that they better brace for it. And just make sure that they can go it alone, so they don't have another financial crisis. That was the lasting thing that the Russians took away from their whole IMF years, let's call it."

The creation of new market financial mechanisms was a critical aspect of the transition from Soviet state planning to a market economy. While in the Soviet period, they were largely isolated from any impact from problems or policies of the worldwide financial system, Russia was clearly a part of that system by the 1998 crisis and therefore subject to the associated risks. This element of risk was driven home again by the 2008 financial crisis, again an event triggered by institutions outside of Russia, but heavily impacting its economy. Reciting these facts is in no way intended to support any policies of the Russian government but does add context and explanation for their efforts to cushion themselves from the impact of global financial markets. It is further context for the decoupling of Russia from that system in the wake of the February 24, 2022, invasion of Ukraine and the embrace of that decoupling by some elements of the Russian elite who are seeking to establish alternatives not controlled by the United States and Europe.

Notes

1 Petr Aven and Alfred Kokh, *Gaidar's Revolution – The Inside Account of the Economic Transformation of Russia* (London, New York: I.B. Tauris, 2013), 83.
2 Alfred Kokh, *The Selling of the Soviet Empire* (New York: Liberty Publishing House, 1998), 39.
3 "Key Facts About the '90s Price Liberalization in Russia," *TASS Russian News Agency*, December 2, 2016, Accessed March 14, 2022, https://tass.com/economy/916534?utm_source=google.com&utm_medium=organic&utm_campaign=google.com&utm_referrer=google.com
4 Kokh, *The Selling of the Soviet Empire*, 30–39.
5 Andrei Volgin and Yury Milner, "Chapter 5: Voucher Investment Funds," in *Russia: Creating Private Enterprises and Efficient Markets*, eds. Ira W. Lieberman and Enna Karlova (Washington, D.C.: World Bank, 1994), 55.
6 Volgin and Milner, *Russia: Creating Private Enterprises and Efficient Markets*, 30.
7 Janine R. Wedel, "Harvard Boys Do Russia," *The Nation*, June 1, 1998, Accessed January 17, 2022, www.thenation.com/article/archive/harvard-boys-do-russia/
8 "Four Reformers in Russia's Shock Therapy," *Geohistory* website, April 4, 2016, Accessed January 28, 2022, https://geohistory.today/russia-shock-therapy/
9 Wedel, "Harvard Boys Do Russia."
10 "Whistle-Blowing on American Corruption in Russia," *Association for Diplomatic Studies & Training*, Accessed January 20, 2022, https://adst.org/2018/05/whistle-blowing-on-american-corruption-in-russia/
11 "Russia Case (and Dust) Settle," *Harvard Magazine*, November–December 2005, Accessed April 28, 2022, www.harvardmagazine.com/2005/11/russia-case-and-dust-set.html#:~:text=The percent20settlement percent20bars percent20Harvard percent20from percent20underwriting percent20either percent20Shleifer's,awarded percent20a percent20 percent2440-million percent20grant percent20for percent20the percent20Russia percent20project
12 "Russia Case (and Dust) Settle," *Harvard Magazine*.
13 Andrei Soldatov and Irina Borogan, *The New Nobility – The Restoration of Russia's Security State and the Enduring Legacy of the KGB* (New York: PublicAffairs, 2010), 12.
14 Soldatov and Borogan, *The New Nobility*, 13.
15 For a full discussion of the Soviet criminal underground and its emergence in post-Soviet business sectors in the 1990s, refer to Mark Galeotti, *The Vory – Russia's Super Mafia* (New Haven: Yale University Press, 2018).
16 "MMM (Ponzi scheme company)," *Wikipedia*, Accessed March 20, 2022, https://en.wikipedia.org/wiki/MMM_(Ponzi_scheme_company
17 Boris Rubtsov, "The Russian Securities Market: 20 Years of Development," 114, Accessed February 11, 2022, https://publishup.uni-potsdam.de/opus4-ubp/frontdoor/deliver/index/docId/6640/file/EFC_Rubtsov_105_118.pdf
18 Rubtsov, "The Russian Securities Market: 20 Years of Development," 114.
19 Rubtsov, "The Russian Securities Market: 20 Years of Development," 114–115.
20 Rubtsov, "The Russian Securities Market: 20 Years of Development," 57.
21 Fred Berliner, "From Wall Street to Red Square: The Birth of the RTS," in *From the Cold – The Rise of Russian Capitalism*, ed. Peter Westin (London: London Publishing Partnership, 2012), 121

22 Berliner, "From Wall Street to Red Square: The Birth of the RTS," 122.
23 Berliner, "From Wall Street to Red Square: The Birth of the RTS," 122.
24 Berliner, "From Wall Street to Red Square: The Birth of the RTS," 122.
25 Berliner, "From Wall Street to Red Square: The Birth of the RTS," 123.
26 Berliner, "From Wall Street to Red Square: The Birth of the RTS," 123, 124.
27 Berliner, "From Wall Street to Red Square: The Birth of the RTS," 124.
28 Berliner, "From Wall Street to Red Square: The Birth of the RTS," 124, 125.
29 Berliner, "From Wall Street to Red Square: The Birth of the RTS," 125.
30 Berliner, "From Wall Street to Red Square: The Birth of the RTS," 126
31 Berliner, "From Wall Street to Red Square: The Birth of the RTS," 127.
32 Berliner, "From Wall Street to Red Square: The Birth of the RTS," 127.
33 "Where dreams take you," *Ruben Vardanyan* website, Accessed February 15, 2022, http://rubenvardanyan.info/en/pages/where-dreams-take-you
34 Bernie Sucher, "Sing When You're Winning: Two Decades of Corporate Governance in Russia," in *From the Cold – The Rise of Russian Capitalism*, ed. Peter Westin (London: London Publishing Partnership, 2012), 225.
35 Sucher, "Sing When You're Winning: Two Decades of Corporate Governance in Russia," 226.
36 Berliner, "From Wall Street to Red Square: The Birth of the RTS," 128.
37 Berliner, "From Wall Street to Red Square: The Birth of the RTS," 128.
38 Berliner, "From Wall Street to Red Square: The Birth of the RTS," 129.
39 Alexander Osipovich and Delta Private Equity Partners, "Banking on the Future of Russia," in *Taming the Wild East: New Russian Entrepreneurs Tell Their Stories* (Alpina Business Book, 2004), 47–48.
40 Osipovich and Delta Private Equity Partners, "Banking on the Future of Russia," 52–53.
41 "About USRF," *US Russia Foundation* website, Accessed February 11, 2022, www.usrf.ru
42 "PE's Doyenne Speaks Out," *evcj*, November 30, 2007, text provided by Patricia Cloherty's staff, May 10, 2021.
43 William Runde, "The U.S.-Russia Investment Fund and the $75-million Question," *Center for Strategic & International Studies* website, November 3, 2011, Accessed February 11, 2022, www.csis.org/analysis/us-russia-investment-fund-and-75-million-question
44 John Lloyd, "The Russian Devolution," *The New York Times Magazine*, August 15, 1999, Accessed April 29, 2021, https://archive.nytimes.com/www.nytimes.com/library/magazine/home/19990815mag-russia-crisis.html
45 Lloyd, "The Russian Devolution."
46 Lloyd, "The Russian Devolution."

4 New Private Sector

Russia Adopts, Adapts, and Integrates

What people don't understand is that, for a period in the 1990s, Russia was clearly one of the most exciting places in the world. And if you were in it, viewing it from ground zero or you were peripherally engaged in it, but you weren't living there, but particularly if you're living there, there wasn't much else that could rival that excitement.

People fell into two baskets. There was the basket of people who saw the cup as half full, or much less than half full. Those people were complainers. For them, Russia was a hardship and dysfunctionality. Those people were hard to be around because everything was a complaint. They didn't have the resourcefulness or the stick-to-itiveness, the positive attitude, or the determination to overcome the many challenges of everyday life.

The other group, the group that stayed that persevered, the group that you're going to interview, they were people who saw the excitement. They believed in the change that was happening, the incremental change that was happening at such a fast pace. And it wasn't transformational overnight, because it was a struggle, but the pace of change was happening. Opportunities were everywhere and the margin in these businesses was wide. Americans were not the only foreign group there, but far and away the largest. It was a mix of different groups of people, some of whom were the Soviet emigres, many of whom were Jewish who came back. Others were folks like me who happened to have studied Russian for whatever reasons and had professional skills beyond the language skills and decided to get involved. Others were people who tripped through Central Europe, which was kind of low hanging fruit, But the real prize was Russia with all its big industrial assets and large market. They saw the pattern, the pattern was clear, move to Russia tackle the Big Mountain.

The expat community was tight knit. There weren't that many places to gather so people got together in a limited number of restaurants, bars and private gatherings. People fed off each other's energy and there was this Bohemian kind of underground culture. People were staying out late. It wasn't that expensive to live.

DOI: 10.4324/9781003182153-5

> To put a frame on it, the oil and gas industry, the metals and mining industry required having government relations. These were the assets that people are getting shot and killed over. These are assets that you better stay away from. They were the big boy stuff that was for the home team. In order to get the export licenses, secure the assets and get access to the pipeline, you had to be able to do things that most of us would never think of doing. So, there are very few foreigners playing that game. There were very few foreigners playing the fast-moving, cash retail businesses because those were also tough businesses where there were mobs and gangs. So, many of us went to the areas where there were kind of open space. and I went to the private equity business, something that I had studied about and done in the West.
>
> The people that I am talking about were not the people who came and headed up Procter and Gamble or Deloitte. I am talking about the people who mixed in with Russians, created small organizations, hired a few experts, mostly Russians and trained them up. They brought this American set of entrepreneurial values and skills, an attitude and they kind of empowered people.
>
> (Rich Sobel, interview on May 13, 2021)

As indicated in the description of the initial voucher privatization and then later in the loans-for-shares privatization, foreign influence in certain strategic sectors of the economy was limited. In other sectors of the economy, the entrepreneurial impact of Americans was quite dramatic during the Yeltsin period. This influence was particularly important in new private sectors that either did not exist in Soviet times, like real estate or were previously significantly different under state control, like hospitality (restaurants and hotels), entertainment and media. Part of this transition was facilitated by the large number of international law firms that also established their presence in Russia and played a significant role in creating the market economy.

As has often been stated in this book, the growth of new private sector businesses was an aspect of the integration of Russia into the global economy and global standards, closely linked with market-driven consumer society. The influence of multinational corporations and individual entrepreneurs was a critical driver of the growth of many of these new businesses, with their influence on the everyday lives of Russian citizens.

Many of these American entrepreneurs acted as the intermediary interface between powerful Russians and Russian organizations and the multinational companies that began to flood into Russia in the Yeltsin period. These entrepreneurs were early market entrants and risk takers who braved the uncertainties, chaos and sometimes lawlessness of Russia at a time when more established Western companies were much more cautious, even as they sought to explore what was to become one of the largest markets in Europe. The entrepreneurs bridged the gap between international business norms and Russian organizations that had been largely separated from international business for more than 70 years. Many of the entrepreneurial foreign startups from the 1990s were ultimately sold to much larger international companies as these companies moved more decisively into the Russian market, as was also the case with the entrepreneurial investment banks discussed in Chapter 3.

The growing expat community in Russia, particularly in Moscow and St. Petersburg, re-created the lifestyle to which they were accustomed and, in the process, introduced modern market economy styles of life to Russia. Initially, they founded small new companies in telecom, real estate, restaurants, and other service industries. As these businesses grew, aspects of that lifestyle were adapted and adopted by Russians in ways that have permanently impacted the structures and habits of daily life for many Russian people.

Telecom: Leapfrogging into the Information Age

The transformation of the Soviet telecommunications sector is one of the most important aspects of post-Soviet Russian modernization, enabling the integration of Russia into global market, allowing for the growth of the new private sector, and changing the style of life of Russian citizens. It is a complex story of privatization of state enterprises and ministries, regulatory reform, and emergence of new private companies. The full story of this transformation is much too vast for a full treatment within the boundaries of this book. However, it is important to include an introduction to the impact of Americans on this sector that helped lead Russians into the information age.

A little background is required to understand the enormity of this transformation. Telecommunications were centralized and served the institutional priorities of the state. The priorities were skewed toward serving the government, military, security services, and to a lesser degree industry, with Soviet citizens the lowest priority. The Soviet Ministry of Communications ran the centralized networks, with the military, KGB and other security services having their own individual communication networks. This system was incapable of transition to the information age and to meeting the demands of a modern economy.

In the mid-1980s only 23 percent of Soviet urban households and 7 percent of rural households had telephones, with huge unfilled consumer demand for telephones. In 1988, the Soviet Union had a waiting list of 14.5 million households, with very long wait times, some reaching as long as 10 years.[1] The entire system was technologically out of date.

The Soviet leadership under Gorbachev realized the importance of telecommunications for a modern economy, but the Soviet Union simply lacked the internal resources, technology, and equipment necessary to modernize its communications. This created business opportunities for foreign telecom companies during perestroika and then in post-Soviet Russia. As in other areas, Russia relied on joint ventures as a means of acquiring needed expertise and equipment, while keeping control over this vital strategic sector of the economy.

In the United States, the 1980s were a time of immense technological and organizational change as the breakup of the AT&T monopoly opened the field for new companies utilizing new technologies. By the late 1980s, some of the new companies began to look at markets in Europe, including the Soviet Union. This was at the same time as people and institutions in the Soviet Union were beginning to look for access to new technologies and were becoming open to Western partners. The beginning stages of this process were described in Chapter 1 with the activities of Joel Schatz, including founding SovAm Teleport and Sovintel. Schatz began his activities motivated by efforts to bring peace between the United States and the Soviet Union. Meanwhile, other US telecom companies were exploring ties with the Soviet Union for purely commercial reasons.

Sprint International – Data Transmission Pioneers

Sprint International was set up to explore potential international business opportunities and through its European office, Sprint Europe, began to explore the Soviet Union as a market. Lee Sparkman, finance director for Sprint Europe, described this initial outreach.

"In the late 1980s we sent a delegation to the Soviet Union to explore providing them upgraded international communications. At that time, they had a total of about 150 international voice lines through four trunk lines managed by the Moscow Central Telegraph." As a point of reference and measure of the relative isolation of the Soviet Union from international communications, the population of the Soviet Union in 1988 was 284.5 million people.

"The Sprint team convinced the Soviet authorities to take one of their voice lines and convert it to Sprint's new high tech, revolutionary data protocol called X 25. This protocol was the basis for all communications between airlines and was the basis for all international trade. In the case of Russia, we built massive networks around the X 25 protocol, even to trade Russian treasury bonds and such. …"

"The company really got set up in the early 90s as a 50/50 joint venture between Moscow Central Telegraph and Sprint. … By the end of the Soviet Union, Sprint controlled 90% of the country's international data capacity."

While Sprint focused on marginally improving the international connectivity of the Soviet Union, others were using a different technology that led to revolutionizing telecommunications.

USWEST – Bringing Cellular Phone Service to Russia

One of the most important technological fixes for the decrepit existing telecom system was the introduction of wireless technologies that allowed for dramatic expansion of service without the time and expense of fixed copper wire connections. The American telecom company USWEST played a critical role in introducing wireless cellular technology in the initial stages of the transformation of the system. Cellular communications became the critical enabling technology for development of a Russian market economy. It opened up communications for the whole range of private companies described in Chapters 3 and 4, all of whose activities would have been impossible without the telecom revolution. Cellular phone service was a big part of that revolution.

As an indication of the dramatic reversal of the telecom situation through wireless communications, "in 2021, Russia had 246.57 million mobile phones, which corresponds to an average of 1.7 per person. In the US, this figure is 1.1 mobile phones per person."[2] The story of how Russia made this leap from 10 year wait times for a telephone to averaging 1.7 mobile phones per person is critical to understanding the transformation of the country.

USWEST, one of seven Regional Bell Operating Companies ("Baby Bells"), was the leader in bring cellular service to Russia. Stan Cramton, VP and general manager of USWEST International (USWI) in Russia recounted that "USWEST started doing business in Russia in the late 80s when it came to an agreement with the Ministry of Communications of the Soviet Union to plan and develop an optical fiber system that was to go east from Moscow to Vladivostok and west to Europe. ... The project included a consortium of every major telecom entity involved in telecommunications in Europe. With its partnership with the Ministry of Communications, USWEST was the leading entity in the consortium."

From the beginning of their involvement in the Soviet Union, USWEST was committed to bringing cellular service to Russia. During the initial negotiations they brought Gennady Kudryavtsev and his delegation from the Soviet Ministry of Communications to Seattle to show them how cellular worked. As Cramton stated, "Cellular was a perfect solution for Russia. Kudryavtsev saw how he could leapfrog all the old infrastructure and just put in cellular." After the dissolution of the Soviet Union, USWEST's cellular activities expanded dramatically to take advantage of the enormous opportunities.

Before the collapse of the Soviet Union, USWEST opened an office in Moscow based on their planning to construct the optical fiber system. "My wife and I moved to Russia in January 1991 and opened the very first USWEST International Office. Then in August 1991 there was the coup and then the dissolution of the Soviet Union in December. In the meantime, we had made a number of commitments, including financing and installing three international gateway switches, one in St. Petersburg, one in Moscow and one in Kiev. We had also convinced the Soviet Minister of the value of cellular in Russia, with the initial project establishing the first cellular company in St. Petersburg, Delta Telecom."

"Then, of course, we had the political turmoil resulting from the 'coup' and many telecom entities left Russia, notably except for my wife and me. Later that year there was a major telecom conference in Geneva with about a thousand people in the audience. The new Minister of Communications Vladimir Bulgak addressed the crowd and said it was nice to see everyone, but the ones he really liked to see were the ones who did not leave Russia during the crisis.

He pointed and said, 'like Crampton.' And that was the impetus for USWEST to accelerate cellular activities in Russia."

Over the next 4 years, USWEST was a co-founder of 12 cellular companies in Russia. Cramton explained their business model, "in every single cellular company, USWEST owned a third, Rostelecom [state-owned telecom provider] owned a third and the Electrosviaz [local telephone provider] owned a third. We never ever had a problem with any of the partners while always adhering to the US Foreign Corrupt Practices Act to the letter."

USWI formed a holding company in Russia called Russia Telecommunication Development Corporation (RTDC) in which USWI was the majority partner. RTDC held USWI's Russian assets and provided assistance in frequency acquisition, technology, marketing, financing, and business training to the Russian staff in all of their subsidiaries.

Cramton also pointed out the importance of the joint venture between USWEST and Rostelecom (WestTelCom) as having installed the first automatic international gateway calling from Russia to the world, 3 state of the art Ericsson electronic switches – 2 in Moscow and 1 in St. Petersburg."

"The opportunities were just unbelievable. Building those international gateway switches and building out our cellular activities were just phenomenal opportunities. We worked as fast as we could do it to make sure we could get the business."

"When we went to Moscow in January 1991 to make an international call you had to go to a booking station, whereas with the installation of the gateway you didn't have to go through this time-consuming procedure. I could sit in my car on my cell phone and make an international call. It was just phenomenal."

"Today, I think there are more phones per capita in Russia than any other country in the world."

In February 1992, USWI set up Moscow Cellular as a sister company to Delta Telecom. Moscow Cellular followed the same ownership pattern as Delta Telecom as a joint venture negotiated with the Ministry of Telecommunications with foreign and Russian partners.

USWI brought Fred Ledbetter to Moscow to serve as the Deputy Director to the Russian director. Ledbetter recalled that "our early customers were only two sorts, based on the high initial cost of service. Our first bill to sign up and to get activated was $4,200, that included the first month of service and the phone was another $1,500. So, one type of customer were foreigners or foreign companies who needed a phone and could not get it. The others were Russians in private business and government who had the financial capability to acquire cellular service. ... Many of our early employees rose through telecoms to manage companies like Microsoft and Google in Russia. It was excellent on the job training for their careers."

Dmitry Kononov, former deputy CEO of Delta Telecom and later CFO of RTDC, emphasized how the availability of telephone service was critical to developing the new Russian market economy. Any multinational entering the Russian market would need communication on a regular basis with its Russian office, which was not possible with the Soviet-era telecom system. Without phone service, it was impossible to efficiently organize real estate markets, restaurants, and the whole range of service industries, down to reserving a haircut. The introduction of phone service enabled every other aspect of private business, not to mention its importance to government agencies.

Around this time, Russian cellular companies, like Vimpelcom, MegaFon, and Mobile TeleSystems also saw the huge opportunities and entered the market. Stan Cramton explained "Russians are smart businesspeople. I have a very high regard for them. They saw what was happening, and so it became a competitive thing to get licenses. All the founders of these companies were part of the telecom hierarchy in Russia. They saw the opportunity and they capitalized on it."

Vimpelcom founded in 1992 by Dr. Dmitry Zimin and an American entrepreneur Augie Fabela, appears in several places in this book. In 1996, it became the first Russian company listed on the New York Stock Exchange as mentioned by Boris Jordan in Chapter 3. Dr. Zimin and his family also became investors in real estate, working with Hines, the multinational real estate developer introduced later in this chapter.

Two other Russian cellular companies were more closely connected with European telecom companies. Mobile TeleSystems (MTS) was a Russian – German partnership pairing AFK Sistema and Deutsche Telecom and was founded in 1993, with commercial operations beginning in 1995. MegaFon was originally founded in 1993 as North-West GSM CJSC in 1993 in Saint Petersburg, beginning operations in 1994 and renamed as MegaFon in 2002. Originally it was partnered with a trio of Scandinavian companies, Sonera (Finland), Telia International (Sweden) and Telenor Invest (Norway).

Ultimately, these three Russian companies came to dominate the fast-growing Russian cellular market. As they were growing, USWEST sold its Russian operations to AT&T connected with the domestic reorganization USWEST itself in the ongoing reorganization of the US telecom industry. AT&T did not want the foreign exposure and sold the assets held by RTDC to a Danish entity.

The irony is that USWEST convinced Russian government officials of the utility of cellular communications for modernizing the telecom infrastructure and then left as the market began to explode. As Stan Cramton remarked, "USWEST left at a very, very poor time and they walked away from a huge potential business."

Radio Page – Moscow Paging

The inadequate telecom system also opened opportunities for American entrepreneurs to fill market niches that later became closed off by developments in Russia. Paging, a much simpler form of communication that filled a market niche before cellular was fully developed, was introduced to Moscow by a pair of entrepreneurial brothers, as a pure startup enterprise. Ken Childs, an ex-IBM marketing expert and his brother Larry took a trip to Moscow in 1990 as the guest of some contacts in the Russian military to investigate setting up an exhibit of Soviet space memorabilia to tour the United States. During the trip, they were introduced to the general director of the Moscow City Telephone Network (MGTS in Russian), with whom they shared lunch and then dinner. As Ken stated, "they were happy to meet with us, because we were Westerners. They didn't know who we were but here were some Western guys wanting to invest in Russia."

The conversation focused on the decrepit telecom infrastructure in Moscow. The Russians were skeptical about cellular due to the lack of transmission standards, access to frequencies, and regulation. Ken recalled that "we were talking about a technology that they hadn't even looked at, which was their introduction to paging. So, we set up a company with MGTS called Radio Page as the marquee first paging company in Moscow."

The Childs set up a Russian company as the joint venture partner with MGTS. Larry became the general director and Ken became the director of marketing, responsible for hiring Russian staff and setting up the business. The Child brothers self-financed the initial capital for Radio Page and arranged for transmitters and antennas from Glennair, a Canadian company. The Russian partner provided the frequency allocation for their pager transmissions.

Radio Page began operations in 1994 covering the core area of downtown Moscow. There were no retail stores for the first couple of years of the business, just direct sales. Ken relied on young Russians who were eager for opportunities to staff the business. "We really tapped into the pool of college age young kids that weren't burdened with the legacy of communism or socialism. They were very interested in everything from blue jeans to working with Western companies. They just didn't have the inhibitions that you saw in older Russians. Once you get networked in and people know who you are, then you get a pool of these people who kept coming forward. … I thought it was going to be difficult for me to hire a marketing crew and set up the office with not speaking the language. Once I had gotten two or three of these young key people, we ended up networking amongst the young folks and ended up with about 300 employees."

The company gradually expanded its coverage area and charged a flat fee of $30 in US currency per month in cash. The number of subscribers continued to expand and at its peak was between 45,000 and 47,000 individual subscriptions. Radio Page expanded into messaging with operators sitting in a room "on these terminals, 24/7, taking calls. They would type the messages and send them out and it became a popular form of communication before cellular took hold."

The client base changed over time but was limited to those who had the money to spend on pagers, just as was the case with the cellular phones. Ken Childs described this customer base, "Initially the market was more fluent people that had cash and sometimes the people that had cash weren't necessarily that honest. … I don't want to say they were bandits, but what they did was to use paging to conduct various types of private business. People were trying to figure out how to sort out using it to their own advantage, where they could communicate with their friends and partners and stuff. … And then we had other customers who were well connected in government. They were younger people, in their 30s that had access to cash. They were people that maybe worked in the mayor's office for Mayor Luzhkov in some capacity."

Asked about pagers as a status symbol he replied, "Yeah very much so. To have a pager and get a message, then look at your pager, it was status to be able to afford a pager." In the telecom dessert of Moscow and before the dramatic spread of mobile phones, pagers were not only a means of communication, but a status symbol.

As cellular phone use began to take off, the pager business began to taper off. Then in 2005, Radio Page received an official inquiry from a powerful Russian entity that Ken Childs believed could have been connected to the security services stating that they wanted to "back door" into the paging network. The way it was phrased left no doubt that this was going to happen. At that point, Ken and his brother walked away from Radio Page, and it was merged into the Russian entity.

The early introduction of cellular technology by USWEST had wide-ranging impact on Russian life; while Radio Page illustrates American entrepreneurs taking advantage of opportunities created by the backward telecom system in the early days of transition to a Russian market economy. The introduction of these and other technologies were part of the creation of a new system of telecommunications based on new private companies and mixed government-private entities that led to dramatic changes in the way that Russians communicated. By the end of the 1990s, these new companies contributed to wholesale change in the Russian way of life that seemed inconceivable viewed from the perspective of the Soviet Union of 1991 and enabled many of the private sector developments described in this chapter.

Real Estate – Building an Industry from Scratch

It is important to restate that there was no private ownership of land and no real estate industry in the Soviet Union. All the office construction was conducted in line with state plans and held in state ownership. As the Soviet Union began to open its economy during the Gorbachev period, international businesses entering that market obtained their office space through state agencies operating according to Soviet standards. All of this began to change during perestroika and then to change even more dramatically in the Yeltsin era with the creation of the new real estate sector of the Russian economy.

In the United States, there is a kind of half-humorous, half-serious saying in the real estate business about the three most important factors for success being location, location, and location. Early in my career in Russia, a Russian colleague explained that the three most important factors for success in Russia were partner, partner, and partner. This is a theme that is repeated throughout the individual stories in this book and one that has relevance in the new real estate sector.

This factor for success in the developing Russian real estate sector was confirmed by Vera Setskaya, one of the early Russian employees of the Perestroika Joint Venture and a 30-year veteran of the Russian real estate market. She explained, "Those who came looking for opportunities to make money saw a niche of the market where there was overt demand and a lack of quality supply for office space. It was a niche that they would never be able to occupy without Russian partners. It was mutual interest and mutual luck for people who found each other as partners to explore this niche."

The demand for commercial office space and quality residential real estate was initially driven by the influx of international companies and the growth of the expat community. But as Vera correctly noted, the ability to take advantage of this demand depended upon partnerships between experienced foreigners and Russian partners. Large Russian institutions partnered with foreigners who understood both the look and feel of Western tastes and who knew the mechanics of leasing. As demand shifted during the 1990s with the growth of Russian economy, the drivers for real estate also shifted toward Russian company clients. As in the finance sector, Russians acquired the skills to manage and develop modern commercial real estate without needing foreign experts by the late 1990s.

In a separate but related development, there was an increasing demand for residential housing driven primarily by foreigners moving into Moscow and St. Petersburg. The initial supply of residential housing came from Russians who had privatized their apartments and obtained a new source of income through rentals. The rental agents were often young Americans with their Russian partners. The Americans were able to find customers looking to rent in the expat community and then got a fee or portion of the rental income that went to the Russian owners. Later, large-scale townhouse developments were constructed for foreigners.

The development of the real estate sector has parallels with the development of the investment banks described in Chapter 3. As the real estate market developed and grew, many of the entrepreneurial companies were sold to international firms as Russia integrated into the world economy, particularly after the 1998 default. Given the importance of finance in the real estate sector, these companies also grew to have a close relationship to private equity funds for real estate finance.

The story of the new Russian real estate sector begins with the perestroika era joint ventures.

Perestroika Joint Venture – First Real Estate Development Company

The founding of Perestroika was introduced in Chapter 1 as one of the significant Gorbachev era joint ventures. Perestroika was formed in 1988 as a joint venture between Delphi International, an American consulting company, and the Moscow State Construction Company (Mosinzhstroi), headed by Andrey Stroyev. Its significance resonates into the early 1990s and beyond in the formation of the real estate sector in Russia.

John Reuther was the first American hired to work in the Perestroika joint venture, as the deputy director. Hiring Reuther was a literal illustration of the Russian historical pattern of seeking out foreign expertise. His father Victor Reuther and his uncle Walter Reuther went to the Soviet Union in the 1930s as skilled workers to assist the Soviets in learning how to operate an automobile production line that the USSR purchased from Ford Motors. Later both became key figures in the founding of the United Auto Workers union in the United States. John went to Soviet Union in 1968 to study Russian and Soviet politics. He then went on to have a varied career as a political operative and sometime home contractor. John was recruited to join Perestroika through Paul von Word, the owner of Delphi International, who was acquainted with John and knew his unique qualifications for this position. Delphi International was a consulting company that was the original American partner in Perestroika. Later as the joint venture sought a partner with more real estate expertise, John and Andrei Stroyev found Earl Worsham, an Atlanta-based real estate developer to become the American partner and Worsham's company bought out Delphi International.

At the time that Warsham replaced Delphi International, John already had plans in place to rehab a building in central Moscow as office space for international companies. The problem he faced was finance. As he recounts, "I had a list of which foreign companies in Moscow might be interested in office premises. I met with their top chief representative and showed him the plans. He liked everything about it and said we'll take it. I told him that at this stage these were just plans because we do not have the finances to do the project. Worsham would not put any money in. He put money into other things but not financing construction. So, we had to find a way to finance this building. The company rep said that they would pay rent for a year in advance. When I explained that this was not going to be enough, he offered to pay five years in advance. Then, I showed BASF, Dupont and Monsanto the plans and told them that the other company was going to pay us five years rent in advance. At this point they all got board approval to pay us six years in advance so that they could get space in the building. This kind of agreement became the means of financing the entire new real estate sector." Given that the private financial sector was in its infancy and Russian financial institutions had no experience with construction financing or mortgages, it is impossible to overestimate the importance of this form of finance pioneered by John Reuther and Perestroika. It was what enabled a private real estate market to begin.

John explained that "everything was going beautifully now. The purpose from the Soviet side of creating a joint venture was to generate hard currency. Stroyev's company was building, and renovating roads and underground utilities and his company needed to buy Germany equipment and so he needed hard currency."

Michael Morgenstern, the next American hire, had a long-term interest in Russia and Russian language skills, having served for many years as the translator for the Moscow Circus when it toured the United States. He joined Perestroika through some attenuated connections to Earl Worsham and had the skills and outlook that Stroyev wanted for the company. "A friend of mine from grad school said that he had a friend in Atlanta whose father-in-law was doing a real estate joint venture in Russia and they're looking for an American who knows finance to go over there and be their finance director. So, to make a long story short, that's how I got introduced to Perestroika. I went over there and in the summer of 89 I moved there."

"Moscow was just starting a renewal and there was a huge market for commercial space. Once we did that first building, everybody saw what we could do. Everybody came to us for something for themselves. The demand from international companies was really, really great."

Michael described the personality and approach of Andrey Stroyev in building Perestroika, "He really had an extreme amount of energy and he wanted to be a kingpin. He had great ambitions. He wanted to change the Soviet system and the period was right for it. I mean he really took advantage of the situation that was occurring in the Soviet Union, at that time and he made a lot of waves. … He had a very strong personality. He was very Western oriented, and he really wanted to try and be Western in every sense; speaking English, the way he dressed, etc."

Asked where Stroyev's drive toward being Western came from, Michael replied, "I never really understood why. He didn't travel extensively. He might have traveled to Germany, or something. I think it was just raw ambition. By that time, there were enough videos and resources in the Soviet Union that he knew, and Russians generally knew, how behind the times they were in a lot of things. Like a lot of Russians, they were tired of Soviet ways of doing things and they wanted change. I think that was more of a motivation for him, rather than having traveled and gained a lot of experience and wanting to copy that. One of the things he was counting on me to do was to set a tone for my department in the company, the finance department and, hopefully, for others to in the company, by bringing in outside ways of doing things, modernizing."

Vera Setskaya was one of the early Russian employees of Perestroika and as such had a unique view on the development of the company and the significance of the American participation.

Originally hired as a translator and assistant to John Reuther, she noted that "Earl Worsham did not speak Russian and the Russians in the Perestroika joint venture didn't speak English. So, a lot of help was needed, not just for oral translation, but also in translation of a lot of documents, starting with lease agreements and ending with all kinds of minutes of the meetings. There were a lot of documents to grasp, to understand and to translate. The Russian staff was mostly doing construction itself. The Americans were more involved with financial things related to leasing and things related to communication with foreigners in Moscow about future lease deals and delivery of premises."

"Stroyev believed in young people. We were all around thirty years old, more or less. For Soviet times, it was unique. Young people would never, never be trusted with anything important. Stroyev had a different mentality. He thought that only young people could learn quickly, could grasp new ideas quickly, and could implement those ideas. He managed to build a team of very young and talented people. He was not mistaken. These young people knew that they were doing something entirely new in this joint venture, understood the goals and ideas and appreciated the benefits. They worked hard and managed to do some really good stuff."

"It was a unique venture from different points of view. It was very smartly built and very beneficial for both parties. The Russian part of the venture was like the skeleton, the backbone. They had access to land on which it was possible to build and were able to get control over some very nice existing small buildings in the center of Moscow. Stroyev and his team did all the engineering, obtained utility connections and managed the construction. They were very, very professional in terms of construction."

"The Americans put the flesh on the bones, so to speak. In the first place, it was important to give credibility to the foreign community in Moscow. At that time, foreigners were skeptical of space built and run by Russians. Politically and ethically, and from a risk standpoint, it was not so easy for us to attract foreigners. The American face on the venture give us what we lacked at that time, credibility."

"At that period, the real estate business as such did not exist in Russia. The word 'developer' and 'development' did not exist. Russians could build an office and fill it with tables, but they could not build an office that would be appreciated and accepted by the foreign community. Americans give us that knowledge of the look and feel in new office space that would be expected by foreigners. It has to do with a lot of aspects, starting with very simple things like, for example floor layout. Our Soviet office buildings were basically a corridor with offices on each side and very bad looking toilets. It was a shock for the Americans when they came to Soviet office buildings and visited our toilets. So, the American influence started with very simple things like office configuration and traffic organization inside the office and extending to much more difficult things like form lease agreements about which we had no idea."

"Property management, nobody knew the word. It was so essential not just to build the building, but to correctly put together the management of the building. There was a Canadian woman that they brought to Moscow for half a year to set up property management systems. Engineering systems, maintenance forms, accounting for property management, all were brought from the West, from America or from Europe, probably from America. And I presume that John [Reuther] contributed a lot into bringing that stuff. Andrey [Stroyev], to give him credit, always knew what was needed and asked for expert providers."

"Earl was just a face to show. He looked very presentable looking, tall, with expensive clothes, all that created the right impression. He would be introduced to the right people by the Russians, and he would say the right words. In my opinion it was just an appearance. But, frankly speaking, I never heard any bright ideas from him, maybe I was not at the right level."

Vera described the market for international companies looking for commercial office space in those days. "Yes, there was a big flow of business to Russia, and of course these companies needed space. There were dozens of foreign companies already existing in Moscow and in St Petersburg, who did not have decent premises in which to work. There was a lack of premises available on the market, so they had to be content with what was offered by the Main Administration for Service to the Diplomatic Corps (GlavUpDK or UpDK). This was not Western-looking space. It was Russian/Soviet-looking space, better quality, but still Soviet-looking."

"Let's put it like this, UpDK was the only option available on the market. A foreign company was not allowed to lease space in whatever building they wanted. They were obliged to get space through UpDK and that's what they did."

"Foreign companies realized that they were very, very carefully watched in UpDK buildings. Clearly, they did not like it. The moment a commercial product started coming on the market and there appeared an opportunity to legally lease space in commercial buildings, they all started leaving the UpDK space and leasing space in the new premises. Among the first tenants who moved to Perestroika's buildings were Dupont, Monsanto and BASF, all of whom had previously been in UpDK space."

Cameron Sawyer was the second general director of Perestroika after John Reuther left after a dispute with Andrey Stroyev. "John Reuther was his first general director and then I replaced Reuther when he left. So, Reuther and I were the ones who did the management of the company and explained how to do it. I wrote all these forms and set up all the legal structures. But Stroyev was the real force behind it. Worsham was just symbolic."

Sawyer had first visited Russia as an exchange student in 1989 and then had gone on to get a law degree. He was practicing real estate law in the Atlanta area. "We had the real estate crash at the end of the 1980s and I didn't have much to do. Unfortunately, we got the work to do all the Resolution Trust Corporation savings and loan workouts, which made us a bunch of bureaucrats. It was just mind numbingly boring. … I hated living in Atlanta. I had a friend, a Russian friend, that I had met in Munich who lived in Atlanta. As a Russian immigrant at the beginning of Perestroika, he had started to travel back to Moscow doing some speculation deals, like they did in those days, buying and selling stuff importing, exporting stuff. … He was doing business with this guy, Andrey Stroyev, who was involved in trading and different stuff besides real estate."

"Stroyev had a falling out with Reuther and Reuther left. Stroyev told my Russian friend that he couldn't really live without Reuther because he could not do this real estate development stuff by himself, with no education or background. He wished that he could find another guy like Reuther to help him. My friend said to me, you've been complaining about how bored you are in

Atlanta. Now that the Soviet system is ending, there are they're going to be unbelievable opportunities in Russia. This is a job you could have if you want it. I agreed to meet Stroyev when he was in Atlanta. That was July of 1991, so just before the August putsch."

"I had pretty much decided to accept the position, but then the August putsch happened, and I thought well you know so much for free enterprise in Russia. I stopped thinking about it and got my nose to the grindstone with my legal practice. Then in October, Stroyev called me and said look it's all over, everything is fine now. Why don't you come on over? So, I went over in October 1991."

"John Reuther and David Geovanis, who developed Ducat Plaza, were the first two Americans in real estate in Moscow. I must have been the third and the fourth was my deputy, a guy named Miles Jones. Miles then went on to start a brokerage company which became Richard Ellis. Then he sold that company, and he started a development company called Griffin where he still works."

"We were building office buildings when I first joined. We were already under construction for Philip Morris and Dupont and some other buildings. Those were renovations of existing buildings. ... Meanwhile, we were also building housing. We built the first townhouses in Russia. It was a project which has since been torn down and high-rise buildings have been built there. We built these town houses, which were prefabricated in Atlanta and the modules were shipped over on a ship. We built a concrete foundation and stacked those modules up to create the townhouses. We built like 60 or 80 townhouses, something like that, and we leased them to all these expatriate managers. ... Stroyev was managing the construction because that was his bag and I was managing all the leasing and design stuff. That was a great project. We finished that about the time I left. I stayed at Perestroika from October 1991 until January of 1993."

"During 1992 after the dissolution of the Soviet Union, it was a new world for a while. We didn't even know what the country was called. ... As we were adapting to this crazy new world, there was hyperinflation going on and during that year, the Turkish company 'ENKA' entered the market. They had financing from Turkish banks, so they didn't need to take six years of rent in advance. They competed with us by leasing space with no rent prepayment and that was tremendously attractive. They were killing us."

"We had great ambitions to create more and more office space because it was so profitable, but our office business was being killed by ENKA. ... I told Stroyev that he had had a great run with collecting the six years of rent in advance, but naturally markets can't sustain that. Perestroika had competitors with financing and would need to shift gears to develop its own financing. ... I told Stroyev that by my accounts he had $30 to $40 million dollars in profits already. He needed to reinvest some of that and meanwhile develop our own banking relationships. We still owned all these buildings that we could mortgage. It was real estate 101."

"Stroyev said no, it's our business and we will not let anyone else into it. He was trying to use all political means to shut down ENKA. That's all he could think about, shutting down ENKA, but not competing with them. This was an absolute case of Soviet mentality destroying this business."

"He also began to have his own political problems. A couple of important people, including the Mayor of Moscow, were involved in the Perestroika joint venture in some way or another, on the board or had some interest. Stroyev got into a quarrel with them over something, I'm not sure about what, but he fell out of favor. Without favor you could do nothing in this field, because land was not allocated on any kind of market basis. It was allocated according to relationships. So, the business started to fall apart. It went so far that Stroyev himself was attacked by maybe tax police. I can't remember what it was, but they were after Andrey himself."

"As the company started to fall apart, I left with my colleagues [Vera Setskaya and Temuri Gelenava], both of whom are still working in our company today 30 years later. We've been working together for exactly 30 years."

"When we left Perestroika Joint Venture, we formed a new company which still exists. It was called GVA Sawyer, part of GVA Worldwide. When GVA Worldwide was acquired by Avison Young in 2021, we became Sawyer Group Holding Company, the Avison Young affiliate in Russia for consulting and brokerage services."

GVA Sawyer – Evolution of Moscow Real Estate Development

"When we started our business, we were trying to build a new world, based on honest market relationships. ... That was the calling card of our company in the early days. We weren't bribing anyone. We weren't cutting in any officials. We were doing it all on a market basis. We were getting our permissions by doing the work, rather than paying bribes. In the first years, it was possible to just buy a building permit. We didn't do that; we did the work."

"We had a very difficult start. We lost our first project because we did not cut in the Institute officials that owned the building."

"Soon, you could no longer buy building permissions. Moscow is very complicated and not quite as corrupt as people think it was."

"And there came the day when you could not get a building permission without doing the work exactly right. Bribery wouldn't help you, except possibly accelerate it. We were one of the few development companies that knew how to do it by the rules. So, we were doing that work on a consulting basis for other companies, including Mayor Luzhkov's wife's development company."

"We developed a brokerage and consulting business. Our brokerage business was never all that strong, but we were the number one development consultants in in Russia for a long time."

"And we built other stuff. We built the first outlet mall in Russia. Then we had a joint venture with Knight Frank to raise an investment fund for Russia in real estate."

As GVA Sawyer developed, so did the sophistication of Vera Setskaya. As one of the founders of the new company, she served first as vice president and then became president in the early 2000s. "When we started working with Cameron, I learned a lot of things from him. In 1993 or 1994, we started the development of the first building in Russia financed 100 percent with private foreign capital. ... I learned that development is not construction, but a financial operation. The idea behind this is that even if you built something, but it does not give you the desired financial result, then you failed. It's an absolutely different way to look at real estate. ... Everywhere in the world, a building is looked at through its existing or potential cash flow. This approach was unknown to Russians thirty years ago. I want to thank those Americans who helped to set up the Certified Commercial Investment Member (CCIM) courses and certification in Russia some twenty years ago. It was extremely useful."

"When I lecture at the Russian School of Management to classes on real estate development, I ask the audience how old this field of activity is in Russia. Usually, nobody can guess. I say that it's 30 years old, starting in 1989 when the first building was built and launched by Perestroika JV. Then I tell them that in England, they consider their property market to be 600 years old. The American market is also several hundred years old. Our Russian market is just 30 years old, nothing in the scope of Russia's history. Yet, we managed to build it from complete absolute zero. Today, nobody brings Americans to teach us how to design and manage space. There are no more such questions. We do it better than Americans I would say. This history of Russia's real estate is a unique page in the history of our country. Already in the first 15 years from its founding, we managed to jump very high and very long."

Hines – Global Real Estate Comes to Russia

Hines is a privately held global real estate development, investment and management firm, one of the largest in the world. The company was an early entrant into the Russian real estate sector, following the familiar pattern of partnering with a powerful Russian partner. In their case the partner was UpDK, which was introduced above as the Soviet entity responsible for providing office space to foreign embassies and international corporations. The founders of Perestroika Joint Venture poached some of their early clients from UpDK because UpDK provided commercial space that was below international standards. UpDK partnered with Hines to radically modernize and change their competitive position in the Russian market.

Lee Timmins is the CEO of Hines Eurasia, the division of the company that covers India, Central Europe and Eastern Europe. He described how and when Hines decided to enter Russia. "Around the time of the fall of the Berlin Wall, one of the board members of Hines was looking at everything from the Czech Republic and Poland to Russia. We ultimately decided that we would open an office in Russia. ... This was before the Soviet Union fell. We did one of the first joint ventures in real estate with an entity called UpDK. This entity was set up back in the 1920s to set up and manage embassy facilities.

… Most people viewed them as a KGB front organization to basically spy on and look after the foreigners. That was why they were set up in the 1920s. What happened is that they had a lot of real estate. They had the embassies and they had excess cash flow that came from the foreign embassy payments in hard currency. They started building a project that was commercially oriented, but they didn't have any idea about how to attract commercial tenants. So, we negotiated a deal that was signed in 1991, before the Soviet Union dissolved. We negotiated a joint venture to take over this project in Moscow called 'Park Place Moscow.' That was before my time but there was a guy before me that negotiated the joint venture. Then, they needed somebody to run it. … I ultimately decided to make a move over to Russia, mostly because I've always had a bit of a spirit of adventure. So, there wasn't any master plan of me going over to change the world or anything of that nature. … That was in April 1993, and I came over on a two-year commitment and 27 years later still there. [The date of the interview was April 17, 2021.]"

"Managing Park Place Moscow was our first project. A lot of the people that we knew said, 'yeah, they signed a two-year agreement, but they will never live up to it. They'll kick you out, etc.' The Russian Government lived up to it to a tee, lived up to it fully. In fact, we extended the agreement a little bit longer. We no longer have that project, but I think we managed it for 22 years."

"Then we did some management projects. We did 'Ducat Place II,' which was a management project. Then by 1996, Hines was doing a global emerging markets private equity fund. It was a concept that was brand new. Nobody had really thought about a real estate emerging markets fund. We ultimately committed about 25 percent of the capital from that first fund into the Pokrovsky Hills project. When the deal was originally proposed, we planned to do the project for about $80 million. Ultimately, due to changes in tax legislation, we invested $100 million of equity in that project."

Pokrovsky Hills was one of the first large-scale gated communities for foreigners in Moscow. Ultimately, it was composed of 207 townhouse units clustered around the Anglo-American School on a woody, hilly site not far from the center of Moscow. It offers three- to five-bedroom townhomes with 24-hour security and its own onsite conveniences.

Lee Timmins described the development process for Pokrovsky Hills. "We knew that the Anglo-American School was desperate for some new, modern facilities. They came to us to ask us if there anything we could do to help. Around that same time, we did a project in Prague where we did the International School of Prague, plus housing as part of the project. It was working very well, so we decided that we could do the same thing in Russia."

"I went to went to the Mayor of Moscow, Luzhkov, and asked for some support. He didn't really give support per se but had one of the city guys help us in finding a site. We went to the US ambassador at the time as well. The idea was to put Anglo-American School together with housing, and then the US Embassy would be the anchor tenant." The financing was analogous to the Perestroika leasing fees paid in advance. "We put the school together with the Embassy. The Embassy as the anchor tenant would lease at least 40 townhouses from us for an eight-year period. Based on those leases, we could put the deal together to acquire the land and develop Pokrovsky Hills, which is ultimately what we did."

The Anglo-American School financed their building through a combination of their own equity and through advance sales of seat fees for places in the school. They went to corporate sponsors from companies established in Moscow and asked for advance payment for a certain number of seats at the school. "The corporate would say I'll commit to five students, and I'll pay you a seat fee of maybe $15,000. So, they would give the $75,000 for the right to have five students in the school. They then got a loan from the Raiffeisen Bank, but they had to get guarantees from three governments, the US Embassy, the British Embassy and the Canadian Embassy."

"We had a few tough moments during the first phase of the project. The price of oil plummeted to about $8 a barrel and we were sweating quite a lot on that. But we kept going and ultimately it turned out beautifully. We ultimately sold it and made about $200 million of profit on a $100 million investment. It was the most profitable deal we had in our entire global emerging markets fund."

"In Russia, we've funded things through three global private equity funds. The total of each of those was about $1.4 billion, of which about a quarter of it was invested in Russia. Then, we had a few what we call separate accounts, where we financed things just with us and one other investor for a single project. … I can give you a couple statistics. The amount of assets that we've developed is about $1.6 billion US dollars. Then we have acquired about $2.2 billion in assets. So we had just under $4 billion in assets over this period in Russia."

"We started development with Pokrovsky Hills, then office buildings, then warehousing and then retail. We bought a large mall and then various other assets."

"After Pokrovsky Hills, our next major investment was our Ducat Place office building. We had great success on that one too. At the time we sold off the Ducat Place office building, it was the single most profitable office deal we had done in the history of Hines globally, throughout the entire history of our firm dating back to the 1950s. So, it was very, very successful."

Hines played an important role in bringing foreign capital into Russia through real estate finance and developed strong partnerships with Russian partners investing in their real estate projects as Lee Timmins explained. "Early on, we had our private equity funds, which would pool capital from institutional investors around the world, pension funds, sovereign wealth funds. These included groups like GM, CALPERS, New York State Teachers Retirement Fund. Later, we had several sovereign wealth funds from Korea, the UN Pension Fund. So, a lot of these global investors came into Russia, for the first time with us. The government of Singapore was an early investor.

Then later, we began having local partners, like the Zimin family that started Vimplecom, one of the largest mobile telephone companies in Russia."

Lee Timmins was very proud of the legacy of Hines in Russia both in terms of their physical construction, but also their contribution to the real estate sector in Russia generally. "We have tried, and I believe, succeeded, in creating great projects. People that used to work for us have now started companies that created projects. Moscow and St. Petersburg are better places as a result. … We've had maybe 1,500 people, maybe 2,000 people that have come through our organization and it could be even more than that. … It's not just people on projects, but it's also bankers engineering companies, contractors, subcontractors. … We started building our projects with international contractors, Italian, Swedish, Turkish. Now our contractors are completely Russian. They are absolutely as good as you find anywhere in the world. … A lot of the Russian contractors we have today started off as subcontractors for the international contractors. Now they started their own firms. They've grown and effectively supplanted the international guys. The same thing happened with banks. The first Russian bank we worked with participated in funding with a large Italian bank and then they learned how to finance projects on their own."

Residential and Commercial Brokers

In parallel with the development of the market for commercial office space, the demand for residential space from foreign expats drove the development of a market for apartments and the creation of real estate brokerages. There arose a set of entrepreneurial brokers offering apartment rentals and commercial space. Many of those interviewed, like Bill Lane, Preston Haskell and Brad Garine, arose very modestly from individual entrepreneurs or small groups and grew into much larger organizations that were acquired by international real estate brokers, following the same pattern as in other new economic sectors. The arc of these companies also illustrates the symbiotic relationship between American and Russian entrepreneurs as it evolved during the 1990s.

Coldwell Banker Richard Ellis (CBRE)

Bill Lane had studied Russian in college and after getting a law degree, he wanted to go to Moscow to look for work. By chance, the husband of the owner of the travel company in Boston where he went to get his visa was looking for someone to run his Moscow office. George Cuker was opening one of the first real estate brokerages in Russia, aptly named First Russian Real Estate and Bill agreed to move to Moscow in October 1992.

Bill described the state of the market in those days. "After 70 years of communism, there was no real estate industry there. Everything was owned by the government. You were told, this is your apartment, and you were assigned to live there. Businesses were given space, but they did not own it. There were no concepts of ownership and leasing like in the US. … George's strategy was to go to some of the former Soviet Institutes that had plenty of available space and cosmetically renovate it. We put a Western face on the space and quote unquote leased it. But you really couldn't lease it because there was no legal infrastructure at the time to lease it. … The market was moving faster than the legislation."

"There were many Institutes that were supported during the Soviet times and then suddenly, the Soviet Union collapses and that's it. Although they lost government financial support, they all sat in these buildings with a lot of empty space. There was starting to be demand, but the few office buildings that existed, like those of Perestroika, were fully leased. Some foreigner businesses that needed more space began using rented apartments, but there was a regulation that said you're not supposed to have an office in a residential apartment. However, plenty of people did that and got away with it. If you are Baker & Mackenzie or a real international company, then you want to try to follow the rules and they needed office space. Those companies had to decide whether to stay working out of a hotel or wait for space to up in one of those few buildings that had the right to lease. The alternative was to take a calculated risk and sign a lease somewhere."

"George went to these Institutes and signed these things call joint activity agreements. As a lawyer from the US, I knew that these almost never had any legal basis, but you get over that pretty quickly. You say to yourself, okay, they aren't real legal agreements, but at least there is something on a piece of paper. … We had another entity, so we leased the space from the Institute and subleased it to the foreign company. … These were not leases because the people who signed them did not own the property, so they had no rights to lease. From the business side, you could occupy this space on this joint activity agreement and take some risk but have a space. If you did not want to do that, there's no other place that you can go other than the hotel rooms."

"We did a couple of deals with Samsung, L'Oréal, the French cosmetics company and a few others. These were big companies that needed office space fast. They made the decision to sign this joint activity agreement and just go with that and the rents were expensive at the time because there just wasn't that much supply."

"Our company was called First Russian Real Estate. I was living in a dormitory and had a fax machine and one phone line. It was very difficult to do anything at all. No mobile phones, too expensive at the time. … So, you just figured it out."

"By chance I met another American guy from Massachusetts, Jack Kelleher, and he joined the company. We began to create cash flow for the company but had a disagreement with George over our terms of employment. As a result, Jack and I left the company."

"We went across the street to my apartment. By that time, I had a three-room apartment and one of the rooms had a desk. George was way behind in the money owed to us, but I had convinced him to give us each $1,000 bucks, a small portion of what he owed us. My student loan payment at that time was around $900 a month so things were pretty tight and difficult. … We went to my apartment, and we flipped a coin, to see whose name would come first on the business card. Jack won so we started a real estate brokerage company in my apartment with the name of Kelleher & Lane. We bought a laptop computer and a fax machine, and we started making phone calls. This was in the beginning of 1994."

"We had our office in my apartment on Tverskaya Boulevard. At that point in the industry. There were a few other expats like us doing similar things. They were in offices i.e., apartments, scattered along Tverskaya Boulevard., Moscow's main street. Each had just one or two or three people. We often lived deal-to-deal during that time, maxing out our credit cards or getting family loans. There were several times that if I didn't close that deal and collect money we would have to leave. Luckily, we navigated those challenging times."

"Initially Jack and I were doing both residential and office brokerage. For residential, there were all these expats that were coming over with benefit packages. A lot of them were with USAID projects, then there were the consultancies, like Ernst and Young, and then there were the law firms. They all had very good budgets to rent apartments. So, we were able to start doing that type of business."

Asked about where the apartments were coming from for the rental market, Bill Lane explained that "sometimes this was through Russian friends of mine or people we had developed relationships with, and they would want to rent apartments. We would find the expats to rent them. Then we just split the fee. It is important to keep in mind that these were almost always first-time landlords. They had never done this before so there was a lot of explaining and hand holding. Almost always we had to explain to the owners that now that they had leased their apartment, they could not simply come to their apartment any time they wanted."

Yeltsin reforms gave Russians the possibility to monetize their newly privatized apartments through renting to foreigners for what was a comparatively very significant amount of money in Russia of those times. "That's a huge part of the story for Russia that is overlooked. This is the fact that Yeltsin allowed people to privatize their apartments. People just don't appreciate what that did for the mentality of people in Russia. These people didn't own anything for 70 years."

"Yeltsin said that you guys can privatize your apartments now. Of course, there was some abuse and some other things that happened just as it would anywhere in the world. People like to talk about this person was cheated, and that and that. But the real story is moving from the past where the government told me that this is my apartment, and I don't own it. So why should I take care of it? Then suddenly, I own this thing. I can sell it. I can rent it or just keep it as mine. It was mortgage free in Russian privatization and that was a piece of the story as well. … Then there was the mentality piece of it which was huge.

People start to realize that I can rent this apartment for a couple of thousand bucks a month. I can just move out to my dacha and rent the apartment."

"We did residential leasing for a little while but then we started to focus on the office sector. We started to meet a few of the other real estate entrepreneurs in the market. Jack and I ended up forming a partnership with two other guys, one other American and a Russian. My original Russian partner is still one of my close friends today. So now, there were four of us and the market was growing so we moved out of the apartment and into an actual office."

"At that time the big global brokerage companies like JLL, Cushman and CBRE had clients like AT&T, General Motors and they all needed office space in Moscow. All the real estate entrepreneurs started to form associations with JLL or Cushman. We formed a relationship with Richard Ellis, which became CBRE. … That was in the mid-1990s. … At that time, the office product in the market started to improve along with the legal infrastructure."

"Hines was one of the early groups in Russia. They initially weren't developing buildings but came in as a property manager in a JV with UpDK, but then they started to develop. You also had a few professional construction companies, like McHugh out of Chicago. Then you had Russian groups that had access to buildings. At that time, you could get one year rent up front. There were some of the most expensive rents in the world. So, you get all that rent up front, developers would use that money to fund construction because banks were not financing construction at that time. A lot of these groups had their own construction companies from the Soviet times. They could very quickly take that money and renovate a building. If you did not want to pay up front and said that you would wait to see the finished space, they would say fine and go on to the next client because someone was going to sign that upfront payment deal."

"We started to grow with the market. We initially were a brokerage, but then we started with construction, construction management, property management and so on. We brought in professionals, architects and other specialists, a few foreigners, but mostly Russians. We started to be construction managers and project managers for some pretty big projects in Moscow. … Most of our employees were Russian and of course, there were some expats. We built the business up to over 100 people, but then we ran into the 1998 crisis when Russia defaulted on its foreign debt."

Before 1998, Lane's company did a great deal of business as the rental agent for the Turkish company, ENKA, that was mentioned earlier in the section on Perestroika. "We did tons of deals with ENKA. They consistently delivered quality space on schedule, something very few of the other construction companies did. They were a great client to have in the market, and that was huge cash flow for us."

"Leading up to the 1998 crisis, foreign companies had been leasing up all the available office space. It was the rare exception when a Russian company leased space in a new class A or class B building. There was virtually no vacancy in the market. At that the market was not big in comparison to other European cities. It was just getting going after 70 years. ENKA was starting to deliver their first buildings and the foreign companies were taking this space right away."

"So, when 1998 crisis comes, the head offices of these companies in London or New York or wherever put a hold on looking for new space. They wanted to figure out what is going on in Russia, so everything was put on hold. Some companies tried to renegotiate their rental terms or sublease some of their space. Overall, there was a lot of uncertainty and some of the market's initial real estate entrepreneurs left Russia. Luckily, and quite unexpectedly, market demand came back much quicker than anyone expected in the first quarter of 1999. This time demand was led primarily by large Russian companies. They had begun to appreciate the benefits of well-designed and well-maintained office space and started leasing large chunks of space overnight."

Then, by the first quarter of 1999, most of the demand began to shift away from foreigners and more real estate market was driven by Russians and Russian companies. "The Russian companies had been watching what's going on and many of them had been privatized then. The Russian banks had money. The Russian oil companies had money. They were all sitting in these old Soviet style buildings but now they wanted to be in the new office buildings."

"Russian companies were flush with cash because they were selling oil for dollars and suddenly there was a strong pipeline of demand for the available office space. So, they started taking space in the new buildings. We did some of the first deals with these large Russian companies in 1999. One of them took an entire building of 7000 square meters, which was a big deal at the time."

"That demand component of the market never went away. It's an important component to the market. If you went to a Class A office building in the mid 1990s, it was 99.9 percent foreign companies. Now it is 50/50, 60/40, 70/30, depending on the building."

There was also a clear transition to Russians running the brokerage businesses and dominating the real estate market that Bill Lane articulated in terms of his own company. "I told my Russian colleagues, I'm not going to be doing this, you guys are. You guys are going to be the leaders in the market."

Looking back on what he considered his successes were, he said "Obviously, the success of selling our business to the largest publicly traded commercial real estate advisory company in the world, yeah that was important. It was also fun and challenging to be part of something during its formation. Monetarily and all that was great, but there was a different category of success that was important. This is the opportunity for our Russian colleagues. They have a profession. They bought apartments. They went on trips. They're spread out all over the market and at senior levels."

Colliers International

Preston Haskell comes from a family involved in construction and real estate development. He was intrigued by the potential opportunities in Eastern

Europe when the Berlin Wall came down. Then he was exposed to the potential of the Russian market when he interviewed with Cameron Sawyer for a marketing position at the Perestroika Joint Venture. He did not get the job but came away enthusiastic about possible opportunities in Russia. In 1993, he and Oleg Myshkin, a Russian émigré friend went to Moscow to explore those possible opportunities. By 1994, they formed what Preston believes to be the first commercial real estate brokerage company in Moscow and eventually became affiliated with Colliers International, New York Exchange listed international real estate giant.

Preston began his real estate business in a manner analogous to the experience of Bill Lane. "I started a very small development company taking apartments and renovating them to lease them out. People working for the World Bank, the IMF or some of the big foreign companies came in and I would do it a lease that would last for say five years at say $1,000 per month. Then these guys would pay me for a year or year and a half in advance, which paid for all the renovation and the furniture. ... It was kind of what Perestroika Joint Venture was doing, but on a much smaller scale."

"Then, I got to know two young Russians, Andrei Barinsky and Vladimir Zubrillian, who are still close friends, and we still have business together. ... They started doing exactly what I was doing but on a bigger scale by taking long term leases on space in Institutes. The first project was actually leased from a theater. The Taganskaya Theater had a four-story building that these guys leased. They renovated it and they needed a brokerage company to help them lease out the space. We said that we could find foreign clients. We found Halliburton and they took most of the building. We also told these guys that we could manage the building so that they did not have to deal with tenants when they called up. In return we received free office space in the building."

"The next thing you know, we made some very good brokerage deals. We got Procter and Gamble to take 7,500 square meters at an ENKA project." The commission from this deal gave them sufficient capital to buy into some larger real estate development projects that his two Russian friends were developing.

"Andrei and Vladimir saw the value in me because I knew real estate. They just didn't know it at all and there was a hell of a need for that knowledge. They had been selling computers and copiers. They got into real estate through an Armenian guy as an interesting business opportunity. I had worked for CB Richard Ellis. Then I went to work for a developer in Atlanta in a very tough market. Through my work in the summers while still at university and the three years after, I was a very experienced real estate professional by Moscow standards. Additionally, I grew up in a family that was in the design and build construction and real estate business. Commercial real estate development was something that I wanted to do from a young age."

"As a result, I was able to understand foreign clients who wanted space in Moscow. We weren't offering the best space because what we had was renovated space in older Institutes. However, we were offering proper property management and a foreign face to deal with in me."

Preston built a strong personal and business relationship with Andrei and Vladimir that carried over into larger projects redeveloping old factory buildings into commercial office space in which Preston was a stakeholder as well as the leasing agent. He had to pay for his share but was allowed into these profitable deals as an equity holder. "They just felt like good fit to me. I needed them because I could not do anything without them. I did not speak Russian. I knew that they needed me as well and we also became personal friends. … But they were fair. They treated me fair. They could have screwed me if they wanted to, but they saw the value, I was creating for them."

In describing the expat community in that period, Preston divided it up into very different groups between those clustered around the American Embassy, professionals in accounting or legal or the like, and the entrepreneurial types. "The diplomatic corps was very specific. If you work in embassies and what not, the embassies in 1993, 1994 hosted functions. There were no real bars so you would go there on Friday nights to have beers. I never really hung out with that crowd. … Then, there was a professional sector which were people that were corporate, accounting or bank, big corporations. You know that sector is a certain type. Then there was the more entrepreneurial sector and real estate is a particularly entrepreneurial thing."

Asked about the impact of the contested election in 1996 between Boris Yeltsin and Gennady Zyuganov, he recounted, "I mean I was glued to the coverage of it. If I was on the inside and if I really understood everything, I would have had a very clear understanding that they were going to rig this thing, no matter what. … Yeltsin, was going to win, even if he was in a coma."

"And I have my different views on Russia today, but Moscow today [June 2021] is a world class city. It is the most livable city by far in Europe, both cost wise and the quality of the inner city itself. Downtown has just fabulous restaurants. The new mayor has done an excellent job with the sidewalks, the walking spaces and decorations during the holidays."

Asked at the time of our interview in 2021 how he thought the real estate market was going to develop and how different that projection was from what really happened, he replied "First up, I never thought it would grow so fast. I never thought that Russians would pick up trends and ideas in the real estate sector worldwide on their own and apply that best practice and best quality, bringing the best architects and so on. I thought Russians always cut corners or this and that. But now what's being built in Russia to me is on par with anything you see in the high-end market of London, New York, and other major capitals around the world. That's truly amazing. I think that the way in which there has been the development of the younger generation of Russian professionals is also really impressive."

Jones Lang LaSalle

Brad Garine is another American entrepreneur who came to Russia as a young man and who built a real estate brokerage that was acquired by a global real estate firm, in this case Jones Lang LaSalle. He was exposed to Russia at an early age. His father was the director for the Occidental Petroleum office in Moscow during the Brezhnev era. His father was posted there for 9 years, and Brad spent some time in Moscow with him during his childhood. Then after graduating from university on the prompting of his Russian stepbrother, he went to Moscow.

"I went originally to pursue a career in trade. I had this interest in import-export. I thought that if I could get my feet on Russian soil, I could be a good conduit for helping do transactions. ... I had arrived in Russia with $2,000 and my apartment rent was $75 bucks. I wasn't out dining at these crazy few restaurants that existed there during those days. ... There were one or two places where foreigners would hang out, like the Irish Bar on Tverskaya. ... So, I lived a pretty frugal life at the time."

"After several months, the money that I had available was literally starting to disappear. So, I said to myself, you know this is going nowhere fast and I spoke to my stepbrother. I told him that I had to find another way to make some income. He told me that he had a friend in the apartment rental business and suggested that I could try to rent out some apartments. ... He then introduced me to this guy who was his childhood friend."

"This guy had basically half a dozen Russian guys that were literally running around renting Russian apartments to Russian people who were looking to find a place to live in Moscow."

"They got the apartments through postings around mailboxes. In those days people who wanted to rent their apartment would post a notice near the apartment mailbox with little tabs hanging off with their telephone number on 10 little cut slips of paper." ... I went to him, I said look, you know I can maybe find foreigners that are looking to rent apartments."

"I went to them and said that I could find foreigners looking to rent apartments to augment their Russian clients. They didn't have any idea how to deal with a foreigner at the time. So, I posted a small ad in the *Moscow Times*, which I think was coming out once or twice a week in those early days. It literally said 'New York broker for leasing apartments, call Brad.' Then it listed the phone number for my apartment. I did not have a pager or a mobile phone. I got a couple of businessmen that were calling because hotel prices were exorbitant at that time. For guys that were really looking to dig their heels into Russia, they figured it would be sensible to find a place to live for a reasonable amount of money in comparison to what a hotel would cost."

"I started to do deals. ... The agreement with the Russian friends of my stepbrother was that we would split fees 50/50. On a $500 deal, we each got $250. When you're 22–23 years old, living in a foreign country $250 bucks could go quite a long way. ... I was back on the money trail."

"Next thing you know, I'm doing $500 deals and then it was $1,000 deals. Suddenly, I'm doing deals like $3,000."

"As more affluent, sophisticated businessmen began to come in, they started to look for apartments with security and a nice entrance. They didn't want to walk into an entrance where there was some drunk sleeping on the floor and the dogs and cats had done their business. … So, the commissions were going higher. Russians understood that they could make significant money for just basically renting out their apartment and moving to their dacha, or to another apartment they owned, or move in with their sister or their brother. … To receive $1,000, $2,000, $3,000 or more dollars per month for Russians in the early 1990's was massive."

"I went out on my own and in a very short period, I was contacted by a young German man and an American woman. They proposed that we work together. At that time, there was only a handful of Americans or other foreigners doing real estate. … We would find apartments that we had pre-identified that would be likable for foreigners. Then we would rent these apartments and we'd renovate them. We put in a very simple cosmetic renovation, basically a whitewash. … You know, structured wallpaper and some better doors. We would get the parquet sanded and make it nice, put in an inexpensive kitchen. These amenities were like gold to foreigners at the time. We gave them something to move into that was a little bit closer to what they were used to at home. It was clean, it was fresh, no cracks in the walls or cobwebs hanging from the corners."

"Anyway, we started to do business for USAID. We got to know the director of the housing department at USAID, and they needed a lot of units for incoming people. … We even did a deal for the USAID Director for Russia at the time. We put together a massive apartment for him. It was a little controversial because the apartment had housed five or six families, living in this massive communal apartment. It was like 300 plus square meters. … I think that there was even a bit of news about it asking why there were two people living in 300 square meters where there had been 50 people living. … That was probably the biggest residential deal that we did."

"Then we flipped into the commercial agency business, and we dropped the whole residential side all together. We decided why spend the time trying to make $2,000 on a residential rental when you could make $30,000 on a commercial rental. … Suddenly you're sitting at a desk or at a conference table across from the head of the Coopers and Lybrand worldwide real estate division. Here is this 57-year-old guy who's been in the real estate market for 30 years finding real estate for their offices around the world. Now he's coming to you because you're the guy."

"Even today when you're living in Russia, you still feel like someone important. I think that this is a part of the problem for some guys that made it their career to be in Russia and to put up with whatever was going on there at that time. They came back to the States, and they were just another snuck. You were a guy with some good experiences, maybe you had a bit of scratch in your pocket, but you were one tiny little guppy in an ocean. In Russia, in Moscow, you were a fish of a different color, and you could have an impact. This is true even to this day, although it has significantly diminished over time."

"You know we were good people, but we were there for the money. It was fun and it was exciting. And we were there to make our fortunes. … Somehow you felt like 'somebody' at 22, 23, 24 years old. Maybe this is just me speaking. I'm not going to speak for other expatriates."

"By the time 1996, 1997 rolled around, we had a huge book of clients. We were one of the biggest commercial agencies there. It was us. It was Haskell. It was the Noble Givens guys. … Most of those guys went on to be successful and the trend was to convert from this foreign-owned, foreign-managed small local real estate company to a multinational affiliated group. People started pairing off with these big international agencies, primarily in the commercial market. Everybody kind of picked partners and went about their business."

Brad Garine's company was called Global ABMP. It developed an association with Jones Lang Wooten. Then Jones Land Wooten became Jones Lang LaSalle and acquired Global ABMP. "So they made the final acquisition in 1997. We remained on as partners of the office there in Russia. We became members of the European board of Jones Lang LaSalle. All these big heavy things that you dream about. … And then 1998 came along, and it was game over." Brad Garine left Russia as the result of the 1998 crisis and came back to the United States. Ultimately, he went back to Russia and got involved in other startup ventures.

Hotels and Restaurants – Modernizing in Western Style

Just as the real estate sector was born initially out of foreign–stimulated demand, the same factors led to a dramatic transformation of hotels and restaurants as this sector adapted to European and US standards. As in other sectors, restaurants began with joint ventures, like TrenMos described in Chapter 1 and then rapidly accelerated with new private ventures in the Yeltsin period that then deeply penetrated the consumer food patterns of Russia society, ranging from high-end dining to fast food outlets.

As the Soviet Union began to open for foreign economic activity in the Gorbachev period, there was a slow growth of the foreign expat community, concentrated in Moscow and to a lesser extent in St. Petersburg. This community had a social life clustered around the US Embassy with basketball games, a bar and holiday celebrations. As the expat community grew, the center of gravity for its social life began to shift to the early foreign hotels and then to an expanding number of restaurants and other recreational outlets like gyms and clubs like the Moscow Country Club. As the Russian economy began to recover in the late 1990s, these early foreign institutions shaped the explosive growth of Russian restaurants, clubs, gyms, and recreational facilities.

Hotels played an important role in the late Gorbachev period as foreigners came to investigate business opportunities and began to open offices. In the Soviet period, hotels played a specific role in tourism and business travel and were closely monitored and controlled by the KGB. Some of the larger Soviet hotels, like the Cosmos, were constructed to accommodate foreign visitors for the 1980 Winter Olympic games. In addition to the Soviet hotels, there were a small number of foreign owned or managed hotels in Moscow pre-Gorbachev.

The Olympic Penta Hotel was opened to accommodate foreign visitors for the 1980 Moscow Winter Olympics. Penta Hotels was originally a joint venture of five European airlines (hence "Penta") that were established in major gateway cities served by those airlines to accommodate flight attendants, pilots and other guests.

The Aerostar Hotel on Leningradsky Avenue was another Soviet-era hotel serving foreign visitors. It opened on May 1, 1991, as a European style hotel. The Aerostar managed by a Canadian company but was Soviet owned.

Both the Penta and the Aerostar served a primarily international clientele and were business gathering points during the Gorbachev period. As business interest in the Soviet Union increased, the demand for accommodations for foreign business travelers, particularly for international class level of facilities and services, continued to grow beyond the available supply.

Radisson Slavyanskaya

As a symbol of the growing Soviet–American business ties, Radisson International opened the first American–Russian joint venture hotel, the Radisson Slavyanskaya. It was significant departure from the existing hotels because it was managed by Radisson International and because it included the Americom Business Center that could accommodate a growing number of international company offices. Once opened, it quickly became the iconic go-to location for business travelers and for business networking between foreigners and Russians. It was originally announced on May 30, 1990, during a visit of Gorbachev to the United States. It was planned as a 430-room hotel, with 165 suites for business offices in a connected business center building. The American partners were Radisson Hotels International of Minneapolis and Americom International Corporation of Irvine, California, led by Paul Tatum. The City of Moscow was the Russian partner. The deal was arranged through a Russian émigré in Minneapolis who had connections in the Moscow government.[3] The ownership structure of the joint venture was set up as the City of Moscow owning 50 percent, Americom owning 40 percent, and Radisson owning 10 percent.

The actual process of opening the Radisson Slavyanskaya illustrates the character of the times and the battles over cash flow that occurred in early joint ventures. The Radisson was soon followed by other foreign and Russian business class hotels, but it had great significance as the pathbreaking hotel venture. The American Paul O'Brien was instrumental for the early-stage operations of the Radisson Slavyanskaya. O'Brien was an experienced professional in hotel/restaurant business who had retired to open his own restaurant in California. In a casual call to the Vice President of Radisson, who he knew from the industry, the Radisson VP asked what it would take for him to come back into the hotel business. Paul replied that "it would have to be something really interesting." When he learned that Radisson was opening the first American hotel in the Soviet Union, Paul replied "wow, that's pretty interesting." Two weeks later, he was in Minnesota at the Radisson headquarters discussing joining the project.

"I got to Russia on St Patrick's Day 1991and I left in December of 2021, 30 years later. … I'll never forget, I was on a Pan Am flight. There was about six people on the flight. When I landed, it was late, around 11 o'clock at night and I did not speak Russian." He took a taxi to the hotel. "I showed up and the hotel was dark. There was a guy with a machine gun out front who did not speak English obviously. Finally, they buzzed me in and was able to reach the Vice President of Radisson who was living there and had been sent to open the hotel. That was how important they considered the project that they sent a vice president. He was an excellent leader. Anyway, he came down and let me in, then took me to my room. I got to my room and the pillows were like straw. It had a black and white TV. The phone was the old dial telephone. … You know, the carpet was terrible. It was just not a good property."

"I went through the whole process of interviewing people, and we had an unbelievable staff when we finally opened. … We hired about 180 people."

"The opening went a little gradual at first. Both sides were supposed to put more money into the venture. The city government never put in any more money and so Radisson did not either."

"So, Norlander who was the President of Radisson, a great guy, and a great leader, called us. He said listen, what can we do to open the hotel. I said, 'we need linen, we need this, and we need that.' He asked what they could do to open fifty or a hundred rooms. I said, 'whatever you send me over I will use to open.' He sent over the stuff by plane, the sheets, the pillows, the stuff to make it a bit habitable."

"So, we opened, and we only charged like S129 per night or something like that. The big famous Soviet hotels are charging $300 per night."

"The day we opened we sold out. And then we continued to sell out and we had all this money coming in. So, Radisson was very happy and asked if we could open another hundred rooms. I said, 'send me this stuff and we will open them.' Within 9–10 months, we had them all open. It was a cash machine. … The most that we were paying the average employee was $300 a month. We paid some managers $500 a month, so payroll was negligible. So, it was a money machine. It evolved to where I was told that it was the most profitable Radisson in the company, and they had some 300 hotels at that time."

"It was Western clientele, not all Americans. In the beginning, there were more Germans in Moscow. … But as soon as the foreign companies started coming in, they'd all come to the Radisson because the Americom Business Center was where they intended to rent an office and set up everything."

"The hotel was one half, and the other half was the Americom Business Center. The Americom Business Center was bringing in big companies like Apple and Xerox. These companies were running their Russia operations out of the Business Center."

The Radisson thus became one of a handful of international branded hotels serving foreign visitors and tourists that also became a critical meeting ground for business.

Expat Restaurants – Transforming Russian Restaurant Dining

The Soviet Union had a comprehensive food and catering system ranging from a limited number of high-end, prestigious restaurants to inexpensive cafes and buffet cafeterias (stolovaya). These were supported by a logistics and food supply system integrated into the centrally planned economy with a structured administrative staff. The quality of the food on offer was often poor and access to high end restaurants was highly restricted. So ordinary Russians did not often go to restaurants. Foreigners found this system baffling, incomprehensible and difficult to navigate.

The expansion of the expat community in Moscow drove the creation of an increasing number of restaurants initially to serve foreigners. Expats wanted places they could hang out that mimicked what they were used to elsewhere in the world. Over time, these restaurants began to include a Russian clientele, but continued to have an American character and served as examples of American life and culture. Two of the icons of American influence in Moscow, Uncle Guilly's and the Starlight Diner were founded by the same group of American expat entrepreneurs, some of whom have already appeared earlier in this book.

The foreign impact on restaurants and the place they played in the new emerging culture of the new Russia had a profound and lasting impact on Russia life. The clearest example is the role of Rosinter Restaurants Holding (Rosinter) and its portfolio of restaurants in leading wholesale modernization of restaurants in Russia.

Along with the restaurants highlighted here, there were other famous and sometimes notorious restaurants and bars that catered primarily to the burgeoning expat community and foreign business visitors but had very little lasting impact on Russian society as a whole. Among expats, one of the most well-known bars was the Hungry Duck, founded by Canadians and famous primarily as a heavy-drinking place for foreign men and Russian women to meet. Equally famous for analogous reasons was Night Flight, a restaurant and bar founded by a Swede and frequented by foreign business visitors who were looking for paid sex with beautiful Russian women. These and similar places played an outsized role in the lore of the wild 1990s among expats but had very limited impact on Russian life and society therefore they were not included in the narrative of this book.

Uncle Guilly's – American Steak House

As already referenced in Chapter 3, Bernie Sucher initiated and helped fund a number of businesses targeting expats that became iconic in the foreign community in Moscow, including the fitness center Moscow Beach Club and the restaurants Uncle Guilly's and Starlight Diner. These projects were all separate businesses under the umbrella of Flying Foods, a partnership of three Americans and one Russian. The American partners were Bernie Sucher, Paul O'Brien, who was already introduced in the section on the Radisson Slavyanskaya hotel, and Shawn McKenna, who came to Russia with a food distribution company. The Russian partner was Oleg Bardeev, a young and well-connected Russian businessman.

Uncle Guilly's was opened in 1993 as an American steak house in a renovated vaulted cellar of a building dating back to the 1700s. The building was very close to Moscow City Hall. Paul O'Brien described the location. "You went downstairs and went in this little door. It was a brick building with little rooms and everything. It wasn't really big, but it was a really cool. ... We opened a 45-seat steak restaurant with a 15-seat bar. We did two and a half million dollars in revenue the first year." The popularity and profitability of the restaurant was a bit of a surprise to the founders. Bernie Sucher described how they originally conceived of it as a place for expats looking for a good quality steak, but quickly it began to attract a Russian clientele as well.

American entrepreneurship operating in the Russian business conditions of those times not only resulted in a highly successful and profitable business but also spawned several copycat steak restaurants in Moscow.

Starlight Diner – American Diner in Moscow

The story that Bernie Sucher recounted about the origin of the idea for the Starlight Diner was that it emerged from an after-basketball discussion of Bernie's US Embassy basketball group about how great it would be to have a Denny's in Moscow to go to after basketball. The idea evolved into a new separate company incorporated in Cyprus as Starlight Development Overseas, Ltd to develop and own a series of diners serving American diner food.

The Starlight Diner became the iconic gathering spot for Americans in Moscow homesick for American style food and a window into American food culture for Russians. Paul O'Brien described the opening of the new diner. "We opened the diner in January 1996 and the first day we opened we had lines. ... We had it built in Florida and shipped it by boat. We ordered the 110-seat model. ... We drove to St Petersburg because the boat was going to come in there. The boat came in and there is no diner. ... They call around and find out that they offloaded it by mistake in Bremen Germany."

"We had to postpone everything. We got trucks and we drove it from Germany to Moscow. We'd already laid the foundation and utilities. We took a seven-ton crane to pick up the three modules and put them on the foundation. We brought six guys from America to put it, together. We were open within two weeks. ... We had lines from the first time we opened. We did four and a half million dollars first year." Ultimately, there were four Starlight Diners scattered around Moscow, with the original one burning down in a fire in 2017.

Rosinter – Modernizing Fine Dining and Fast Food

The career of Henrik Winther in Russia dramatically illustrates the profound and continuing impact of Americans on changing how Russians viewed restaurants and the development of popular restaurant culture. Born in Dallas, Texas of Danish parents, Henrik, and his family moved back to Denmark at an early age. Then when he was in his early teens, the family moved to Southern France where they managed a hotel and restaurant on the Cote d'Azur. Later, he returned to the United States and worked for several restaurant companies, including Marriott.

By 1990, he was back in France managing the family business when he saw an ad for a restaurant director in Moscow that changed his life. "It was in the International Herald Tribune. Those ads were like one and a half lines in length. So anyway, it was enough to catch my attention. I called him up and one thing led to another, they wanted me to come to Moscow."

The ad had been placed by a Venezuelan entrepreneur of Russian background, Rostislav Ordovsky-Tanaevsky Blanco. Winther explained how Rostislav Blanco's motivation for starting a restaurant was quite different than that of Paul O'Brien and other expat entrepreneurs. Blanco was not specifically interested in restaurants as such. His interest was in finding a way around the inconvertibility of the ruble at that time. As Henrik explained, "He came over in 1988 or 1989 and started up Kodak distribution in the Soviet Union. He had a problem in his Kodak business. He wanted to sell Kodak products for rubles. But this was a problem because at that time you could not convert rubles into dollars to pay his supplier. ... But a law was passed allowing for opening up hard currency restaurants. The idea came to him to open a hard currency restaurant with dollars from the restaurant going to pay Kodak and the rubles from the Kodak sales going to pay for the expenses of the restaurant. ... Primarily it was a currency convertibility issue that he wanted to solve."

"Rostislav had a friend in Spain that he brought over to help him open his very first restaurant. ... But at the point when he brought me over, it was because he needed more currency conversion. He needed more restaurants. He was not a restauranteur. He is an entrepreneur. So, I joined him in Rosinter, and I opened over 400 restaurants over the next 17 years throughout Russia and the CIS, but primarily in Russia."

"Rosinter quickly grew into its own business. In 1993, we opened the American Bar and Grill, the Santa Fe, Patio Pizza, Conti's sandwich place and Rostik, the Russian fried chicken equivalent of KFC. ... By the end of 1993, we had probably about 25 restaurants or so. By probably 1996, we got up to 100 restaurants. It was going quite fast, and it was hard to make sure that the wheels didn't fall off the wagon."

"There was no reservoir of knowledge or knowledgeable people to run a professional restaurant in European or Western style. They were just not there. So, it had to be done with foreign expertise. We brought in a lot of Americans and Europeans, but they were deeply handicapped by not speaking Russian. So, it's always kind of a difficult trade off. This was the case up until the default in 1998. I think we fired about 75 foreigners in 1998. Most of the restaurants were already managed by Russians by that point in time.

"When we began Russians thought a restaurant was a Soviet restaurant. So, what is a restaurant that's not Soviet? They just could not fathom what that should be. They just did not get what a restaurant was supposed to be. You could try to explain it to them, and you can try to demonstrate it to them. But for them, it was just kind of abstract words didn't take on a place in their imagination that they could strive for."

"So, we had to start at a very basic level, training, teaching, and involving. It's not only technical skills, but it's the emotional part of being in the service industry. We know that in Soviet times they never smiled, only crazies smiled. ... For us to have staff that are energetic, smiling, talkative, relaxed was very difficult, but nevertheless objectively we had to just go ahead and systematically create them."

"We created a school of hospitality. It was an internal development program for all positions. We needed to fill new positions in all new restaurants. We needed maybe 500 managers and directors a year. ... So, we needed a big throughput. Then obviously you have turnover of staff. Competitors loved to hire our people because they were the only people that learned something about the hospitality industry. People that we trained, educated, and brought into our thinking system were high value targets for anybody else that wanted to open a restaurant in Moscow. The only alternative was to take another foreigner at a foreigner's salary. And well, we know where that goes."

In discussing the most difficult aspects of training, Henrik pointed to "the most ingrained is this lack of smiling and enthusiasm. It's something that took a lot of my efforts early on. It must have been in 1994, something like that. I had been wanting to have people to wear name tags as is normal in Western restaurants. ... It was impossible. People quit, refused, walked off work. They didn't want it. They were scared that people would know what their name. They were fearful that the distance between them and the guests might be less and that was very threatening to them. We're talking about some deep-seated cultural obstacles, barriers, due to the isolation of the country for the previous seventy years."

"When you go to a restaurant it is not only to eat. You also go there because you feel good while you're eating. So, it's such a critical part of the experience. It was our unique competitive advantage that we gained through the 1990s. We were the only restaurant company that was driving standards, consistent standards. It didn't mean that we were perfect all the time, no way, by far. ... The standard level of the foreign restaurants in Moscow in those days was still immature and low budget. We just did things right, so that became a competitive advantage. Now that's all changed. But in those days, it was a big part of our business model and therefore all the focus we had on training and human development."

Henrik Winther and Rosinter not only created a new culture of service orientation among its staff, but also created its own infrastructure to supply its rapidly expanding network of restaurants. "Going back to 1991, 1992, 1993, in those early years when we were expanding to 25 restaurants, we couldn't buy anything in a regular supermarket. There were no supermarkets. We were forced to open our own warehouse distribution center. We bought a warehouse, a big one, and fitted it out."

"A distribution center was important for our business because we bought everything, the wine, the alcohol, the meat, everything in Europe and shipped it into Russia. ... Well, I shouldn't say everything. We did buy Russian vegetables and fruits, but a lot of the key products were imported. Even for those fruits and vegetables that were bought locally, there were no suppliers of fruit and vegetables in the local market. There was no distributor you could just call up and say can you bring me seven cases of tomatoes, please. So, we set up this distribution system or facility to just service our restaurants. It grew into a whole different business that was then later sold off. Today it is still in business under a different name."

"We also had to have lots of cars. We had a lot of foreigners, and they were all helpless. So, everybody had to have a car with a driver for distribution to the restaurants, there was also the need for a lot of trucks. So where do you get those cars serviced? Well again, there was nobody you could really call to do that quality wise. So, we had to set up eight automotive repair service facilities, huge hangars with trucks in and out getting repaired for the road. We had a whole group of Soviet cars that were shared and that broke down all the time. There was a lot to do there."

"Then there is the bakery where we would buy bread for the restaurant. If you cannot find bread, there's nobody to call. So, you go out there and you make your own bread. ... And then you set up a big bakery and production facility. Then you needed to distribute all this bread to all the restaurants, again more trucks, and more drivers and so forth."

In addition to shaping and modernizing supply chains, Henrik Winther had a quirky and interesting impact on what food choices there are in Russian restaurants. "Why in every restaurant in Russia today is Caesar salad on the menu? It's a popular salad worldwide but it's not on every menu in every restaurant in that country, like in Russia. It is actually a funny story. The very first restaurant that we opened, Le Chalet, was kind of fine dining, and our best-selling specialty salad was Caesar salad done table side. The waiter would bring out the egg, capers, the mustard, etc. He would fix the sauce, put in the cheese, toss the salad, and serve it. It was really a fantastic salad because I had done it in United States for years before that. And every waiter was required to know how to make it."

"So, when anybody was about to open a restaurant, the first place they would go to find employees would be my restaurant because they had at least had some training. ... So, I had high turnover of staff. When these new restaurants began, no matter what they were doing, they always had to consider what was going to be on the menu. Always, the staff would say Caesar salad because they knew how to make it. It meant that in the 1990s every restaurant had Caesar salad because there was this little pool of expertise that was seeded at the launch of the Russian hospitality business. It just took off and infiltrated the whole industry. It's an obvious example, but there's a lot of other things that we did in corporate policies that spread through the industry."

"One of the issues that I have driven home very strongly and consistently for the last 30 years is customer service. It was so obvious in the 1990s that it was so critically needed that something had to change. But it was never a broadly accepted business practice in Russia. I guess maybe people didn't have to, or they weren't able to undertake such fundamental training. Most of the restaurant change in those days was just in a couple of small restaurants. … What I see today is that the focus on customer service and guest contact has found some fuel. … I see that, in that sense the Russian restaurant hospitality business has in many ways leap frogged Europe and United States in service awareness and service."

In addition to operational and menu impact, Henrik Winther also contributed to changing the target audience for restaurants by developing Russian fast food and casual dining. "Going into the fast-food segment with fried chicken [Rostik's] was a big play for a broad customer base. Even though our other restaurants were priced in convertible currency, fast-food was sold for rubles." Then later in the 1990s, after Russia had begun to recover from the crash of 1998, the company was involved in the Sushi craze that swept through Russia. "In 1998, we opened the second sushi restaurant in Moscow. It was one of the very first affordable casual dining sushi restaurants, called Planet Sushi. … I think that within five years we probably had 40 Planet Sushi restaurants."

In assessing his impact on the restaurant business, Henrik Winther spoke of the general context. "It was very exciting, because you were doing something that you knew nobody had done before. You are a pioneer. Every step that you took you knew that nobody stepped there before."

"It was not a matter of opening restaurants, that was the easy part. It was opening distribution and supply for the restaurants that was important."

"The whole point is that no matter what the task was when I opened my restaurants, it pulled along a whole pool of other service businesses that in Europe or America you normally would just make a phone call for. This internal system included the training school that we discussed. It became a major project that we were able to pump out these hundreds and hundreds of trained managers. It was a very big, exciting project, and I was feeling that I was changing the Soviet Union. I was changing the country from the Soviet Union into a new world and new way of thinking. In that sense, it was very satisfying. There was a certain acknowledgement that this was happening. Still when you are in the midst of it, maybe it was a little hard to understand a historical perspective on what you are doing, and what the impact is. As the years went into the mid 1990's, and the later 1990's that whole kind of introspection became more and more clear."

Entertainment and Media – Embracing the American Cultural Invasion

In contrast to the real estate, hotel and restaurant sectors, the American influence in the entertainment sector was not driven primarily by demand from expats. It was the result of entrepreneurs seeing the opportunity for private companies to enter the space that had been the exclusive preserve of the Soviet Union and to present Western-style popular culture to Russian audiences in non-political, but immensely impactful venues of radio, TV, and print journalism.

As already discussed in Chapter 2, there was a very large-scale, US government-funded effort through Internews to develop a professional independent news industry in Russia. It was part of the effort to create and support new civil society institutions and that could arguably be considered an effort to reshape Russian political life. The new private media world also suffered through the so-called media wars of the 1990s in which oligarch-controlled private media outlets were part of the battle for power and influence in the Yeltsin period. In distinction, the entrepreneurs in this chapter by and large sought to avoid politics and to focus on business opportunities. It may be that these business media companies had greater long-term impact on Russian life than the directly politically oriented efforts of Internews. This is yet to be determined, but the impact of the companies profiled here on everyday Russian life is unquestioned.

One of these business entrepreneurial ventures was highlighted in Chapter 3 in the interview with Drew Guff of Russia Partners, which created Russian MTV. This chapter will look at similar projects in movie theaters, FM radio, TV and print media that were primarily targeted at market opportunities created by the transition from the Soviet system to a market-based new Russian economy.

In the movie theater, FM radio, and independent TV examples to follow, there is a repeating pattern of American entrepreneurs bringing Western technology and business methods to Russia that is absorbed and assimilated by Russians over the decade of the 1990s and ultimately ending up in Russian ownership.

Kodak Kino Mir and Kinostar De Lux

Paul Heth is a military veteran and entrepreneur who came to Russia at age 29 to develop trade in timber products. As he recounted, he was floating on the sea of capitalism with the mindset that anything is possible. He also emphasized that he always was respectful of his Russian counterparts and polite in his dealings. But he was there for the business opportunity and had no agenda to change Russia. Over time, he became of the major modernizers of the Russian movie industry.

When the timber project failed to develop, he was in Moscow looking for other opportunities. He came up with the idea of opening a movie theater that would show American movies, primarily to expats. He then negotiated a lease with Paul Tatum for the conference space at the Radisson Slavyanskaya in 1992 or 1993 where Heth regularly screened movies under the name, American House of Cinema. Later he became a victim of the power struggle over control of the American Business Center already discussed in the section about the Radisson Slavyanskaya. When Paul Tatum was murdered, the new Chechen general director of the Americom Business Center representing the City of Moscow revoked Heth's lease. This forced Heth to move his movie theater business to the Penta Hotel, where again the primary audience were expats looking for entertainment in their own language.

In the process, Paul Heth had his eye on a much bigger market opportunity in the movie industry. The Soviet Union had a legacy of a very large, professional film industry financed by the government. Soviet citizens had long established habits of attending movies in large numbers, averaging from 33 to 35 visits per year, although the theaters themselves were austere and very basic. With the dissolution of the Soviet Union, government financing of the movie industry collapsed, with an ongoing decline in both the number of new Russian films and closing of movie theaters. Foreign films, dominated by Hollywood films, entered Russia in pirated video cassettes that made Russia the piracy capital of the world.

For Paul Heth, these conditions brought an opportunity that he was able to realize through a chance meeting with a Kodak film sales executive in Moscow. Kodak had had relatively strong sales of film to the Soviet film industry that were now dramatically reduced. Paul proposed that instead of providing the raw material for movies, Kodak should partner with him to provide movies directly to the Russian public. Together they developed Kodak Kino Mir, the first modern film theater in Russia. When it opened in 1996, it kick-started a revival of the Russian film industry.

Kodak Kino Mir had an American theater atmosphere with a flashy lobby, stereo sound, Coca Cola, and popcorn in a 600-seat theater. Kino Mir opened with the movie "The Rock," starring Sean Connery. The lines were out the door to get into the theater. The first year they had one million visitors and were the highest grossing movie theater in the world. At one point, they grossed 50 percent of all movie revenues in Russia.[4]

In later years, Paul Heth partnered with Sheri Redstone to create a new company, Kinostar De Lux that began to develop movie megaplexes as part of the malls created by IKEA. He also became involved in financing and developing new Russian movies and was still operating in the industry at the time of the interview in 2021.

Radio Maximum and CTC TV

Peter Gerwe was introduced to Russia as the producer of the US Festival featured in Chapter 1. After graduating from university, he went to work for Steve Wozniak and cut his teeth in the media business producing the US Festival. In the process, he got to know James Hickman as well as the Russian side of the space bridges of the 1980s, GOSTELERADIO and the Ministry of Communications. This led to an entrepreneurial career in Russian FM radio and independent television.

Gerwe recounted that "my first trip was in 1984 in conjunction with producing the US Festival." Later he and James Hickman looked for ways to continue their Russia adventures. "... with Hickman, we started doing all this kind of stuff like selling film for rubles to convert rubles to convertible currency. There was a lot of wild stuff between 1984 and 1990. ... Then by 1990 with perestroika, all kinds of stuff started opening up. ... I said let's do a radio station." There were no radio stations at that time operating on standard Western FM frequencies. The Soviet Union had operated FM radio on different frequencies. So, Peter opened his own company, StoryFirst Communications and started Radio Maximum, which was one of the two first FM radio stations in Russia. The other one was Europa Plus, which was started by a French company. As Peter expressed it, "The key thing about it, which was interesting was that you could start things from scratch that you could then build." And build, he did.

"So, our station was called Radio Maximum. We launched on December 25, 1991, the day that Gorbachev resigned, and the Soviet Union dissolved. This is a true story. We were supposed to launch on January 1, 1992, but we decided to start a week early and just continuously play Beatles music. The first song played was 'All You Need is Love' and the second was 'Back in the USSR.' *Moscow News* was our partner. We went on air and about an hour into the broadcast one of the big bosses came in and told us that the Soviet Union just broke up. I thought he was kidding. He wanted to go on air immediately. I said, 'wait a minute, no news, no news.' So, we negotiated this terse two sentence statement of what had happened that we played at the top of every hour."

"We really did not do any advertising at all to publicize our station. Everyone knew about Radio Maximum right away, anyone who was cool. They were already making dual band receivers for sale in Russia for a year or two but there was nothing there on FM. ... Then you have Madonna, the Beatles and everything. It took off like a rocket."

"It was owned by Westwood One Radio Networks and Harris Corporation and me. Westwood One was the biggest radio software programming company in the world, a billion dollar, NASDAQ listed music programming company. Harris Corporation was one of the biggest producers of transmitters in the world."

"When I was putting the project together, I went to these guys and said 'hey, I can get radio licenses and let's build radio stations in Russia. Let's build one in every city.' They said great idea. The funny thing was that the Westwood One guy said 'we don't really need you. We will do it ourselves.' So, he got on his private plane and flew to Moscow with his wife. His wife is a famous radio personality, and they stayed at the most expensive hotel in Moscow. She went to take a bath and turned on the water, which came out yellow. She freaked out, completely lost it. Then they went to the first few business meetings, and they got questions like, 'what is FM radio and how does it work?' He then got back on his jet that afternoon and flew back to the US. He called me from the plane and said, 'go do your deal.'"

At that point, Peter Gerwe started building partnerships in Russia for new radio stations with the backing of Westwood One and Harris. Westwood One provided programming and sent an expert to Russia to assist Peter. Harris was providing new transmitters for the local radio stations. "Harris started shipping transmitters. The Ministry of Communications guys saw people getting a brand-new Harris transmitter and it is like a Rolls Royce rolling into their showroom. So now, I was friends with all of them. They were calling me to say that they wanted one of those."

As Peter Gerwe began to make a name for himself with the expansion of the FM radio network, Radio Maximum, his involvement with the Ministry of Communications led him into the private television business. "We launched Radio Maximum in 1992 and my name started to get out. Six months later, I get called into a meeting. I had lots of meetings with the Ministry of Communications guys where they would not give you their names or their cards. They just sat there, didn't say anything, or ask a question. There was one guy who ran the meeting. So, I was in one of those meetings. There was this guy sitting there who told me that he was from St. Petersburg and had the first 24-hour private TV station license in the country." Peter Gerwe ended up partnering with this guy and building a TV station in St. Petersburg.

"So, we built a TV station. It was the most painful experience I ever had. Then we moved on to build eight stations around Moscow. It took me a whole year and we paid to rewire the whole city. We really did not turn on our station for a year while we were testing and testing until we had perfect reception. Then we launched CTC Network. We thought that we would have maybe 50 stations as affiliated stations under agreement in our network by the end of the year. As it turned out, by the end of the first year, we had 300 affiliated stations and 85 percent penetration of the Russian market."

"All the Ministry guys were grabbing licenses and building their own stations, but they did not have any programming. We provided them with programming as our network affiliates. It was just entertainment. We did not have any news. We had better penetration than half of the TV networks that got all the press coverage. Nobody ever talked about us. We were happy with that. ... We did a movie every night at nine o'clock, very simple programming. I think Hill Street Blues was our first American series. ... Then we started producing local Russian TV series. ... And those were really big. That's what really made the company."

As CTC continued to grow into the third largest TV network in Russia, it came under increasing pressure from Yeltsin-era Russian oligarchs, particularly as a purely foreign-owned network.

In 1997, the Russian oligarch Vladimir Gusinsky, who owned the rival network, NTV, contacted Gerwe and stated his intention to buy out CTC.[5] "So, we had meetings with people like Gusinsky, saying 'oh you're so smart, but you should sell it to us now.'" After Gerwe refused to sell, Gusinsky hired all of CTC's senior staff in a bid to cripple the network, but he failed.[6]

A different kind of pressure came from being such a visible foreign-owned TV station and having such a prominent role in the Russian market. "We operated under licenses from the Russian government. There were some guys that I knew in the licensing division, including one, who was a very honorable man. ... He said that he could not just keep giving us licenses as an American company. This was not right. So, we came up with a whole new strategy by doing a deal with Mikhail Fridman's Alfa-Group. The Alpha-Group bought 25 percent of the network. They did not want more because they wanted to be able to say that they only had a minority stake. ... They were the best partners, just the best, great people."

Like others profiled in this book, the 1998 crisis had a huge impact on CTC Media. "We cut the staff from 1000 to 200. Then we stayed at the level of 200 staff as the market came back. Our revenues shot up and we just kept a low overhead." CTC Media also got a boost in the aftermath of 1998 by a group of investors, including Delta Capital Management.[7]

By 2006, CTC Media was listed on the NASDAQ and conducted an initial public offering valued at $2.3 billion. The company valuation went up to $4 billion at its peak. Peter Gerwe completely left CTC Media and has followed other ventures through his company StoryFirst. By 2015, CTC Media was sold to a Russian company owned by Russian billionaire Alisher Usmanov and his business partner Ivan Tavrin because of the 2014 Russian legislation restricting foreign ownership of media companies to no more than 20 percent. This transfer of ownership completed the transition to full Russian control for political reasons. It does not in any way negate the impact of American introduction of foreign technology and business methods in the 1990s that deeply impacted how Russians entertained themselves through FM radio and through their home television.

Moscow Times and *Cosmopolitan*

As has been stated and restated repeatedly, the focus of this book is on the influence of Americans on Russia in the 1990s, while acknowledging the important impact of Europeans and other foreigners. However, the impact of Derk Sauer, the Danish journalist and publisher, who was the founder of the *Moscow Times* and publisher of the Russian version of *Cosmopolitan* must be included because of their importance to the story of those times.

Derk Sauer initially came to Russia in 1988 to publish the very first glossy English language magazine in Russia, *Moscow Magazine*. This magazine was a joint venture between his employer, VNU, a Dutch publishing company and the Russian Union of Journalists. "It was in both English and Russian language. The English version was for distribution in hotels and the Russian version in kiosks. It was basically like *New York Magazine*. ... It was actually quite an interesting magazine, but it was not a real commercial enterprise."

"The journalists from the Union of Journalists were not real journalists. They really didn't contribute anything. This was really at the beginning of glasnost and perestroika. They all had this crazy idea that if you work with a foreign company then you immediately get rich. So, the first thing they asked is when do we go on vacation. ... They thought, now we work for an international company, so we don't have to work. Work was not on their mind at all. ... *Moscow Magazine* was launched in the spring of 1990, and it lasted a year and a half."

The Dutch publisher pulled the plug on *Moscow Magazine*, but Derk and his wife had no intention of leaving Russia. He started an English language newsletter with information about where to shop and similar things. This led him to start his next venture, *Moscow Times*. "We estimated that, at that time there were about 30,000 expats in Moscow in 1992 and we thought there was a market opportunity for an English language paper."

Derk started the *Moscow Times* with a Dutch friend using his personal savings. They went to the Radisson Slavyanskaya and made a deal with Paul Tatum before the hotel and the Americom Business Center even opened to get office space for the new publication in return for promoting the Radisson Slavyanskaya. They then made another barter deal with the Soviet newspaper Pravda to print their paper in return for Dutch cheese know-how for the Pravda-owned dairy farm.

"Of course, it turned out to be much more difficult than I had ever imagined. ... The idea was for free circulation. We were probably the first free circulation newspaper in the world. Later that became a model with Metro newspapers and so on. But the idea was free circulation supported by advertising. ... With all the foreigners that came into Russia, most of our readers were Russian because it was a very good tool for them to get in touch with Western companies."

Despite having carved out an innovative role as a pioneering newspaper for the growing expat community and for linking Russians to the expanding job market with foreign companies, the *Moscow Times* struggled financially. "We could not cover the costs. For two years, we were really, really struggling. ... And then my wife said that we should start a women's magazine." At that time in Russia, there were only two women's magazines in Russia, both holdovers from Soviet times, *Farm Women* and *Factory Women*.

Derk elaborated on his wife's idea and proposed that they should introduce *Cosmopolitan* to Russia. "We chased Hearst all over the world to try to get this license, which was very tough because they just had done an unsuccessful joint venture with *Izvestia*. ... They were very skeptical and had a very bad experience. But we convinced them and that saved us. *Cosmopolitan* was launched in 1994 as a joint venture with Hearst. ... It was launched two years after *Moscow Times* and was far more successful financially." Derk's wife Ellen was the Editor of *Cosmopolitan* in Russia.

Despite being a joint venture with Hearst's *Cosmopolitan*, the team in Moscow created a lot of their own content. "Most of the photography was from *Cosmopolitan* and some articles. But from the very beginning, we did a lot of our own content, Russian content. It was very hard to adapt articles from the Hearst publication to Russian life in those days. The Russian style of living of women was so different from the US that you could not just copy or translate articles. You had to find your own angle to it. The topics were the same, fashion, sex, lifestyle."

"*Cosmopolitan* basically created the market for magazines in Russia. There was really nothing else there. The Soviet women's magazines were sold through kiosks, very old-fashioned and very slow. ... What we did was to put ads in the newspaper that you could buy boxes of the magazines directly from us. ... This magazine was such a sensation that young people, young kids would buy a box and they would go to the Metro station or stand on the street in the center of Moscow to start selling *Cosmopolitans.* Then they came back and bought two boxes and then they came back and bought three boxes. The first edition was 50,000, but in a year, we went to almost a million copies a month."

"Some of these boys later became some of the biggest distributors of magazines in Russia. They began with one or two boxes, then they bought a little truck, then 10 trucks, then they shipped *Cosmopolitan* to the Russian Regions and then they became real distribution companies. So, a whole new form of distribution was started by *Cosmopolitan*."

"And the same can be said of the advertising industry because there was no advertising industry. There was no fashion industry, so there were no fashion photographers and there were no fashion designers. Everything was built on the success of *Cosmopolitan*. We had magazine issues with 800 pages and 600 of them were advertisements. It was like printing money."

"For several years we had no competitors. We started launching our own competitors because we knew that we would not be in such a privileged situation forever. This was too good to be true. We launched *Harper's Bazaar* and then *Men's Health*. Then about three or four years after we launched *Cosmopolitan, Elle* came to the market. They were out first competitor."

"After one or two years, *Moscow Times* became a small part of our operation. It all started with the *Moscow Times*, but it only ever became break even at best. But these magazines were so profitable that we could afford to keep spending on the *Moscow Times*. ... We grew from like 20 people to well over 1000 employees in a couple of years."

While *Moscow Times* was well known for its politically independent reporting and for the many high-level professional journalists who worked on it, Derk Sauer was adamant that *Cosmopolitan* had a much greater impact on Russian life. "The impact that *Cosmopolitan* had during that period cannot be overstated. *Cosmopolitan* was the first to write openly about sex and sexual relations between men and women in Russia. Domestic violence was an issue that for the first time was discussed openly. We had tons of letters from readers saying for instance that 'after reading *Cosmopolitan*, I decided to throw my husband out of the house. I'm fed up with being abused.' We wrote extensively about abortion. In those days every Russian woman had like I think an average of three abortions. It was it was a form of birth control."

"All young women in Russia read *Cosmopolitan*. They shared the magazine. It was expensive for them, especially in the Russian regions. They would buy one copy together and it would go from hand to hand. It was just the Bible for young women. ... And the impact was amazing."

Reflecting on the impact of the independent media in those days, Derk Sauer stated that "you look at the net result now of independent free media, even though it is basically closed. But if you look at how people think and behave, how they consume, how they use the Internet, YouTube and social media, to a large part it is a result of what they got through the independent media. Well, I think the new generation is, I would say, even more hungry for what's going on in the rest of the world. ... Technology, of course, has changed everything. When I started, there was no technology. We still used to print the newspaper. Now everything is technology. It's all digital. We don't print anymore. The technology has changed everything in the US and Europe but also in Russia. Technology has changed the lifestyle and the mentality of people. Even for more authoritarian societies like Russia. It's impossible to suppress it."

Rose Creative Strategies

John Rose and his partner had an advertising agency in Boston, Massachusetts founded in 1984, which represented companies like Marriott, Bausch & Lomb, and the City of Boston. Just as Derk Sauer and his wife were the founders of independent English language journalism and of the magazine industry, John Rose was the initiator of American-style advertising in Russia and likewise became involved in Russia somewhat by chance. His partner in the agency met some Russians on a flight in 1988. The Russians were working for *Moskovskaya Pravda* and has just gotten permission to start the first magazine that could accept advertising. His agency began consulting them. That led to a joint venture to create a new magazine called *Moscow Business* and to founding of first a branch of the Boston agency in Moscow in 1989. Later he founded Rose Creative Strategies in Moscow.

John's motivation was mixed between recognizing a business opportunity and doing something adventuresome, completely off the beaten track. "Just the idea of doing something so offbeat. People thought we were crazy. ... But we were trying to do something that was totally different. The other thing was that I certainly saw the inevitability of this business in Russia. Though at the time there was zero advertising, I could see that it was coming."

"In the early, early days, there were really no consumer products that were being produced by Russian companies. But international companies were becoming interested in the market. ... For us, it started with Kodak, one of our clients at the time. We brought them to Russia to make some introductions to publishers. There was virtually no advertising when we arrived. There weren't a lot of magazines but there were some newspapers. And we started doing print ads. So, we were one of the catalysts for advertising in Russia. We did a lot of firsts. Meaning, we did the first radio spots for Fanta. We shot the first TV ads for Sony. We literally constructed the first outdoor advertising in those early days, the first big walls that you saw for Coca Cola or for Baskin Robbins or any of those other big billboards and rooftops in those very early days. … That was us." John Rose was also the founder of the Russia chapter of the International Advertising Association. In addition to Coca Cola and its Fanta brand, he represented other international companies like DuPont, GlaxoSmithKline, Samsung, Sony, and Volvo in the Russian market.

"We went through a couple of waves of foreigners, depending on what the country needed and how it was evolving. … The first wave followed the big multinational brands, the service companies, the lawyers, the accountants, the advertising guys. We were all sort of on the front line."

"At first, the international companies didn't want to have a whole lot to do with the small Russian agencies that were sprouting up. Too many obstacles, from language to just lacking sensibility about what was needed. The Russian agencies didn't know what strategy was. They didn't know how to build a marketing plan. They didn't understand all the groundwork. They only saw what came out the other end. A lot of people got into the business, like a lot of Russians were going into a lot of businesses in those days. It really had nothing to do with their love of what they were doing. There was no passion. It could easily have been any other business. That's why you saw a lot of Russians moving from business to business because it didn't matter what they did as long as it made them money. … They didn't grasp the concept of building a career. That attitude would eventually change of course."

"That also meant that we also had no talent pool from which to hire. So, we hired people out of printing houses to work on production. We would hire people out of the film industry or TV production, to learn how to produce commercials. We even hired a doctor to work on a pharmaceutical account because she could make more money working with us than at a hospital. We had to teach them everything. But they were quick learners."

"In the mid-1990s, like 1995 or 1996, somewhere in there it became very competitive. … All the multinationals were coming in and some of the big gun agencies entering the market. We were their training ground for staff. They would come in and offer our people twice as much as we paid them. We had trained them up for these agencies to recruit. That was a challenging period. But we ended up with a lot of alumni and we stayed friendly with pretty much everybody. A lot of our early people got into very high-powered positions at companies and other agencies."

At that point, just as with the real estate agencies already described above, international giants in advertising began to acquire the small pioneer agencies as a way of market entry. John Rose sold his company to a large French advertising company that became part of ad giant Omnicom. But a few years later after a series of corporate changes, he ended up owning it again.

He discussed the trajectory of attitudes toward foreigners, particularly Americans in those years. "Early on, there was clearly a fascination with Americans and with Westerners in general. Russians are not known for humility. But they held it in check, and they were more willing to learn. At a certain point, it became 'a little knowledge is a dangerous thing' kind of situation. It wasn't that we went through any nasty anti-American sentiment, at least that I experienced. I do think it was more like we don't need you guys as much as we needed you before. They felt that they had learned enough, and they started to want to prove themselves. In a superheated economy, when everybody is making money, everyone thinks that they are a genius. And you tell yourself that you must have learned everything you need to know. In fact, you probably know more than the foreigners know now. That's the kind of attitude that I think became pervasive."

As the experience and skill level of Russians working for multinationals continued to grow, there was economic pressure to replace expats with Russian nationals. "The expat cost me a lot more money than a Russian guy. At a certain point, they decide we don't need to do this expat anymore. Expats were getting big compensation packages, hazard pay, relocation expenses, housing allowances, drivers, schooling, etc. Those packages became enormous and unwieldy. At a certain point that breaks down. So, there were several different influences or drivers let's say for Russians replacing expats."

"The other thing that happened was the crisis of 1998 and the pause in activity by multinationals in the Russian market. It was a difficult awakening, but also an opportunity for Russian brands to compete with international competitors. Suddenly Russian companies that you may not have heard of became important. For instance, the Russian company Wimm-Bill-Dann became a big yogurt and milk producer. ... There was a pause in the market and imports were not coming into the market at the same pace. And suddenly they were becoming much more expensive because of the exchange rates. So, an opportunity was created, much the same kind of opportunity as was created recently with the sanctions [2014 Crimea-related sanctions]. ... You create a vacuum. Russians are very good at filling vacuums. ... These catastrophes created opportunities for the Russians."

"I think the Russians were very good at assimilating as much information as they could from various sources, certainly early on, mostly American. I don't know that I can say that it's mostly American anymore. I think that there are a lot of influencers here now. I think the Russians have adopted what they need. They pick and choose what they think they need."

"So, for instance, if a Russian is creating a company or taking a company public they look more towards the US because it is the most stringent market. They figure if they can meet the high bar set by the market in the US then they will be taken more seriously. They needed to act like that and learned how to manage to get up to that level."

"I wouldn't say that they've rejected the US model. I just think that they've adopted as much of it as they could. They're trying to create their own model, which has a lot of different kinds of influences both the East and West. They have adopted whatever suited them depending upon their kind of business. In my business, there is a lot of US modeling because it is where the advertising business originated. I think that drives a lot of it, so there is a US-centric aspect to it. There's a lot of big US companies that have managed to become very big enterprises here. Out of their ranks came a lot of Russians who then went to work for other companies, whether they're Russian or whatever. So overall, I think we managed to pollinate the market pretty well."

International Lawyers – Facilitating Global Integration and Advising Emerging Russia

International law firms and individual attorneys played an important role as facilitators for multinationals entering the Russian market and as advisors to Russian reformers. Many prestigious international law firms were early entrants in Russia, including Coudert Brothers, White and Case, Baker & Mackenzie, Cleary Gottlieb, Steptoe and Johnson, Latham and Watkins, LeBoeuf Lamb, Salans, Squire Sanders and several others. Some of these firms have changed their names subsequently, so the name of the firm at that time will be used for reference here. Unfortunately, it was impossible to include all the rich experience of the 1990s that were in the attorney interviews. As a result, this section will focus on four pioneering attorneys and their experience in the Gorbachev and Yeltsin periods and their varying motivations for working in Russia. Some came for business opportunity, and some came for the opportunity to participate in constructing a new Russia, or some mixture of the two. The range of different and simultaneous motivations reflects the broader diversity among the expat business community of the time.

LeBoeuf Lamb

John Huhs was one of the very early American lawyers in the Soviet Union. He graduated from Stanford with a JD and an MBA in 1970. He wanted to get into international transactions without the long apprenticeship that typically was required for young associates in major law firms. Instead, he went to work for Satra Corporation, acronym for Soviet-American Trading Corporation, as a legal and business consultant in New York. Satra was founded by an American entrepreneur of Armenian-Turkish background, Ara Oztemel, and was a major trader in chromium ore from the Soviet Union. In 1971 the Mack Truck company of Allentown, Pennsylvanian was negotiating with Soviet authorities to build a new "green field" truck factory in Tatarstan, the Kamaz truck factory. Satra had an office in Moscow and became Mack Truck's consultant as a result of their expertise in the Soviet Union.

As John remembered, "Satra rented rooms in the Metropole Hotel and opened an office in 1970. … I spent most of 1971–1973 in Moscow."

"In 1972, Nixon and Kissinger went to China and Russia. They signed all the commercial agreements with the Soviet Union and the era of Détente bloomed. … Our phones lit up and we were working six-day weeks with fifteen hours per day. It was just bedlam. … I was serving as a business/legal advisor putting transactions together."

John left Satra Corporation in 1973 and spent several years working as a national security advisor to Presidents Nixon and Ford in the White House. In 1976, he joined with a well-known American attorney, Sam Pisar (stepfather of US Secretary of State Anthony Blinken), who also specialized in Soviet affairs, to form the firm Pisar and Huhs. They continued to handle business with the Soviet Union including the opening of McDonalds in Moscow and Tallin, and representing major international firms like Revlon, Seagrams, the International Olympic Committee and many industrial companies. John joined the LeBoeuf Lamb law firm in New York in 1989 to help them develop an international practice, with a Soviet practice being one of the first elements.

"In 1991, we established the first office for LaBoeuf Lamb in Moscow. Coudert Brothers preceded us by about a year. … Then in 1991 the IMF engaged us to help them establish a representation in Moscow. We negotiated space for ourselves and the IMF in the same building next to the Russian 'White House' (Parliament)."

When the Soviet Union dissolved, the LaBoeuf Lamb Moscow office was overwhelmed with work. "We had more work than we knew what to do with and devoted ourselves 18/7 professionally to handle it. Our clients didn't want to give up what they've been doing in the Soviet Union merely because it no longer existed as an entity. They were doing some interesting things. Pratt and Whitney, for example, was helping establish a jet engine factory out in Perm. … And Boeing was one of our largest clients, including the establishment of the Boeing Technical Research Center in the McDonald's building in 1992."

"The majority of the LaBoeuf Lamb clients in Russia were foreign multinationals, but that began to change by 1995–2005, when some large Russian companies began engaging international law firms, like LeBoeuf, Lamb for their overseas as well as domestic transactions."

Even before that, John Huhs was involved with a cultural and commercial phenomenon that originated in Russia, which was not well known, but has subsequently been chronicled in several books. "In 1989 and thereafter, we represented Nintendo to license Soviet video game 'Tetris' from the Soviet foreign trade organization, 'Electronorgtechnica.' Nintendo wanted Tetris for its Nintendo entertainment system and for its new handheld game called 'Gameboy.' They loaded a Tetris cartridge with every Gameboy they sold. It was phenomenally popular, within a year, I think, sales exceeded 50 million individual units. Nintendo also convinced the Russians to engage us to negotiate their foreign Tetris licenses (to the extent they didn't compete directly with Nintendo), which ultimately exceeded over 50 individual licensee companies."

"LeBoeuf, Lamb merged with Dewey, Ballantine in late 2007 to create the Dewey & LeBoeuf firm. The Morgan, Lewis law firm acquired the Dewey & LeBoeuf Moscow office in 2012."

Chadbourne & Parke

Like John Huhs, Robert Langer was one of the cohort of lawyers who were active in the Soviet Union prior to its breakup and witnessed many of the seminal events of late 1980s and 1990s that form the backdrop of all the activities highlighted through the interviews in this book and who therefore has a unique perspective on those events.

He started studying Russian language when he was sixteen. At University of Michigan, he selected Russian as his foreign language and the first person he met in Russian class in 1978 was Bernie Sucher, who was first introduced in Chapter 3 and appeared again in this chapter. Robert then went to Tulane to study Soviet law and went to the Soviet Union on an IREX grant in 1985, before getting his law degree. "I was hired as a lawyer by Chadbourne & Park in January 1987, at the seminal moment for business in the Soviet Union when Gorbachev signed the decree on joint ventures. … At the time my firm had no interest in the Soviet Union, but I got them to send me to the Soviet Union in 1988 for a conference on joint ventures."

"I came back in 1988, then in 1989 one of the partners in our firm got a call from a guy in Austria, who asked about setting up a joint venture law office in the Soviet Union. He said that we had a potential partner there with a Soviet law association. … So, I spent 1989 and the beginning of 1990 negotiating a joint venture law office that was registered in May 1990."

As a result of this presence in Moscow, Robert became involved with the joint ventures being formed by Americans and Russians in the late perestroika period. "There were a couple of consortiums that were being set up. … Folks were trying to get together to do these big joint venture projects with the City of Moscow. One of them, Dennis Sokol, ended up founding the American Medical Center." This was the short golden age of joint ventures when the August 1991 coup and the dissolution of the Soviet Union called everything into question.

Robert's position in Russia was further complicated by the fact that he was just an associate, not a partner, and had no say in how the firm spent their money. "In order to sell it to the partnership, I had to convince them that this is a good business opportunity. You also must remember that there was a tremendous amount of cachet in international offices. I think technically there were only two foreign law firms that that had offices there when I moved over, Baker McKenzie and Coudert Brothers. We were the third international law firm in Moscow and the first joint venture."

"There was a lot of excitement about Russia and a lot of uncertainty. At the end of 1990 or early 1991, US Commerce Secretary Robert Strauss came to see for himself what was transpiring in Russia. Robert who knew Strauss remembered that 'Bob famously said, if I had $100,000, then I would invest $10,000 in Russia and if I had $500,000, I would invest $10,000 in Russia.'"

The firm decided to maintain the office in Moscow. Meanwhile, the events leading up to the dissolution of the Soviet Union changed the entire business landscape. "When we woke up in January 1991, now you're in this new thing. Remember the first thing that the Russians did was adopt a decree that said, all Soviet laws are remain in force, unless superseded by a new Russian law. ... They needed that to keep civil society going. ... You couldn't just get rid of all laws. You had to keep them going, so that's what they were doing. They were doing two things at the same time. One thing was reengineering laws like the Civil Code and then adopting a whole host of new laws in 1992."

Asked about whether he was involved in drafting new laws, he responded "Not me as much as some of the other academic folks. A whole bunch of people came over, definitely Sachs and his team. ... I was in a little bit different position than them because I wasn't sent over there to help build the new country. I was sent there earlier, quite frankly, our role was to make money from the news."

"There were a lot of folks who were flooding in there who were willing to take that kind of risk. Whether they saw the opportunity or just felt the opportunity or were making it up as they went along, I don't know. ... I mean some people would say we were almost building the aircraft as we were flying it. They were flying and they were okay with that. As lawyers, we just kept pointing out that we're going to crash, we're going to crash, we're going to crash. ... That's the difference between some of these other people who are coming in and a lawyer, like myself."

The internal battle over privatization and converting to a market economy came to a head in 1993 with the Yeltsin-ordered military assault on the Soviet-era hold-over legislature, the Supreme Soviet and its headquarters building known as the White House. Robert expressed the general support of most Americans for Yeltsin because politically they supported the transformation he was attempting. Unlike many others, Robert also looked at this assault from the point of view of a lawyer. "The shelling of the White House, I mean from a legal standpoint is a very interesting issue. What Boris Yeltsin did was a complete power play. I cheered it on because my theory was that if you don't destroy the old system, you are not going be able to create the new one. ... The Supreme Soviet was operating under the law which had not yet been changed. The Supreme Soviet has the right to change the Constitution and remove the office of President from the Constitution."

"There was all this stuff that was going on tied to the privatization that was going on then, but this was a major, fundamental fight. The Supreme Soviet said that they were going to essentially write out of history the President of the Russian Federation. Yeltsin said no. He said I've got the guns and I'm going to disband the Supreme Soviet. I'm going to write a new constitution. This is really shortening history."

"What he did was eminently illegal. Having said that, once he disbanded the Supreme Soviet and forced through his new constitution, which was very president-focused, it really gave the impetus for a new Parliament to start adopting some real laws. Giving a little bit more measure of stability if you can call it that."

Robert was part of the process of facilitating the entry of multinationals into Russia that drove the growth in the expat community and the new sectors described earlier in this chapter. Robert moved to the firm of Akin Gump Strauss Hauer & Feld at the invitation of Bob Strauss and then joined K&L Gates in 2010. He had a rich history in Russia representing among others, Citibank, EBRD, Nestle, and Vimpelcom. In addition, he was one of the founders of the American Chamber of Commerce in Russia.

Now located outside of Russia, working for another law firm and abstaining from any work there due to sanctions, he was asked to look back on lessons that he learned from this long and deep experience. "I learned that we all went over there with the idea that wouldn't Russia be great if they just had some 7–11 stores. You can fill in the blank with some others like Dunkin' Donuts or your favorite New York bagel store. The thing you learn being in Russia for so long is that Russia would be great if they could take just the good bits from other countries and leave out all the other crap."

"There were a lot of folks like me and other Americans going over there, who were basically telling them to adopt our system, our system of democracy, our system of checks and balances our constitution, you know what I mean. I'm a lawyer that's why I'm focusing on the legal part of it. But you realize over time that isn't really going to fit them."

Steptoe and Johnson

Like many other attorneys interviewed, Randy Bregman had a long-standing interest in Russia and in the Soviet Union that opened opportunities for him in the Gorbachev period. "An old friend, Sarah Kerry, contacted me and said they needed somebody to run their office in Moscow. … It must have been 1991. That's when I moved to Moscow, in the summer of 1991. Steptoe & Johnson already had an office in Moscow at that time. They had a joint venture with a Soviet law firm. … My first job was to terminate the joint venture because it just wasn't working. … My wife and I were excited about moving to Moscow because of my long-term interest in Russia and of course, our interest was piqued by perestroika."

"After the fall of the Soviet Union, there was a period of transition. A lot of the work was registering companies and then negotiating joint ventures. Most of our clients were American companies doing deals with Russian companies. … There was also a good deal of what I would call consulting work that was not legal work. … We were kind of an outpost. When our clients came, they didn't read Cyrillic. They didn't understand how the system worked at it all and how it was changing. I think most important was how it was changing because the goal was to find ways for them to take advantage of opportunities and to be creative with the changes, to develop something that wasn't there. So, we were providing a strategic view and consulting within a legal framework."

"It definitely was not just a job. I did feel a lot like we were building a new Russia. I felt that we could help, not by telling them what to do, but because we knew we had experience with a market economy. … It wasn't so much to just transfer US laws to Russia or even modify the US laws. It was a way of thinking about how law works so that is relevant for them. … I think Steptoe did maybe a little bit more than others, just because both Sarah and I had such strong personal interest in Soviet Union. So, we would get involved in programs, some of them way before that the time was right for them."

"We did several big seminars about privatization before Russia even had a privatization law. … We brought in big Russian companies for these seminars. At that time, Russian state enterprises were a way of life. The general directors would say, if they privatized, who is going to care of the workers? At the time they had extensive vacation plans at resorts for workers and health care was built into the system. The general director was a little bit like almost a feudal lord. There was almost an ideological and a physical resistance. … I don't think that their main question was how you do privatization. It was why do we do it and what's going to happen to our country if we do. … Some of them were called "Red Directors," but this title has the connotation of being Soviet in the bad sense of the word. Most of these guys had taken on this responsibility. They benefited from the system and I'm not saying that they were idealistic. But it was an ideological system and that was the first issue to deal with. I think the privatization law and the privatization campaign were a way for the reformers and the government to start doing things, rather than persuading and really winning over the Red Directors."

"Back in 1991, 1992, they weren't hostile to privatization because I don't think they really understood it, or else, maybe they would have been. They just wanted to know what this means, how is the company going to look. They were quite cordial. It was only when you started bringing in financial people to say that they had to change how your finances work, which means the Red Director does not have as much control as the shareholders that he must report to, where before they had one shareholder, the government."

As recounted earlier, the reform period was more than just a series of legal questions. It was a period of political and occasionally violent struggle over the direction of the society. Like other foreigners at the time, Randy took the conflicts in stride. "At one point, the managing partner of Steptoe called me in Moscow while all this street fighting was going on. On the phone in the background, he could hear the cannon shooting because we lived on the Ring Road and we were very close. He started talking about extra hazard pay. So, it almost was to my advantage, this sound in the background. … At the time, I felt that it was part of the growing pains for creating a new system and that there was a clear struggle between reformers and Red Directors. I think if anything I underestimated how hard it would be to take Soviet Communism into a market economy and democracy. Much of it was the culture, even though most people rejected Marxism-Leninism, they had lived through the Soviet experience."

Randy discussed the process of Russification of the international law offices, particularly his own. "Well, it started off when I first moved there with two of us and I guess when I left it was up to 30 lawyers and paralegals, most of whom Russian were. When I left, I would say maybe 20 percent were Americans or Canadians."

"Russians learn quickly. After four or five years, they had learned how to do a lot of this work themselves. And it's a natural development that they would do it themselves. I felt there was a brief period where they could learn, and we had something to teach. ... It was broader than just training in the office. Several law firms had long-term exchanges, that is a lawyer from the Russian office would work in a home office of that firm in the US for three to six months. I think it was sort of return total immersion into a system. ... There was a whole framework for this kind of training for Russian lawyers and Russian lawyers wanted to do it because they saw how much money US lawyers made."

After working in the Soviet Union and Russia for almost ten years, Randy Bregman decided that if he was not going to be limited to only practicing in Russia, he would need to leave the country and resume a more diverse international law career. It explained this decision. "We were living there for four and a half years and then I was going back and forth every two weeks or so. As much as we had good friendships and good relationships there, it was just not our country. I would never be fully a part of it."

Latham Watkins

Richard Conn was responsible for opening the Latham Watkins office in Moscow in the very early 1990s, a bit later than the other attorneys who appear in this chapter. Like the others, he had a personal interest in Russia through his study of Russian language, literature and chess and had been closely following developments in the Soviet Union. When the Soviet Union collapsed and the Yeltsin group came to power, he lobbied Latham Watkins to set up an office in Moscow. "I went to the head of the firm and said that this guy Boris Yeltsin is just coming into power. You may not know this, but I speak Russian fluently. ... I basically said, 'I think I can probably make some good things happen. We'll have some clients here, maybe in the US, who need support over there. Russia is trying to transition to a free market democratic structure. I'm sure that there will be some opportunities, perhaps to be helpful in that and basically, I'm crazy enough to do it.' He was very supportive and let me do it. I guess the way I thought of it that there are many other sorts of self-selected types, who had an idealistic view of what they could accomplish in Russia. ... No, I can't say that in the forefront of my mind was that our clients are dying to get our services in Moscow and St Petersburg. That was an adjunct to it, and of course I took great care to spend a huge amount of my time building a client base. But in terms of my own personal interest that drove me to go there, it really did not have anything to do with the idea that it's a good business decision for me personally or that our clients desperately needed us in Russia. But the two things tended to go hand in hand, you know building good relationships in a country generally allows you to function more smoothly. … And I just thought, I wouldn't say an obligation, but I felt that it was the right thing to do to try to be helpful to a Russian Government that at least as I perceived it, was trying to move in a direction that I felt I wanted to support." This fundamental idealism was embodied in how Richard described his career while he was resident in Moscow from 1992 to 1995 and his subsequent involvement with Russia.

Richard spoke to the collegial relationship among the Western lawyers in Moscow and the degree of cooperation among them within the chaotic early post-Soviet years. "We had a wonderful camaraderie among the law firms that were on the ground there. We would get together for breakfast meetings, usually at the Radisson. Many times, in those meetings, I would say that I thought of us as one firm in the sense of the work we were doing to help the Russian government. … Yes, we competed for clients, but unless you've lived it to some degree, it's a bit of a frontier mentality. …"

"I remember conducting discussions of which laws we were going to obey and which ones we were not. I know that sounds like a strange thing, but you know, there was a period where orders would come down from a specific government ministry during the transitional period and you had to decide, was that a real thing or was that a mafia group basically, trying to get information on your clients, trying to shake them down. I mean there are all sorts of complications that lawyers in the West would never have to even consider. If you get an order from the SEC, you comply with it. You never think to yourself, gosh I wonder if those guys were being paid off to try to see our bank accounts. In those days, there was a lot of that, and the Russians would educate me and others on these games that were being played and how to be savvy about those games."

Richard described the kind of help that his firm provided to the Russian government, particularly the Anti-Monopoly Committee. "Part of our work was helping them with their activities, dealing with the Supreme Soviet and the transition that was taking place from the Soviet structures to the new Russia structures." Richard described this relationship as a kind of quid pro quo. "The Anti-Monopoly Committee was providing us office space and we were thanking them by doing pro bono work. … There were many different pieces of legislation that were involved with what I'll call the remnants of the Supreme Soviet. It was all rather gray, at that moment. There was the ongoing transition, but we still had the Supreme Soviet down the street in what's called the White House. We had the Kremlin being occupied by people who were anti-Supreme Soviet." The deadlock between the Supreme Soviet (the holdover legislative body from the Soviet Union) and the Kremlin ultimately resulted in Boris Yeltsin ordering an armed assault on the White House in 1993 as has been referenced previously, followed by the adoption of a new Russian Constitution.

Richard provided his perspective on the political crisis in Russia that led to the assault on the Supreme Soviet. "It's only looking back that I can get some perspective. I did feel that the movement in the country was going to be away from the Soviet structures. Nobody was paying me for this, I was just doing what I thought I should do. … So, I was thinking more about what pieces do you need to accomplish this transition, what laws do you need and how do we operate to get these orders all in place in light of the fact that you had a Supreme Soviet who was not going to cooperate with all that. This is how we began all the process of the 'ukasi,' the orders, the edicts, coming down from Yeltsin's team, which were, in my view, necessary at that time, even though one can argue there's a dictatorial aspect. … But what really hit me during that phase was that I really felt the limitations of law in the sense that, when you're living in an environment which is sort of a jungle and there is no order, there are no real courts that function then laws are important. We spent a lot of time thinking about what precedents we wanted to set and how we were going to structure things and all that. But I have to say, I sort of appreciated back then that there was a period where we had no choice but to move forward without the ratification of a legislature."

During the assault on the White House, there was street fighting and gunfire in various part of Moscow. Richard recalls that "I wanted my family to be safe, and I remember machine gun fire outside the apartment where we were at the time. We moved out to a community outside of Moscow very rapidly. Before we had furniture, we were sleeping on mattresses, and I would go in with the driver to get groceries and other supplies. … At the same time, we were closing deals. I remember working with Baker & Mackenzie and we had a conversation on where we should have the closing. We were representing Citibank on some deal, and we were discussing where to meet where there were fewer snipers."

Richard reflected on the important role that American lawyers played as advisors to Russian officials and the perception of them as neutral, honest brokers. "Russians could not have that same level of confidence at this time period talking among one another. There was a tremendous amount of distrust. And I think Americans, certainly the groups that I dealt with there, were very proper and viewed as people of great integrity. They were seen as people who were there to help. I'm sure we also had folks who were representatives of different governmental agencies who may have also been there to help, but also had other agendas."

"The information and advice we were giving, I think, was very helpful to them. We were also involved with IMF funding with all sorts of different major economic programs that helped in the country to form and to be successful. We were also vital in terms of helping bring business into the country."

"No matter what had transpired, no matter what Yeltsin's team tried, I'm sure there would be plenty of room for criticism. But I think they were genuinely trying to do the right thing. This how I think of the right thing, which is to create an environment where people had their rights protected through legal structures like courts. And that they had private property. I keep saying that the challenge of transitioning from a nation state that had no property rights to one that does should not be misunderstood or underestimated. That is a massive undertaking, and I don't know if there's a clean way to do that."

Richard moved with his family back to the United States in 1995 but continued his involvement with Russian legal matters by flying in and out of the country as needed. In response to the question of how he felt about the situation in Russia in 1995, he responded, "I thought the job was done, not by just by me, but by all of us, and by the government, of course, and all the people who were working on reform. I was very optimistic how the investment banks were operating, and we had a lot going on in the economy. Years later, I was absolutely shocked to see that, although we had worked with them to put this wonderful infrastructure in place, unfortunately, essentially the FSB forces, came back in and took control of industry."

This chapter has been meant to introduce the important role of Americans in the private sector of the post-Soviet Russian market economy. Unfortunately, there were other sectors and other entrepreneurial pioneers that had to be left out in areas like telecommunications, logistics, transport, bottled water, and retail. Americans and other foreigners contributed to changing and modernizing Russian life in all those areas and more.

Notes

1 Robert W. Campbell, *Soviet and Post-Soviet Telecommunications – An Industry under Reform* (Boulder, CO: Westview Press, 1995), 16.
2 "Telecommunication in Russia," *WorldData.info*, www.worlddata.info/europe/russia/telecommunication.php, Accessed January 15, 2023.
3 "Moscow Hotel Venture Is Set," *New York Times*, Section D, page 22, May 30, 1990, Accessed July 22, 2022, www.nytimes.com/1990/05/30/business/moscow-hotel-venture-is-set.html
4 Anna Franklin, "Kodak to Sell its Kino Mir Moscow Flagship Cinema," *screendaily.com*, December 4, 2001, Accessed July 30, 2022, www.screendaily.com/kodak-to-sell-its-kino-mir-moscow-flagship-cinema/407685.article
5 Alex Osipovich, "Big Adventures on a Small Screen," *Passport Moscow*, September 2004, Accessed August 3, 2022, www.passportmagazine.ru/article/120
6 Osipovich, "Big Adventures on a Small Screen."
7 Osipovich, "Big Adventures on a Small Screen."

5 Russia Turning Away

What Americans Thought, What Americans Misunderstood, and What Remains

"If you have enough strength, brains are not needed."

"Hopes die last."

(Two Russian folk sayings translated by the author)

At the time of writing of this book, President Putin has led Russia into war in Ukraine and active military, social, and cultural confrontation with the West. With this dramatic change of course, we are left with the question of what impact the 1990s had on current Russia? Are there lessons to be learned from this period that are of value moving forward or was this period an historical anomaly that has no relevance for the future of relations between the United States and the West with Russia? This book is intended as a contribution to answering these questions without claiming to be the exclusive or complete answer.

Flawed Understanding

There were many different interpretations of reasons for collapse of the Soviet Union at the time it took place so it would be incorrect to say that there was unanimity in the US foreign policy establishment or among the public in the United States and Europe. However, it would also be fair to say that the majority opinion agreed with the quote from Zbigniew Brzezinski that opened this book in the introduction. The USSR lost the Cold War and Russia was a diminished economy that was in his words in "de facto Western receivership." While clearly the USSR lost the political and ideological aspects of the Cold War, the characterization of its economy as being in receivership was incorrect.

The consensus view of post-Soviet Russia led to varying degrees of Western hubris and superiority that contributed, by the mid to late 1990s, to some Russians pushing back and telling Westerners to "stop telling us how to live." On a policy and geopolitical level, this flawed view arguably led to errors in political relations with Russia, underestimating and denigrating Russia's economic

DOI: 10.4324/9781003182153-6

and political place in the world order. The impact of political relations is beyond the scope of the book but emanates from the same flawed model.

In creating the new post-Soviet Russian Market economy, modernization echoed and repeated Russian historical patterns dating back to Peter the Great. In a relatively short period of time, Russians drastically altered their economic institutions and assimilated Western business practices as they sought to overcome the stagnation of the late Soviet period. They were assisted in this process by American aid programs, consultants, private foundations, and private business. The future of Russia is yet to be determined but the country is not turning back to the past as contended in the quote from Fiona Hill and Angela Stent that began this book, at least in its economic foundation.

Clearly, the Russian political order under President Putin has turned out not to be as Americans in the 1990s expected or desired as he has demonstrated in practice the common Russian folk saying about strength and brains. However, the fundamental economic changes that Americans participated in have remained largely in place, along with many of the changes in Russian life that they helped pioneer, leaving hopes for the future as expressed in the other Russian folk saying quoted.

Americans' Intentions in 1990's Russia

As demonstrated by the interviews, foreigners played a very important role in defining and implementing many of the Yeltsin-era reforms, with top-level policy decisions made by Russians.

While Brzezinski and others in the US political establishment considered the Soviet Union to be a defeated power, it was not defeated in the same way as Germany and Japan in WWII. There was no military occupation or economic reconstruction under direct foreign control. The events from the August 1991 coup attempt to Gorbachev's resignation and the dissolution of the Soviet Union on December 25, 1991, were primarily driven by the internal power struggle within the Soviet Union and the victory of the Yeltsin reformers over a divided and demoralized ruling Communist Party.

In these circumstances, the Russian reformers reached out to the West for support and technical expertise in implementing their goal of destroying the foundations of the Soviet planned economy. These reformers saw the use of Western support and technical expertise as an aspect of modernization and improvement of their country, not as a capitulation or transfer of political power. The reformers had their own strong notions of what generally they wanted to happen in Russia. They just wanted help to implement it.

US government programs in Russia included those that were intended to support the Russian reformers in the transition to a market economy and those that were focused on creating and supporting independent civil society organizations to mimic American society. As described in detail in Chapter 2, the US government aid programs were diffused through a whole range of Cabinet-level agencies, but most importantly through USAID-funded programs, under the Freedom Support Act. As indicated in interviews, the US programs were largely reactive to specific requests by Russian government officials under Yeltsin and reflected the diverse approaches and competencies of the US agency and its contractors who implemented these programs. It would be naïve to omit the activities of United States and foreign intelligence services who participated directly and indirectly through aid programs in those years, but these activities are outside the purview of this book.

Significant aid also came from European and international sources like the EU Commission's program, Technical Assistance to the Commonwealth of Independent States (TACIS), the World Bank and individual national assistance programs from the UK, France, Germany, Finland, Sweden, and others.

The exact methods for accomplishing the broad objectives of the Freedom Support Act were left to subcontractors who submitted proposals for USAID funding, often consulting groups or large non-profit organizations that had a history of working with USAID around the world. They each had their own approach and methodology that they had used in USAID-funded projects in other countries.

Despite the lack of coordination between programs and the many competing reform programs and approaches, the USAID-funded programs had a substantial impact on Russian legislation, new institutions, and business practices as described in Chapter 2.

Overall, these American programs in Russia reached deeply into Russian life, as illustrated by the Peace Corps interviews and the broad reach of BISNIS across the entire country. Study in America programs like those administered by American Councils provided access to the professional education that young Russians then used in replacing foreign experts over time. Other exchange programs like Business for Russia, Community Connections and Project Harmony gave Russians the opportunity to broaden their knowledge of the world outside of Russia and accelerated their ability to imagine a new modern Russia. Internews taught Russians how to organize media as a business and sought to implant their journalistic standards in an emerging independent private media sector. This is not to mention the knowledge and skills transfer programs developed through private foundations, US professional associations and government institutions at all levels.

All these activities ventured much deeper into Russian life than is generally recognized, certainly much deeper than Americans have allowed other countries to reach into our society. Consider for a moment how Americans would react to a network of Chinese business development centers across the country dedicated to finding business opportunities in the United States for Chinese companies, analogous to the BISNIS program set up across Russia by the US Commerce Department. Consider how Americans would have viewed a Chinese or Russian version of the Peace Corps showing up in Cincinnati or Omaha. How would Americans react to a foreign government sponsoring travel for Americans to their country to train them in the values and techniques of that country, analogous to the thousands of Russians recruited to travel to the United States in programs run by American Councils and Business for Russia, among many others. All these programs seemed normal and benevolent within the model of Russian receivership.

The reference to receivership is not meant to impugn the motives of the Americans who ran these programs, some of whom were interviewed for the book. Most Americans in these programs were motivated by a genuine interest in helping Russia and Russians. They expanded the world of experience and knowledge of the Russians who participated in these programs, accelerating the transfer of knowledge needed for modernization of Russia. However, in the end, all these programs were expelled from Russia as the window to the West was shut. Those who thought that Russia would become a liberal democracy with a vibrant civil society had their hopes dashed by accelerating Russian nationalism under President Putin.

There were varying degrees of belief among Americans about the permanence of Western influence in Russia. Generally, businesspeople interviewed were much less certain about the longevity of the changes of the in 1990s. Richard Sobel, a Principal Banker at the EBRD from 1992 to 1994 and Director, Emerging Markets, Baring Asset Management who was also a founder and senior manager of the $160 million Barings First NIS Regional (PE) Fund from 1994 to 1997, spoke about how to evaluate the success or failure of American efforts in Russia. "I would be careful not to romanticize it, like we all thought we were going to change Russia politically or that we thought we were going to remake Russia in the American image. I think that would be naïve and that would be miscast. But I do think that we all felt that we were going to make Russia better from a private sector and capital markets standpoint."

"In the period after the coup, there was this euphoria, like this honeymoon period, where the Russians believed that they had thrown off the yoke of communism and they believed that anything was possible. They believed it more than we believed it, but they weren't that ready for it. And it was hard to tell them no, no it's not going to work like that. There's a lot of hard work to do. So, their expectations many times were unrealistic about how fast they could get to a better place. And what the West did or didn't do that contributed to Russia not making it to where they hoped to get in the 1990's, I think that's another book. But it's not fair to say that the Americans lost Russia. It was never ours to lose. What I would say is that in that period of the 1990's, an enormous transfer of positive experience took place and money was made, but it was an unsustainable broken time."

Russians' Intentions in 1990's Russia

While Americans thought that they were managing the reconstruction of a defeated enemy through its diverse aid programs, Russian reformers were following the historical script of Peter the Great and Stalin in using foreign expertise to modernize, without giving up control of the key Russian strategic assets.

This view of Russian agency and control was confirmed in the interview with Cameron Sawyer, the Deputy General Director of the Perestroika Joint Venture and co-founder of the GVA Sawyer real estate firm, profiled in Chapter 4. Sawyer had a unique insight into the inner circle of the Russian reform leadership through membership in the Reform Club. "When I first moved to Russia, I had some connection to Chubais and Gaidar. Those guys had a club, called the Reform Club and I was invited to participate in their monthly meetings. It was about 25 to 30 people. We met once a month to discuss the future and concrete policies. I was sitting with Gaidar and Chubais discussing all this stuff. So, I witnessed that they also had market romanticism. Everyone thought that all you must do is privatize. It did not matter whose hands it gets into, just privatize everything as fast as possible because the market will sort it out. That was the basic idea."

"Those guys just didn't have a clue about the orgy of corruption that would erupt based on those policies. I mean it was disastrous in the end. But that was what we thought. What I thought was the same thing as what Chubais and Gaidar thought because I was sitting with them every month and knew what they were thinking. ... We would discuss things like whether they wanted a social market economy like they have in Germany or Sweden. They hadn't forgotten all the ideals of the Soviet Union. They felt that Russia could not afford it, so they first had to build a solid market economy. Then they could start to think about stuff like their ideals."

"I can tell you from meeting with those guys once a month for about a year and a half that they had very strong ideas of their own. They were in no way driven by the ideas of consultants. They were using consultants only to figure out how to implement these ideas."

"And our mistake, our collective mistake was believing that it's not really that important whose hands it gets into just if it's privatized. The Soviet Union seemed to be this massively powerful monolith. We concentrated too much on the creative destruction part of it. Let's just tear this down and then something beautiful will come out of the ashes of it. That was a mistake that all of us made. No one really understood what would happen."

"Yeltsin was kind of the leader of the market romantic movement. When he was elected over a strong challenge by Zyuganov [Russian Presidential election of 1996], we thought that was the vindication of all those ideas. We thought it would get better and better. Unfortunately, what happened was that Yeltsin increasingly withdrew and the country began to be run by this clique of oligarchs around Yeltsin. Things became less to do with making democracy work and getting the market economy work and more and more to do with building this kleptocracy. ... The other thing that it's important not to forget about that period is that we had a real lack of law and order. There was a huge amount of crime in those days at all levels. Yeltsin was not managing to deal with that. The police and the services were all utterly corrupt and were paid by criminals. There was a real Wild West in those days. We hoped that this was a short-term problem that would go away once the country started to get a grip with democratic institutions being built. It didn't because those institutions didn't get built."

Yeltsin won the title of being a democrat because of his staunch opposition to the Communist Party and his determination to remove it from power. Ultimately, he and his colleagues failed to create a liberal democracy. Whether their intention to create a political democracy was as strong as their desire to dismantle the Soviet system of public ownership of productive property and replace it by a system of private ownership is a question for further debate. However, as described in Chapter 3, Yeltsin's continued rule depended upon the financial support of the new oligarchs in the election of 1996. This limited circle of beneficiaries of the privatization of state property were hardly interested in creating and supporting democratic institutions.

As the process of political change and creation of a market economy proceeded in the 1990s, the economic condition of most of the Russian people became catastrophically worse. During the Yeltsin years, the real gross domestic product per capita declined by more than 40 percent, substantially worse the decline in the United States in the depths of the Great Depression.[1] Inflation peaked at over 2,000 percent in the early 1990s.[2] Life expectancy declined from 68 in 1990 to 65 in 2000.[3] As their standard of living dramatically declined, they were aware through the vibrant and active mass media of the growing collection of wealth in the hands of the new oligarchs. The declining standard of living led to passive discontent and cynicism about the new market economy.

One countervailing factor providing some measure of popular support noted by Cameron Sawyer was the Russian decision to privatize apartments free of charge. This was different from the Polish and Czech privatization of apartments where people became tenants with rent gradually increasing to market levels. He pointed out that "despite the terrible economic times up to 1998, people were at least secure in their housing, which made a big difference in how much risk people could take in their economic lives. This also preserved a certain amount of continuity of privilege among the formerly privileged members of the nomenklatura [Soviet-era elite]. The housing allocated to them was considerably better than what average people got, and after privatization, this became a valuable asset. This allowed many of the suddenly unemployed people to maintain a decent lifestyle, in some cases renting out their good Moscow apartments and living on the rent at their dachas. At no time during the 1990s was real estate cheap that was well-located in Moscow. My first apartment in Moscow, on Nizhny Kislovsky Pereulok, was a case like this. My landlord was a academician and department head at the Institute of Marxism-Leninism. He and his wife lived quite well during this period at their dacha on the rent I paid them."

Russia was characterized by weak institutions throughout the 1990s. A neglected but key aspect of the institutional weakness was the restructuring of the KGB and division of its functions among competing new institutions that opened the political landscape to oligarchs, mafia, and regional power centers to grab property and power. Then in 1995, Yeltsin reorganized the security services again and gradually reunified its functions under the control of the Federal Security Service of the Russian Federation (FSB) and most significantly appointed Vladimir Putin as the head of the revitalized FSB in July 1998.

In August 1999, Yeltsin turned over the government to Vladimir Putin and the FSB and power ministries clustered behind Putin in return for amnesty from prosecution for bribery for him, his family and close colleagues. Given the chaos of the Yeltsin years, it was not exactly clear at the time whether this was a good or bad transition in power. By the end of the 1990s, Putin and the FSB put an end to the era of mafia domination of sections of the Russian economy and brought a renewed system of law and order.

As one of the Western businesspersons interviewed expressed it, "Western people who never lived in Russia just really don't understand who Putin is or was and his significance. They don't understand anything about him. He was great in the first years. He seriously cut down the corruption that we dealt with on a day-to-day basis. We now know that one of the mechanisms of that was that he was consolidating power in his own hands, instead of letting it be widespread. But what we saw was a reduction of everyday corruption and an immediate improvement of law and order. That was basically the end of the mafia. At the beginning of Putin's first year, there was still something that you might call mafia. By the end of Putin's first year, you did not have to deal with the mafia to run an ordinary business."

As Putin gathered strength and brought his own version of order to Russian society, he curbed the power of the Yeltsin era oligarchs, the mafia and regional power centers. His power to a certain extent was built on the Russian perception of the Yeltsin era of the 1990s as a period of corruption, crime, disorder, and declining standard of living and on the growing self-confidence of Russians in mastering their own economic destiny without the necessity of Western oversight. From this point of view, the window of the Peter the Great-like opening to the West began to close in the aftermath of the 1998 financial crisis, even though foreigners were not necessarily aware of it.

Window to the West Begins to Close – Russification

By the end of the 1990s, the combination of Russians traveling abroad for education, foreign internships, and experience working in foreign companies created a growing pool of Russians to fill professional and managerial positions in Russia. There was a growing feeling that they no longer needed foreign tutelage and could compete as businesspeople and entrepreneurs in the market. By the time of the 1998 financial crisis, a critical mass of new Russian businesspeople had been formed. With the mass exit of foreign expats in the wake of the financial crisis of 1998, there was a natural process of Russians replacing expensive foreign talent. This process was mentioned repeatedly in interviews in Chapters 3 and 4 that referenced the impact of the 1998 crisis.

In parallel with growing Russian sophistication regarding market economy business, there was a substory of Russian resentment of foreign hubris, superiority, and expectations of a superior standard of living. Michael Morgenstern, Finance Director of the Perestroika Joint Venture, discussed in Chapters 1 and 4, and later a participant in an oil joint venture in Siberia, explained how the friction over Russian versus foreign staff developed in the 1990s reform period. "The idea of Westerners coming to teach Russians how to do things was rubbing really, really thin. My deputy at Perestroika, who was a very smart guy, and a very quick learner could quickly do almost everything I could. He resented the fact that I was making a salary much greater than he was. That kind of resentment was suffused in almost every single joint venture that I know of. In Siberia, it was even worse because you had all these shoot-from-the hip oil guys from Texas bringing their own housing and their own food into a small town of 15,000 people in which some people were living in cleaned out oil drums for housing. ... Russians found out that there was nothing the foreigners were doing that they couldn't do or learn themselves. The discrepancy in compensation and treatment was so great that it started to cause more problems than it was worth. It added onto the overall underlying sense of dissension and disenfranchisement among the Russian population in general." Once again, we can see the limits of the notion of receivership.

Michael Morgenstern continued, "Russians that I know gained a lot from the experience of working with foreigners or at least working for us, having society opened up to other ideas and other ways of doing things. ... Now, they have their own companies and have been very successful taking from the Western model. ... The need to bring in Westerners was a stopgap. But in terms of Western influence because Russia is the way it is, you always have this fight between something nationalist and looking at something broader. It hasn't changed anything from the time of Peter the Great. Some parts of society are influenced by Western ways and motivated to excel because of it, then there are other parts that do not accept those ways and probably never will accept them." The natural process of highly educated Russians quickly assimilating business skills through working in foreign firms and then starting their own companies was repeated in all the industry sectors highlighted in Chapters 1, 3, and 4, financial institutions, real estate development, restaurants, media, entertainment, and law.

No Turning Back – Structural Economic Transformation

Despite Putin's rejection of the Yeltsin era political reforms, there has been no fundamental return to the Soviet past in the basic Russian economic structure. Government control of the economy has increased, but central planning has not been restored. The destruction of the basis of the planned economy through privatization has remained in place. Russians are oriented around mobile phones and computers, maybe even more so than Americans. Individuals still have ownership of their apartments and dacha plots. Small business, while not as important as in the West, continues to exist. The Russian version of a market economy was successfully constructed during the 1990s and many of the economic fundamentals of that time remain in place, even as political democracy failed to take hold in Russia.

Peter O'Brien, former co-Head of Investment Banking (Russia), Morgan Stanley and Chief Financial Officer of Russian energy company SIBUR until resigning in March 2022, described how Russia has developed quite significantly from the 1990s and the complex relationship of foreigners to that process. "If we want to make some judgement about how the US treated Russia, whether it was because they followed US advice or a combination of that with the chaos at that time, there is certainly some reason to blame Westerners that gave advice on how to transition from a Communist or Socialist society to a market economy because that transition certainly did not serve all Russians. To expect a transition where things can be privatized, everything happens on a market basis and there are government institutions to regulate and oversee the market proved optimistic and naive. ... I also think that it's still only been 30 years and a lot of what we found in the early 1990's was rundown, uncompetitive industrial concerns, other than natural resources. ... To come here in the early 1990's and assume that in a few years there will be a market economy where businesses know how to interact and decide to make capital investment decisions to build new factories because they are confident that they can pull all the parts and people together, then actually sell them and get paid, it was crazy. It takes time." Whether Russia will get that time or better still how long that time will stretch into the future has been called into question by the invasion of Ukraine. Nonetheless, to this date, Russia has not returned to a planned economy, renationalized private property or sought to restore the economic autarchy of the Soviet Union. The fundamental reforms of the 1990s in establishing financial mechanisms of economic regulation and creating an active private service sector still remain basically in place.

Financial Sector – Shareholders and Private Equity versus Banks

As described in Chapter 3, new capital market institutions were created in the 1990s that changed the role of money and the means of capital allocation for the post-Soviet Russian market economy. The creation of these institutions rested upon privatization of family housing and of a section of state enterprises. This was one of the main priorities of the Yeltsin reformers and was accomplished with significant assistance from US consultants, including Harvard's Institute of International Development and the team from Credit Suisse.

As part of the destruction of the Soviet planning methods through privatization, stock exchanges began to emerge on a kind of ad hoc basis. Americans played in dominant role in professionalizing stock trading and creating the infrastructure for a Western-style stock market.

Alongside the stock market, an entirely new segment of private financial institutions led by pioneering American entrepreneurs in Renaissance Capital, Troika Dialog, UFG and others created the investment banks that dominated this market. Later these firms were absorbed by larger international financial institutions as part of the integration of Russia into global financial markets. This integration is one of principal reversals resulting from the invasion of Ukraine.

There were also a small, but significant number of private equity investors, like Delta Capital, Russia Partners, Fleming and Baring Vostok, who worked with powerful Russian partners to finance the modernization of state enterprises or to finance new companies being formed by other American and European entrepreneurs.

Meanwhile, the banking system remained primarily in the hands of the emerging Russian oligarchs.

The expectation among American consultants and financial entrepreneurs was that the stock market and private equity would play the same dominant role in capital allocation and economic power as in the United States. Russian reformers and political leaders allowed foreigners to invest and make profits through the stock exchange, but they were not willing to allow foreigners to gain control over principal assets of Russia in strategic sectors. This different understanding of the Russian modernization program was demonstrated by the exclusion of strategically important state enterprises from the initial round of privatization and then limiting participants in the 1996 loans-for-shares, second round privatization of strategic assets to only Russian oligarch banks, except for the friends of the Russian reformers, George Soros, and the Harvard Endowment, who were allowed to participate.

This tension within emerging capital markets between the foreign-dominated stock market and the Russian-dominated banks characterized the different understanding of the path forward for the new Russian market economy. Daniel Wolfe, a veteran of the Russian financial sector as Chief Operating Officer, Troika Dialog Bank; Senior Managing Director & General Counsel, Alfa Capital Partners; Member of the Board of Directors, Renaissance Capital, and other financial industry and business positions, expressed the American attitude toward financial markets at that time, again prior to the invasion of Ukraine. "We all thought that the markets would become more and more important and play their important role in the economy. … But the banking system is important. How entrepreneurs feel is important. How the legal system shakes out is important Politics is important. So, it's all important. … Now we look with hindsight and think it could have been better. Russia could have been bigger and more integrated with the rest of the world. It could be more friendly with the Europeans and the US. All in all, I think it's pretty amazing how far Russia has come in the last 30 years. I mean look at the capitalizations of Russian companies. They are much bigger and almost identical to their Western counterpart companies by and large. … It would have been hard to imagine this even in our most optimistic days. The disappointing side is that you have an economy that's still quite dominated by the state and companies in the state sector. That's probably the biggest disappointment because there was a time when that was less true. That's a major negative."

Putting this another way, the Russians adapted the Western model of financial markets to fit their own interest. Initially, they did so by maintaining control of strategic assets through banks controlled by oligarchs. Later control has been through strengthening of the central government under President Putin. Still the financial institutions and allocation of capital in the post-Soviet Russian market economy is far from the Soviet-era planned economy, even though it differs from the free market economies of liberal democracies.

Private Sector and Private Life

In the 30 years between 1992 and 2022, there were dramatic changes in the structure and operation of institutions of everyday Russian life. These changes were heavily influenced by the Americans interviewed herein, their colleagues and other foreigners who were active in Russia in these years. In this period, there were enormous changes in the life of Russians through modernizing the service and consumer goods sectors, bringing them in line with the Western consumer style of life.

Russians keep in touch with friends and relatives and interact with government services through mobile phones. Russians buy and sell apartments. They shop in malls and big box stores, although these forms of retail shopping channels are currently threatened by sanctions that have removed Western brands from Russia. They listen to music on FM radio and watch movies at multiplex movie theaters. They have a range of restaurants from fine dining to fast food from which to choose. Russians are top-notch professionals in real estate development, advertising, accounting, and law. In all these areas, pioneering entrepreneurs described in Chapter 4 created new companies in Russia that seeded or inspired Russian owned and operated competitors. The post-Soviet generation has grown up with these changes and have a lifestyle or aspirations for a lifestyle that was shaped by these new private service sector industries.

Apart from the big structural changes in the new private sector, there are any number of smaller changes in Russian life introduced by Americans and foreigners, including the introduction of the ubiquitous Caesar salad by Henry Winther, Siberian corn and soybean seeds by Mike Cooper and a new self-awareness of Russian women through Russian *Cosmopolitan* by Derk Sauer.

The exodus of foreign companies from Russia in response to the war in Ukraine could lead to isolation of Russia again, but this is far from a settled conclusion. Russian firms have absorbed and adopted a great deal of management and production expertise from the West. They have created Russian copycat versions of several international brands. Anecdotally, many of franchises of companies like McDonalds and others leaving the Russian market have been sold to Russian franchise holders who are not changing the structure and style of the companies, just the name. It is likely that much of the impact of the foreign private sector will remain, even without the foreigners, through the activities of this modernized Russian private sector. This would have been impossible to conceive of in 1992 but is at least worth consideration in 2022 because of the impact of foreign private business on post-Soviet Russia.

Looking Forward

As of the time of writing of this book, the future shape of geopolitics remains uncertain. The globalized world of the 1990s may be permanently fractured into competing and antagonistic blocs, with Russia and China composing one pole of this realignment and the United States and the West another. No matter what shape the future takes, Russia will continue to play an important role in the world. Understanding its interests and patterns of behavior remains an important part of statecraft and diplomacy. Looking back to the Chaika watch factory described in the introduction, it is critical to remember that Russia has a long and turbulent history of persistence, periodic uncertainty, and revival. To use the vernacular of our times, Russia will not be cancelled.

If we assume that some form of dialogue will resume between the United States and Russia someday when political conditions allow, it is worth preserving aspects of the experience of the 1990s to inform this new dialogue when it takes place. Taking the long view of the arc of Russian – American interaction during the roughly 30 years covered by this book, there was success where there were mutual interests and mutual benefits. One-sided or misunderstood interests resulted in conflict and failure. This importance of mutual benefit is clear from the beginning of the citizen diplomacy, space bridges and joint ventures of the Gorbachev era through to the financial investments and new private sector of the Yeltsin era.

Where the relationship was based on the notion of receivership, teacher-student or mentor-mentee, there was much less chance of success than where there were true partnerships that met the needs of both sides.

We should also note the latent basis for citizen diplomacy in the life experience of thousands of Russians who came to the United States on exchange or training programs and the thousands of Americans who worked in Russia or travelled there in the Yeltsin and Putin eras, plus the highly educated diaspora of Russians who have fled since the invasion of Ukraine. However, the potential for citizen diplomacy from the exchange programs of the 1990s is diminishing as this population ages and distances itself from that past period, without a new generation having similar experiences. Furthermore, there has been a determined effort by the Russian government to block any foreign influence through use of the designation of "foreign agent" for those perceived to be too close to foreigners and by limiting of travel and business visas by both the United States and Russia. The gap between what Americans and Russians think we know about each other and what we really know will continue to grow without actual contact. If and when contacts renew, the lessons of the 1990s will be important in how we view and treat each other. Partnership, not receivership will be required.

Linda Giudice spoke of the difference in perspective between receivership and partnership in her experience in Russia. She went to work full time for a joint venture tobacco company in Moscow on behalf of a US venture capital fund in December 1992 and stayed until December 2003. In the early 1990s, the Soviet Ministry of Foreign Economic Affairs invited multinational companies to Russia to help correct critical production shortages.

Reflecting on the question why Americans went to Russia, she said, "For different people there were different purposes. ... There's a difference between people who went for business and people who were sent to advise on policy, like writing the land code. Most of the entrepreneurs were interested in making money by taking advantage of economic opportunities. Many of these expats were just starting out their careers; there was a lot of trial and error."

"When I first arrived in Russia, I thought we (Americans) had something to teach our Russian counterparts. As the months and years passed and certainly by the time I left, I didn't feel that way at all. I told my Russian colleagues that I learned as much from them as they did from me. I felt like it was about a partnership. It was about taking the best from one another, and it was only through my own professional maturity that I came to learn that it was relationships that really mattered." As an aside, many of her Russian relationships still endure today.

When describing the earliest days of the joint venture, she said, "There were some very tense moments between the Russian and the American counterparts, a fair amount of distrust. ... There was one very colorful example when the deal almost fell apart. I remember a critical conversation in Russia that brought the key players back to the table. ... You were really trying to make something happen, not just as an American for the benefit of Americans. I really thought that it was a good deal for the Russian counterparts as well. You stood up for that integrity and you were able to bring the parties back together. Sometimes that's what it took. I mean the relationships were full of mistrust. It took a lot of work on the ground and staying power to really work at those relationships. To make something happen, there's a lot behind it and a lot of different approaches. What we did was to make it economically beneficial, meaning Russian counterparts legitimately received shares, employment contracts, consulting agreements, salaries, and bonuses. We tried to treat them fairly for their participation and this really mattered. ... I think that transformative cultural change happened, and we ended up with a bit of a mix of both cultures. That's where I consistently come back to the same themes of partnership." In this emphasis, her own perspective and experience came to be quite different than the notion of a Western receivership model.

"It occurs to me that the transformational period was unique and perhaps once in a lifetime. ... Russia was a country that was relatively closed, and then it was relatively open. I wouldn't necessarily say that Americans led the charge, but often that period is viewed as sort of the American romance. I don't know that we'll ever see that again because the dynamics will never be the same again."

History will undoubtedly not repeat itself in the exact same form, but many of the Americans, like Linda, who experienced Russia in those years were profoundly changed by that experience. They had the opportunity to fully explore Russian society and life and to know Russians as real people, not stereotypes or memes.

Responding to the question of whether Russia has rejected the Western model, Linda answered, "My answer to your question pains me in some ways because of what has happened in the last 20 years since I left there. The US–Russia relationship has changed dramatically, and the level of distrust has returned and even grown. Russia started seeing itself as a Eurasian power, as opposed to caring about America or a Western model. They care about being this power broker in the Eurasian sphere and the whole dimension of US–Russia relations has pretty much changed. We might see this dysfunction for a very long time. It may be permanently fractured."

Unfortunately, the above insights expressed well before the February 24 Russian invasion of Ukraine are proving prescient. The invasion itself has cast a shadow over the original intent of the book and indeed over the entire period covered by this book. In the fall of 2022, it is difficult to write anything about Russia that includes positive statements about Russian people, culture, or achievements without being suspect of supporting the invasion itself. This collective condemnation of all things Russian prevents us from sorting out which segments of Russian society to condemn and which segments with which to seek common ground. As painful and difficult this will be for both Americans and Russians, it is an unavoidable necessity in a world demanding collaboration to solve global problems of disease, climate, war, and hunger.

The book has been prepared with the sincere hope that the war in Ukraine will end soon and the process of rebuilding ties with Russia in areas of common interest and common benefit can begin again, with some small contribution from the insights gleaned from these interviews and analysis.

Notes

1 Paul Krugman, "Wonking Out: The Nightmare after Gorbachev," *New York Times*, September 2, 2022.
2 Krugman, "Wonking Out: The Nightmare after Gorbachev."
3 Krugman, "Wonking Out: The Nightmare after Gorbachev."

Index